Anthology of Musical Structure and Style

Mary H. Wennerstrom
Indiana University

PRENTICE-HALL, INC., ENGLEWOOD CLIFFS, NEW JERSEY 07632

Printed in the United States of America

10 9 8 7 6 5 4 3 2 1

ISBN 0-13-038372-4

Editorial/production supervision and interior design by Diane Lange
Page makeup by Meg Van Arsdale
Cover design by Dawn Stanley
Manufacturing buyer: Ray Keating

PRENTICE-HALL INTERNATIONAL, INC., *London*
PRENTICE-HALL OF AUSTRALIA PTY. LIMITED, *Sydney*
PRENTICE-HALL CANADA, INC.
PRENTICE-HALL OF INDIA PRIVATE LIMITED, *New Delhi*
PRENTICE-HALL OF JAPAN, INC., *Tokyo*
PRENTICE-HALL OF SOUTHEAST ASIA PTE. LTD., *Singapore*
WHITEHALL BOOKS LIMITED, WELLINGTON, *New Zealand*

Contents

Preface

This anthology is intended as a source of musical examples for the study of Western music in theory and literature classes. It is not intended to be a historical anthology; and thus many pieces that would normally be included to illustrate the history of musical development (e.g., organum) have been eliminated. The entire history of Western music is represented somewhat equally, although the period before 1700 receives less emphasis. The compositions were chosen not only because they would be useful in a study of harmony, counterpoint, and form but because they represented important or typical examples of music literature. Another criterion for selection was that as many compositions as possible relate to other works in the anthology—either by use of the same materials (e.g. cantus firmus, chaconne progression), by different manifestations of the same compositional principle (e.g. fugue), or by specific stylistic and compositional connections. These relationships are mentioned in the commentary on each composition and are drawn together in topical units in the study guide.

The anthology is divided into five units on the basis of arbitrary time divisions (before 1600, 1600–1760, 1760–1830, 1830–1900, and since 1900). These divisions roughly correspond to the typical "style" categories, but there has been no attempt to handle the difficult problem of whether, for instance, Beethoven is a "late Classic" or an "early Romantic" composer. A neutral time grouping seemed preferable; in only one or two instances is a composition placed in an "incorrect" category (see for instance Gesualdo's madrigal, written after 1600, but placed for comparison with vocal works of the sixteenth century). Within each time period the compositions are arranged basically chronologically by composer; only in the settings of chorale tunes in the second unit did it seem better to ignore chronology.

This volume includes 168 musical excerpts, numbered by section (I.1., I.2. . . . , II.1, II.2. . . . , etc.). The compositions are mostly complete; only a few are excerpts of longer compositions. Duplication with existing anthologies was avoided as much as possible; most of the works in this volume are not found in similar anthologies. Other factors considered in the selection process were the availability of recordings, or the ease of performance of the example, and the desire to represent as many different genres as possible within the limitations of space. Thus this anthology gives more emphasis to some genres almost ignored in other collections (e.g. opera) and about 30 percent of the works are given in their original form in open vocal or string quartet score or in full orchestral score. In only three or four cases is an orchestral score presented in piano reduction.

In addition to the music itself, the book includes a general introduction to each unit. In this introduction suggestions are made for the study of structure and style and a few reference sources pertinent to the time period are listed. There is no attempt in the listings to be complete; general histories of music, general anthologies, and anthologies which provide no commentary are eliminated. Each composer is then discussed briefly in connection with the specific works included, and some suggestions for analysis are given.

Translations are included for all foreign texts. These translations are not intended for singing (except in the case of the chorale translations) but are intended to provide a sense of the meaning of the text. In many cases the original rhyme scheme has not been preserved. The translations are a mixture of existing translations and ones adapted or newly written for this volume. In this area I acknowledge the help of Thomas Binkley, who was helpful in deciphering the archaic German texts.

At the end of the volume is a study guide. The purpose of this section is to provide suggestions for students and teachers about ways of approaching these compositions. Possible analytical questions are listed, and the works are grouped by topic, e.g. by formal type, texture, or harmonic vocabulary, moving from more obvious to less obvious examples. This guide is obviously not complete and users of the volume are free to organize the compositions as best fits their needs. The index provides a much more complete listing of specific references. A chronological listing of the composers in the anthology is also included.

It is intended that this volume provide enough material for the normal undergraduate basic curriculum in music theory (harmony, counterpoint, form) and/or music literature, including courses in form and analysis and in twentieth-century techniques. The examples range from simple keyboard pieces which can be studied by beginning students for diatonic harmony and simple phrase structures to complex examples of larger forms. This anthology is the product of many years of teaching theory and theory/literature courses of different kinds, spanning the earliest music to the most recent, and includes musical examples and analytical approaches which have been successful with a wide range of students.

I would like to express my appreciation for all the ideas and support given to me by my students and colleagues at Indiana University. I would also like to thank Virginia Whaley, who assisted in the preparation of the manuscript; Diane Lange, Prentice-Hall editor; Leonard M. Phillips, my ever-supportive husband; and my parents, Marie and Walter Wennerstrom, to whose memory the volume is dedicated.

I hope the study of the works in this volume may in a small way provide a new appreciation of the fascinations of musical structure and of the diversity of compositional styles.

Mary H. Wennerstrom
Bloomington, Indiana
June, 1982

I

Before 1600

The examples in this section range from monophonic chants and secular songs to the complicated counterpoint and chromatic harmony of the late sixteenth century. All of the examples are given in modern notation, although a few examples of original Gregorian notation are shown. It is best to remember that these compositions were originally written without bar lines and, for the most part, were in separate parts (not in score). In many cases editorial accidentals are added above the line because the composer did not indicate all the accidentals that were probably performed. Text underlay is another problematic area; in some compositions it is hard to determine just where the words should be placed. Of course, dynamic markings, tempo gradations, and other interpretive indications were not commonly used during this period.

These manuscript problems indicate that we should analyze these pieces with the realization that we are not looking at the original notation and probably do not understand all the performance conventions that would have been natural to a medieval or renaissance musician. Variations in twentieth-century editions, for instance, often make such comments as "four-bar phrase" and "chord progression from B♭ major to C minor" questionable.

As we study more carefully the performance practice and the theoretical background of this era, we find that there were highly developed systems of rhythmic and pitch organization and complicated compositional procedures. Great demands probably were made on the performers, perhaps including a high degree of improvisation and more instrumental performance than is indicated. In any case it is wrong to view this music as being simply a preparation for later music. We should apply basic concepts of musical materials and style to study each work on its own terms: what are the melodic characteristics of the lines? How is form created? What rhythmic patterns recur? What vertical sonorities are used and how do they relate to each other?

The compositions in this section have been chosen to illustrate as many different procedures and genres of the period as possible and to provide opportunities for comparative study of different treatments of the same cantus firmus as well as several examples of a type of piece. They have also been chosen for their relationships with works after 1600, either in choice of cantus firmus or in similarity of compositional procedure. More specific questions about individual compositions and their relationships with other pieces are included with the work itself or in the study guide.

A selection of general books and anthologies that cover specifically this period is given below. All are helpful for reference and for a study of this music.

BROWN, HOWARD M., *Music in the Renaissance.* Englewood Cliffs, N.J.: Prentice-Hall, Inc., 1976.

DAVISON, ARCHIBALD T., and WILLI APEL. *Historical Anthology of Music*, Volume I. Cambridge, Mass: Harvard University Press, 1959 (revised edition). An early and still widely used anthology of music before 1600, with commentary on and translations of 181 examples.

GREENBERG, NOAH, and PAUL MAYNARD, *An Anthology of Early Renaissance Music.* New York: W.W. Norton and Co., Inc., 1975. 41 pieces from Dufay through Josquin des Prez, with discussion of performance problems and notation. The introduction is a useful summary of tempo, musica ficta, ornamentation, etc.

HOPPIN, RICHARD H., *Medieval Music.* New York: W.W. Norton and Co., Inc., 1978. With an *Anthology of Medieval Music.* (Music up to 1400)

REESE, GUSTAVE, *Music in the Middle Ages.* New York: W.W. Norton and Co., Inc., 1940.

———*Music in the Renaissance.* New York: W.W. Norton and Co., Inc., 1959 (revised edition). Very comprehensive reference book.

SEAY, ALBERT, *Music in the Medieval World.* Englewood Cliffs, N.J.: Prentice-Hall, Inc., 1965.

Most music before 1600 was highly influenced by the modal system and the melodic characteristics of Gregorian chant. The contour of chant, its melodic intervals and procedures, and its tonal orientation were important factors in the development of polyphonic music. Examples I.1 through I.6 are six of these chants; I.1 and I.6 are given both in neumatic and modern notation. The standard twentieth-century source for Gregorian chant is the *Liber Usualis,* edited by the Benedictines of Solesmes (Tournai, Belgium: Desclée Company). In the *Liber Usualis* each chant is classified modally in the standard eight-mode system by a number before the chant. These numbers have been omitted here. The Solesmes edition also includes more specific rhythmic indications.

The chants given here should be analyzed for modal classification (most clearly determined by the last note and the range of the chant), for melodic patterns and intervals used (some patterns recur frequently as melodic formulas in a large number of chants, particularly those in the same mode), and for form (repeated sections and phrases, variation techniques, etc.). Also important is the overall contour and shape of the melodic line. These chants form the basis of several other works in this anthology. For comparison, see:

I.1: V.23
I.2.: II.41
I.3: I.10, I.19:
I.4: I.10, I.19
I.5: I.23, I.24
I.6: I.18.

Another chant is given in I.14.

I.1.

Kyrie from Missa "De Angelis" (Mass VIII)

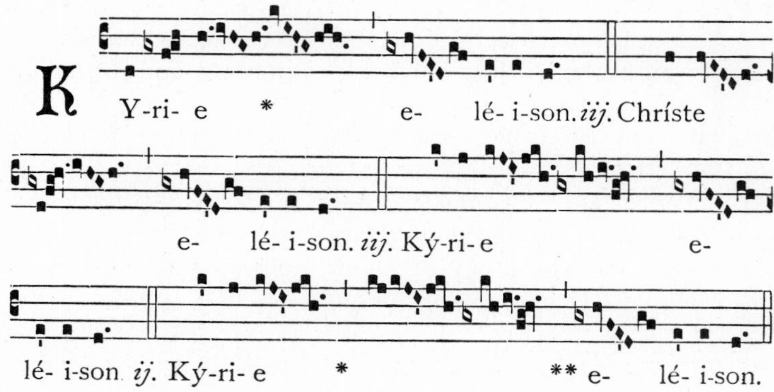

Lord, have mercy upon us. (3 times)
Christ, have mercy upon us. (3 times)
Lord, have mercy upon us. (3 times)

I.2.

"Victimae paschali laudes" Sequence

Let Christians dedicate their praises to the Easter victim.
The lamb has redeemed the sheep; the innocent Christ has reconciled the sinners with the Father.
Death and life have fought in wondrous conflict; the leader of life reigns living after death.
Tell us, O Mary, what did you see on the way? I have seen the sepulchre of the living Christ, and His glory in rising.
The angelic witnesses, the veil and the garments. Christ, my hope, has arisen and goes before His own into Galilee.
We know in truth that Christ has arisen from the dead: be merciful unto us, O victorious king. Amen. Alleluia.

I.3.

"Alma redemptoris Mater" Antiphon

O sweet Mother of the Redeemer, who still keeps the open gate of Heaven and who is the star of the sea, help the fallen people who strive to rise up; Thou who gave birth to your holy son, while nature looked on in wonder. Thou, who were a virgin before and after, receiving that "Hail!" from Gabriel's lips: have mercy on us sinners.

I.4.

"Ave regina caelorum" Antiphon

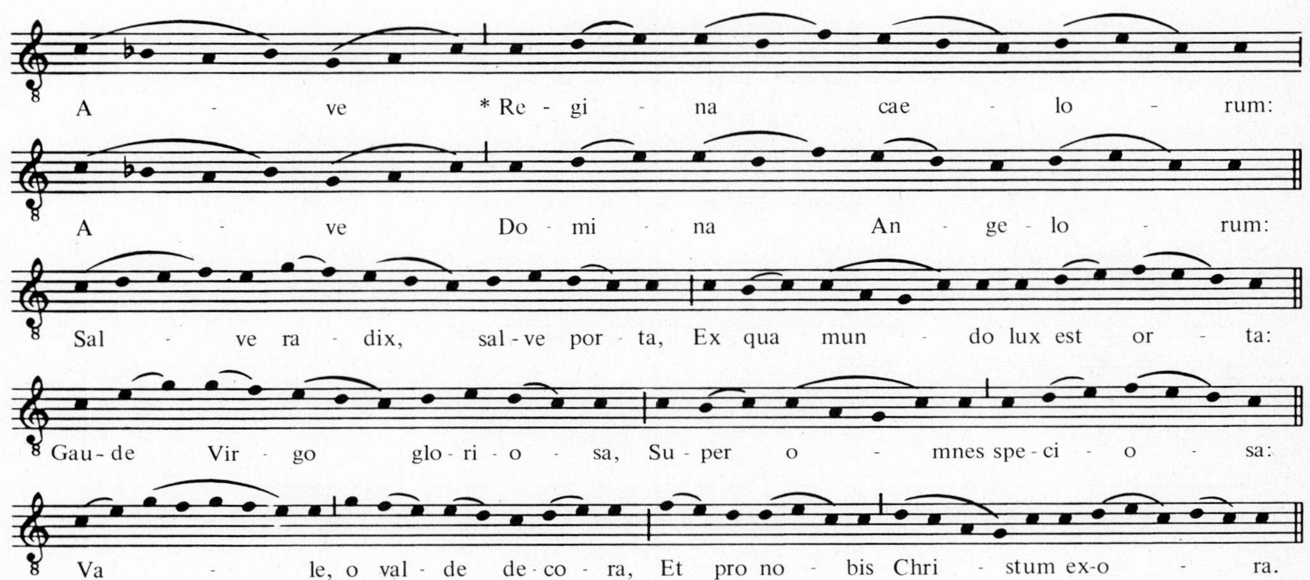

Hail, Queen of Heaven! Hail, mistress of the angels! Hail, holy root and gate through which light rose over the earth. Rejoice, O glorious Virgin, that surpassest all in beauty! Hail, Lady most comely: pray for us to Christ.

I.5.

"Veni sponsa Christi" Antiphon

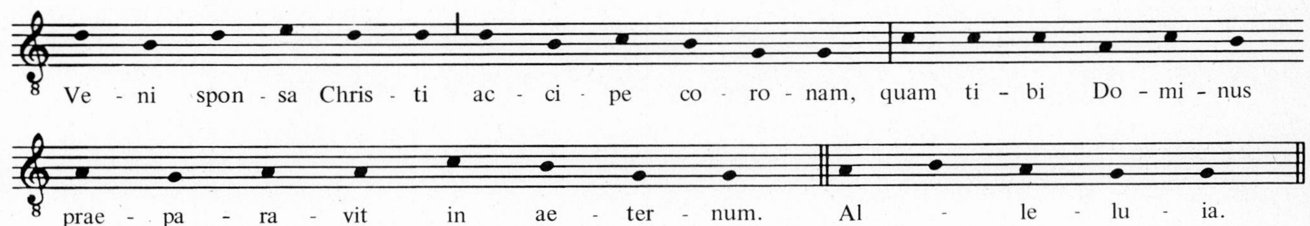

Come, thou bride of Christ, receive the crown which the Lord hath prepared for thee forever. Alleluia.

I.6.

"Pange lingua gloriosi" Hymn

The same music is sung to several verses of text. Only the first of six rhymed stanzas (by St. Thomas Aquinas) is given here.

Let my tongue tell of the mystery of the glorious Body and the Blood, the Gentiles' king who shed a noble womb for the ransom of this world.

Examples I.7, I.8, and I.9 are monophonic secular medieval songs. Some of the many verses of text are not given. These examples exist in a variety of modern rhythmic notations, most of which show the influence of the repeated rhythmic patterns of the rhythmic modes. These examples can be studied for form (I.7 is a lai, and I.8 and I.9 illustrate the bar form) and for their scale basis. Notice the mixture of major scales with the church modes and with pentatonic material.

I.7. Moniot d'Arras, trouvère, 13th century

"Ce fu en mai"

5

1. Ce fu en mai, Au douz tens gai Que la sai -
2. Cors o - rent gent Et a - ve - nant, Et molt trés
3. Tot be - le - ment et dou - ce - ment chas - cuns d'ans

1. It was in May, that time of gaiety,
when the season is so lovely
that I rose up and went my way
to where a fountain played.
In a blooming orchard
I heard the sound of a viele.
I saw dancing there
a maiden and a knight.
2. Speaking softly and sweetly
they danced many times,
while in kissing and caressing
they derived much pleasure.
Down a path beyond the tower
hand in hand they went.
Beneath the blossoms they played
the game of love at their pleasure.

3. Gracefully and sweetly
each one of them enraptured me.
In as much as God briefly
sent me this joy,
why do I feel pain and torment?
I will give great thanks to them,
and will pray to God to protect them.

I.8. Wizlaw von Rugen, Minnesinger (1268-1325)

"Nach der senenden claghe můz ich singhen"

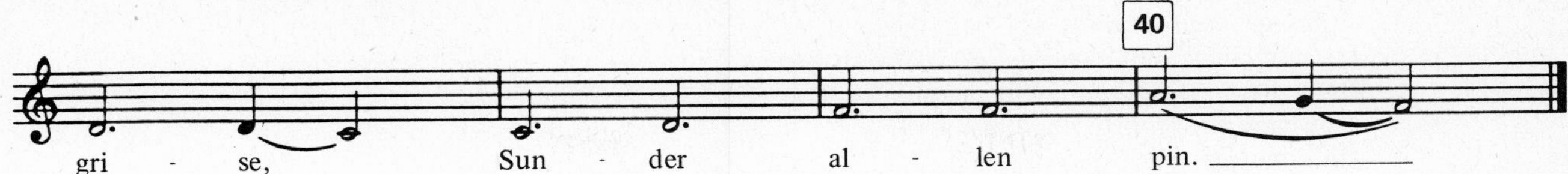
40
gri - se, Sun - der al - len pin.

I must sing a longing lament. If I could bring myself joy, so I might live without trouble; I would be one who bears joy. I would like to be in high spirits; then I would overcome all longing so that I, in a praiseworthy manner, may grow grey in good cheer, into old age, without any grief.

I.9. Wizlaw von Rugen, Minnesinger (1268-1325)

"Ic parrêre dî dorch mîne trôwe"

The text is a reconstruction of the Low German original.

4

Ic par - rê - re dî dorch mî - ne trô - we, de ic dî lêf - lik
her - te - trû - de, se mîn ên - var frô - we, tô al - ler gô - de

1 2

sach vor mî - nen ô - gen, we
schîn - bar und un - dô - gen.

7 9

mach vor - gô - den dî - ne gô - de, wen got, der gô - de,

12

di be - hô - de? des be - darf ic wol, sal ic mî ne - ren vor

15

dî - ner min - ne; dit mach ic swe - ren.

With my faithfulness would I adorn thee,
since my eyes first saw thee in thy beauty.
Love, be mine, and never let me mourn thee,
thou paragon of virtue and of duty.
Oh none can merit thy affection
save God who grants thee His protection;
this I too must have or soon must perish
of love for thee whom I would hold and cherish.

I.10. Anonymous, 13th century

Motet "Ave, regina celorum/Alma Redemptoris mater/Alma"

(from Montpellier Codex; also #5 in Bamberg manuscript)

This example illustrates an early type of polyphonic music. The bottom line (tenor) is based on the opening of the chant "Alma Redemptoris mater" (see Example I.3). The upper two lines (*motetus* and *triplum*) each have different text. In this case they are both sacred texts (see Examples I.3 and I.4), although they could also be secular texts. The tenor should be studied for its melodic and rhythmic repetition. In the fourteenth century the tenor's repeated pitch pattern (called *color*) and the repeated rhythmic pattern (called *talea*) became longer and more involved and were the basis for the fourteenth century isorhythmic motet (see Example I.12). The procedures are the same in this example, but are less complex.

Notice the narrow range of the composition and the overlapping of phrases. What sorts of vertical sonorities occur at the beginning and ending of phrases? Do these sonorities set up a tonal center?

This composition should be compared with I.12, a Machaut motet using similar isorhythmic and isomelodic procedures, and with I.19, a Josquin motet on the same texts.

-ta, 4. ex qua mun- do lux est or- ta: 5. A- ve4) [vir- go]
-ti, 5. sur- ge- re qui cu- rat po- pu- lo: 6. Tu que ge- nu- i-
glo- ri- o- sa, 6. su- per o- mnes spe- ci- o- sa:
-sti, 7. na-tu- ra mi- ran- te, 8. tu- um san- ctum ge- ni- to-
7. Va- le, val-de de- co- ra,
-rem: 9. Vir- go pri- us ac po- ste- ri- us,6) 10. Ga-bri- e- lis ab o-
8. et pro no- bis sem- per Chri- stum ex- o- ra.7)
-re 11. su- mens il- lud a- ve, 12. pec-ca- to- rum mi- se- re- re.7)
fol. 322v

Motetus (Alma Redemptoris mater)
O sweet Mother of the Redeemer, who still keeps the open gate of Heaven and who is the star of the sea, help the fallen people who strive to rise up; Thou who gave birth to your holy son, while nature looked on in wonder. Thou, who were a virgin before and after, receiving that "Hail!" from Gabriel's lips: have mercy on us sinners.
Triplum (Ave regina celorum)
Hail, queen of Heaven! Hail, mistress of the angels! Hail, holy root and gate through which light rose over the earth. Rejoice, O glorious Virgin, that surpassest all in beauty! Hail, Lady most comely: pray for us to Christ.

Compositions I.11 and I.12 are by Guillaume de Machaut (c. 1300-1377), the most well-known French composer of the fourteenth century. He was also a famous French poet, and I.11 illustrates one poetic form of the time: the *virelai.* I.12 is one of Machaut's isorhythmic motets. The two compositions give some idea of the variety of Machaut's style, from monophonic writing to complicated polyphonic textures. They also illustrate his continued use of medieval sonorities and modal rhythmic patterns, with the innovative addition of syncopated rhythmic patterns and chromatic lines.

I.11. Guillaume de Machaut

"Foy porter"

Fourteenth-century virelai, (only first portion of text given)

1. To keep faith and honor, seek peace, to obey, fear, serve and honor you is my desire until I die, lady without peer.

2, 3. My love is so great for you that one could sooner dry up the sea and restrain its waves than stop me from loving you.

4. My thoughts, my remembrances, my pleasure, my desire — are all upon you and I will not forget you.

I.12 is an isorhythmic motet based on a tenor (bottom line) that is as of yet unidentified, although it is similar to many chant segments (e.g. "Pastor bone" in the Antiphon "Sacerdos et Pontifex" for the reception of a Bishop). Study the tenor line for the pitch pattern that is repeated (the *color*) and the rhythmic pattern that is repeated (the *talea*). This edition has a wrong pitch in the tenor in the first statement of the pattern; the correct version can be found from studying later statements of the pattern. This motet is particularly interesting because of what happens at measure 97; how does the tenor from here on relate to the first section of the composition? The top two lines should also be examined for evidences of isorhythm or of repeated rhythmic patterns. This motet was probably written for the election of Guillaume de Trie as Bishop of Rheims in 1324; compare it to the less complex thirteenth-century motet (I.10).

I.12. Guillaume de Machaut

"Bone pastor Guillerme/Bone pastor, qui pastores/Bone pastor"

Isorhythmic motet (1324)

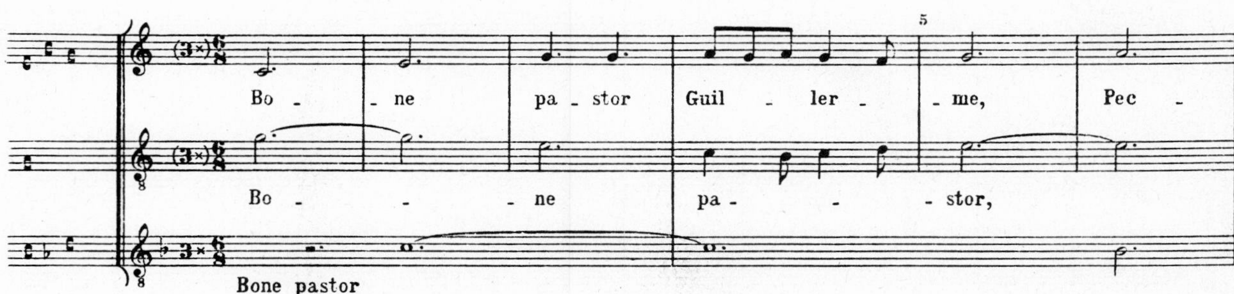

Fa - ven - te sed Mi - ner - va Vir - tu - tum est ca - ter - va
- cis per mo - res Et per
For - ti - ter ar - ma - tum. Por - - tas ur - bis et po - stes
ge - nus Et per fruc. - - - tum stu - di - o - - - -
Tu - e mu - nis, ne ho - ste Ur - bem po - pu - len - tur Mun - dus, de - -
- rum To - len - tem men - tes y - - mo - -
- mon et ca - ro, Mor - su quorum a - ma - ro Plu - ri - mi mor - den - tur.
- rum Ce - lo te - nus, O, Guil -
Mi - - tra que ca - put cin - git Bi - no cor - nu de -
- ler - - - me, te de - cen - ter

60
65
-pin-git Du-o te- - - sta-men - ta, Que mi-tri-
Or - - na - - - - tum rex, qui po - ten -

70
75
-fer ha-be-re De -bet tanquam cin -ce-re Men-tis or-na -men-ta.
-ter Cunc - ta re - git, Su-e

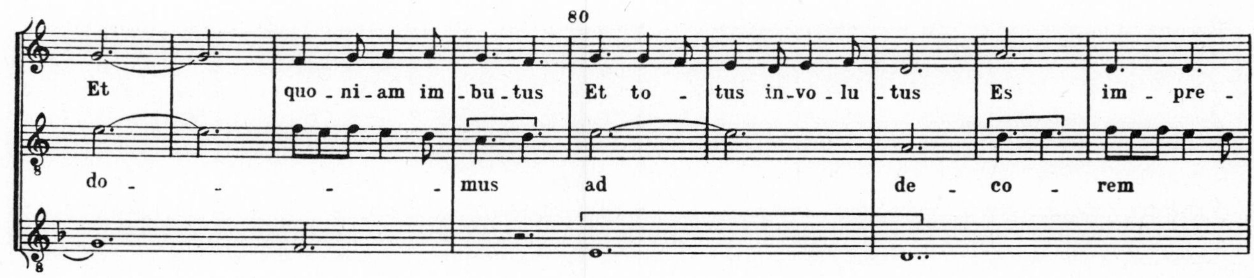
80
Et quo-ni-am im -bu-tus Et to - tus in-vo-lu -tus Es im - pre -
do- - - - - mus ad de - co - rem

85
90
-li -ba- -tis, Fer-re mi-tram est dig-na Tu -a cer-vix, ut
Re- men - si - um in pa- - - sto - -

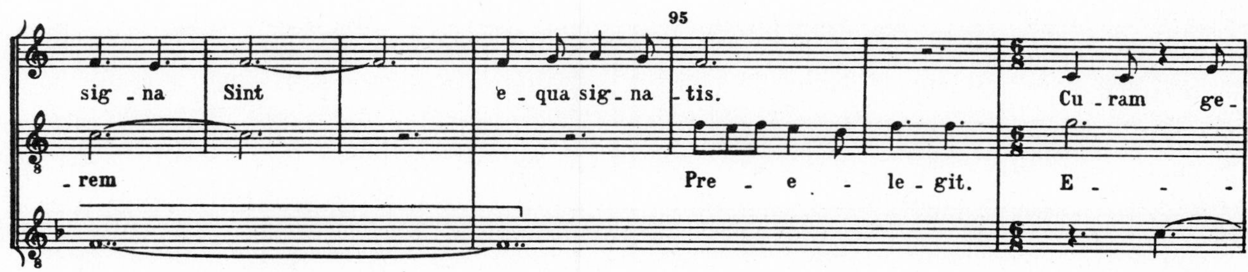
95
sig-na Sint e-qua sig-na -tis. Cu-ram ge-
-rem Pre - e - le-git. E - - -

-rens po-pu-li, vis ut queant sin-gu-li Va-gos pro-fi-ce-re Pri-
-le- -git te, vas ho-ne-stum, Vas
-ma par-te ba-cu-li At-tra-he-re; Par-te qui-dem
in-sig-ne, De quo ni-
a-li-a, Que est in-ter-me-di-a, Mor-bi-dos re-ge-re; Len-tos par-te ter-ci-
-chil sit e-ge-stum Ni-si
-a Scis pun-ge-re. O-ves pre-di-ca-mi-ne Et
dig-ne. De-dit te,
cum conver-sa-mi-ne Pas-cis lau-da-bi-li, De-mum e-ro-ga-mi-ne Sen-si-bi-
vas speci-a-le Si-bi re-

Triplum

Bone pastor Guillerme,	Good shepherd Guillerme,
Pectus quidem inerme;	To be unarmed
Non est tibi datum;	Is not given to you;
Favente sed Minerva	With the favour of Minerva
Virtutum est caterva	With the fulness of virtue
fortiter armatum.	You are strongly armed.
Portas urbis et postes	The gates and doors of your city
Tue munis, ne hostes	Be protected by you, so that the
Urbem populentur	enemy / May not overrun the city,
Mundus, demon et caro,	The world, the devil and the lusts of
Morsu quorum amaro	the flesh / By whose bitter attacks
Plurimi mordentur.	many have been stung.
Mitra que caput cingit	The mitre that surrounds your head
Bino cornu despingit	Depicts with its two horns
Duo testamenta,	The two testaments,
Que mitrifer habere	which the wearer of the mitre must
Debet tanquam cincere	have / As the ornament of a pure
Mentis ornamenta.	mind.
Et quoniam imbutus	And, because you are steeped
Et totus involutus	And enveloped in
Es imprelibatis,	Excellence,
Ferre mitram est digna	Worthy to bear the mitre
Tua cervix, ut signa	is your neck, so that the sign
Sint equa signatis.	And the signbearer are equal.
Curam gerens populi	You carry care for your people
Vis ut queant singuli	You want the individual
Vagos proficere	To help those who stray
Prima parte baculi	And with the first part of your
Attrahere;	crook. / To draw them to you.
Parte quidem alia,	With the second part, however,
Que est intermedia,	Which lies between,
Morbidos regere;	You will conduct the sick,
Lentos parte tercia	With the third part
Scis pungere	You will spur on the slow ones.

Oves predicamine
Et cum conversamine
Pascis laudabili
Demum erogamine
Sensibili.

You commend your sheep
And direct them
And nourish them with praise
And at the last
With understanding aid.

Det post hoc exilium
Huic rex actor omnium,
Qui parcit humili,
Stabili dominium
Pro labili.

After this suffering
May the King who effects all things,
Who spares the humble,
Give a constant kingdom
For the inconstant.

Motetus

Bone pastor, qui pastores
Ceteros vincis per mores
Et per genus
Et per fructum studiorum
Tolentem mentes ymorum
Celo tenus,

Good shepherd, you who surpass
other shepherds / In morals
And in lineage
And in the fruits of study
Which carry human thoughts
Up to heaven,

O Guillerme, te decenter
Ornatum rex, qui potenter
Cuncta regit,
Sue domus ad decorem
Remensium in pastorem
Preelegit.

O Guillerme, you who are so fitly
Dressed, the King, by whom all
that is powerful / is ruled,
Has selected you
To grace his house
To be the shepherd of Reims.

Elegit te, vas honestum
Vas insigne,
De quo nihil sit egestum
Nisi digne.

He chose you, an honourable Vessel
A distinguished Vessel, from which
nothing is poured forth
That is not worthy.

Dedit te, vas speciale
Sibi regi;
Dedit te, vas generale
Suo gregi.

He gave you, as Vessel individual,
Himself, the King,
He gave you, as Vessel universal,
His flock.

I.13 is by Francesco Landino (Landini) (1325-1397), the best-known fourteenth-century Italian composer. It illustrates a secular musical and poetic form, the *ballata* (taken from the French *virelai*).

I.13. Francesco Landino

"Giovine vagha, i' non senti"

Fourteenth-century ballata

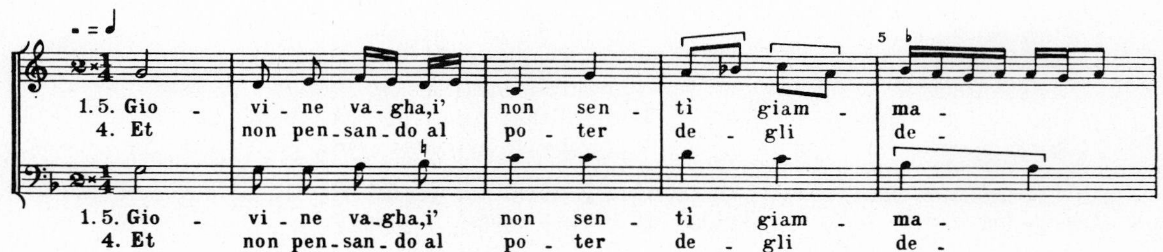

1. Comely maiden, I had never felt love's virtue, but you, the highest good, have placed it in my heart, your servant.
2. When first my eyes were mirrored in yours,
3. I saw Love inside and in seeing it I became pure.
4. And not thinking of the power of the gods I was like a child, but then I found within my breast the golden arrow.

A detailed article that is helpful in studying Landino's music and in understanding fourteenth-century contrapuntal principles in general is "Landini's Treatment of Consonance and Dissonance: A Study of Fourteenth-Century Counterpoint" by Carl Schachter, in *The Music Forum*, Volume II (New York: Columbia University Press, 1970).

Compositions I.14 through I.17 are from the first half of the fifteenth century and represent three different compositional procedures: 1) secular song, 2) simple sacred setting of a cantus firmus, and 3) a more complex contrapuntal setting of a cantus firmus.

I.14. John Dunstable (c. 1380-1453)

"Ave maris stella"

Setting of a plainsong for the office

Dunstable's 3-voice setting is meant to be sung with alternate verses of the hymn "Ave maris stella". The monophonic chant is retained for verses 1, 3, and 5. How does Dunstable treat the chant? In which voice or voices is it placed, and how is it presented? How is the triad used in this setting? The cadences in this setting are typical of the time, and show a stepwise approach to the cadential sonority (e.g. measures 17-18) as was typical in the thirteenth and fourteenth centuries, plus a newer V-i cadential motion (see measures 5-6, with crossed voices).

1. Hail, star of the sea, gracious Virgin Mother of the Lord most high, portal of the sky.
2. By Gabriel's "Ave," establish peace below and reverse Eve's name.
3. Break the captive's fetters; Pour light on blindness; expel our ills and bring us good.
4. Show thyself a Mother; offer Him our sighs, who for us was born and did not despise thee.
5. Virgin of all virgins! Take us to thy shelter. O most gentle, make us chaste and gentle too.
6. As on we journey, help our weak endeavor. Till we rejoice with thee and Jesus forever.

I.15 is a secular song by Guillaume Dufay (c. 1400-1474). This song could be compared in form, rhythmic content, and pitch structure to the secular songs from the fourteenth century (I.11 and I.13). Study particularly Dufay's cadence structures, his use of triads, his opening rhythmic motive, and the textural relationship between the voices.

I.15. Guillaume Dufay

"Bon jour, bon mois"

Burgundian chanson (mid-1400s)

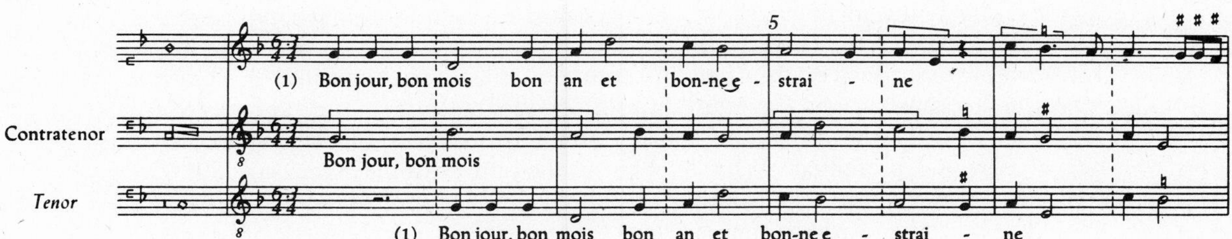

Good day, good month, good year and lovely gifts
May you receive from Him who has all things:
Riches, honor, health, and joy without end,
Good fame, lovely lady, good wine,
To keep the creature hale.

I.17 is a movement from one of Dufay's masses. He was the first composer to set the complete text of the Ordinary of the Mass in several ways. This mass, the *Missa L'homme armé*, is based on the fifteenth-century popular tune shown in I.16. This tune serves as a cantus firmus for many fifteenth- and sixteenth-century compositions; Dufay uses it in a rather traditional way in this mass movement. In which voice does it occur? How is it presented? What happens to the cantus firmus in measure 80? The treatment of the cantus firmus and the relationship of the four voices in this Kyrie should be compared with the cantus firmus usage and texture in the Kyrie of Josquin's *Missa Pange Lingua* (I.18) and Palestrina's Kyrie (I.24).

Dufay's complete mass consists of the Kyrie, Gloria, Credo, Sanctus, and Agnus Dei, each movement using the "L'homme armé" cantus firmus. The cantus firmus appears in retrograde in the last Agnus Dei.

I.16.

"L'homme armé"

Fifteenth-century melody

I.17. Guillaume Dufay

"Missa L'homme armé"

Kyrie (c. 1455-60)

10
lei - son. Ky - ri - e e -
lei - son. Ky - ri - e e -
e e - lei - son.
ARMÉ
lei - son. Ky - ri - e e -
15
lei - son. Ky - ri - e
lei - son. Ky - ri - e
Ky - ri - e, Ky - ri -
lei - son. Ky - ri - e
20
e - lei - son.
e - lei - son.
e e - lei - son.
e - lei - son.

B
25
30
Chri - ste e -
Chri - ste

35
lei - son.
e - lei - son. Chri -

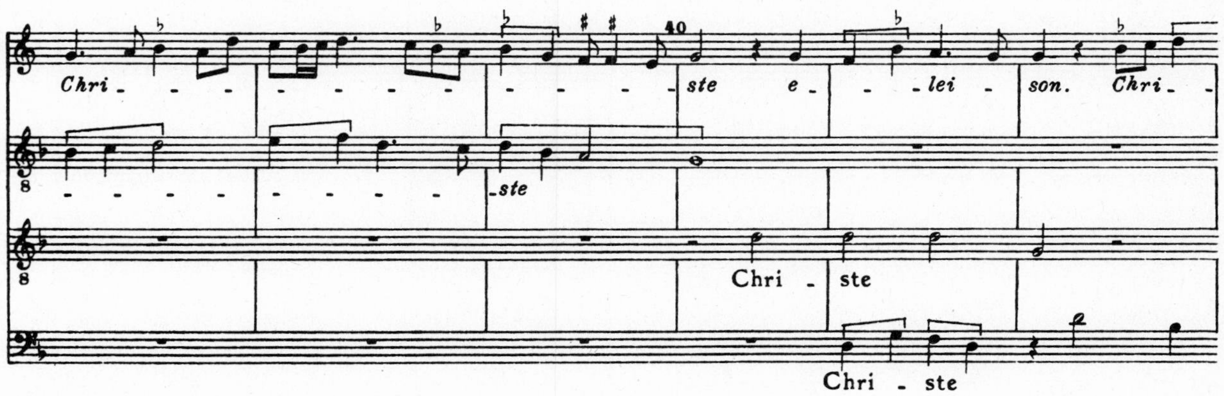
40
Chri - ste e - lei - son. Chri -
ste
Chri - ste
Chri - ste

45
ste
e - lei - son.
e - lei - son.
Chri - ste
e - lei - son.
Chri - ste
50
e - lei - son.
Chri - ste
e - lei - son.
e - lei - son.
e - lei - son.
C
55
60
Ky - ri - e
Ky - ri - e
Ky - ri - e
65
e -
e -
e -

Lord, have mercy upon us. Christ, have mercy upon us. Lord, have mercy upon us.

I.18, I.19 and I.20 are three compositions by Josquin Des Prez (c. 1440-1521). They illustrate three different types of pieces: 1) a mass movement from late in his life, 2) a motet from his earlier years, and 3) an instrumental piece.

I.18. Josquin des Prez

"Missa Pange Lingua"

Kyrie (early 1500s)

This mass is a setting of the text of the Ordinary (Kyrie, Gloria, Credo, Sanctus, Agnus Dei) and is based throughout on the Gregorian chant given in I.6. The way that Josquin uses the chant creates a textural unity among all of the four voices. The cantus firmus should be traced throughout this movement in detail. How do the cadence notes of the chant relate to the cadential sonorities that Josquin has chosen? Compare this Kyrie to Dufay's Kyrie (I.17) and to Palestrina's Kyrie (I.24) for treatment of the cantus firmus, pitch materials, and texture.

From *Werken van Josquin des Prez, Missen* Vol. IV, ed. Prof. Dr. A. Smijers, Vereniging voor Nederlandse Muziekgeschiedenis, 1963.

45
e - le - - - - - - - i -
- i - son, e - le - - i - son, Chri - ste e -
e - le - - - i -
- i - son, e - le - - i - son, e

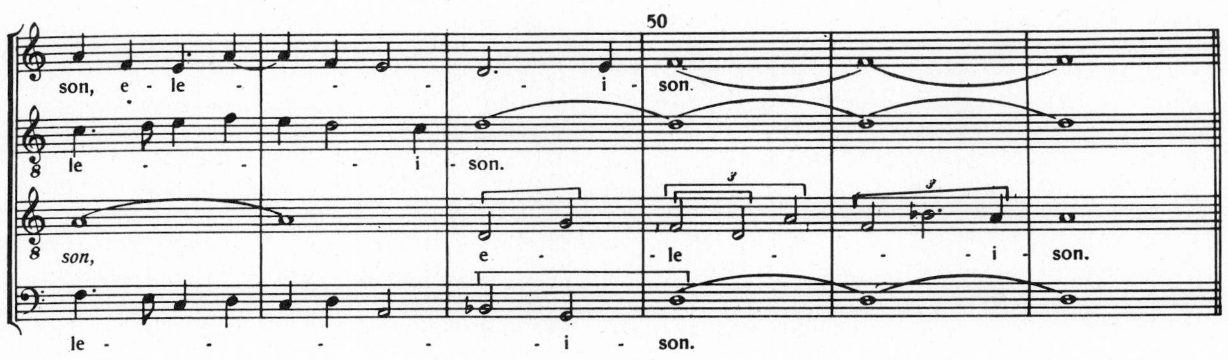
50
son, e - le - - - i - son.
le - - - i - son.
son, e - le - - - i - son.
le - - - - - i - son.

55
Ky - ri - e e - le - - - - - i - son,
Ky - ri - e e - le - - - i - son,
Ky - ri - e e - le -
Ky - ri - e

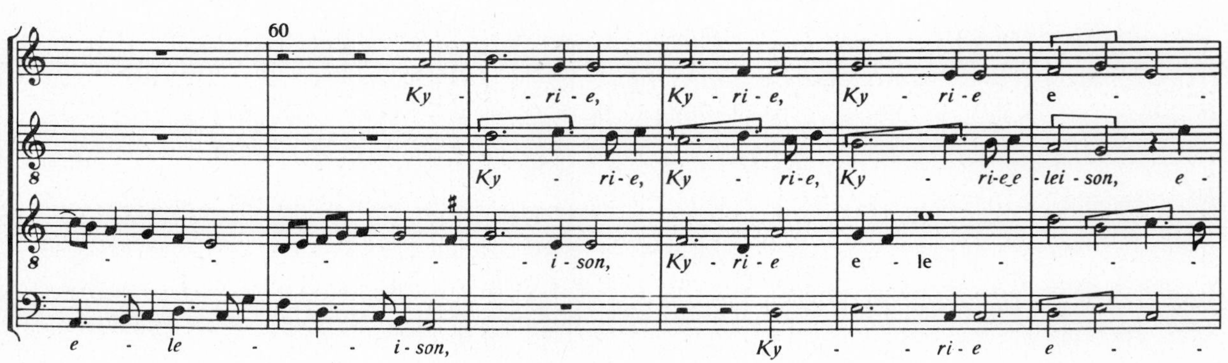
60
Ky - ri - e, Ky - ri - e, Ky - ri - e e - -
Ky - ri - e, Ky - ri - e, Ky - ri-e e - lei - son, e -
- - i - son, Ky - ri - e e - le - - -
e - le - - i - son, Ky - - ri - e e - -

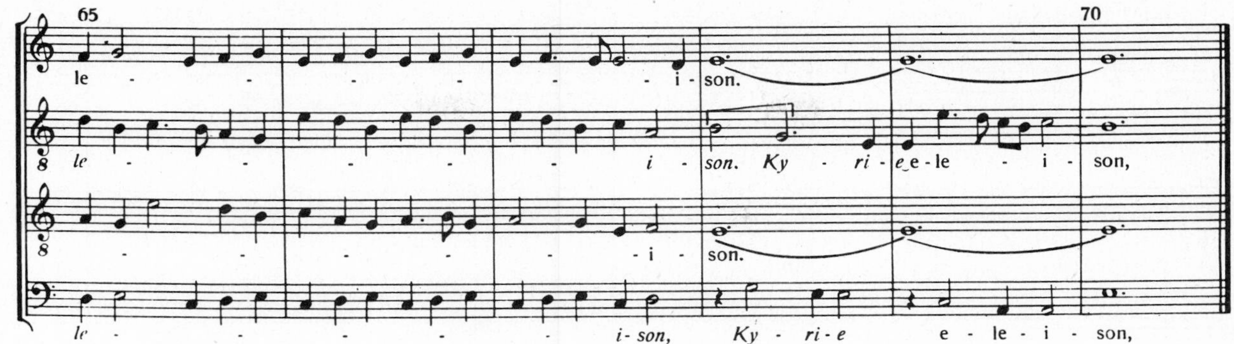

Lord, have mercy upon us. Christ, have mercy upon us. Lord, have mercy upon us.

I.19 is one of Josquin's earlier motets. It is based on the two Gregorian chants given in I.3 and I.4, the outer two lines of the motet paraphrasing "Alma Redemptoris mater" and the inner two lines paraphrasing "Ave regina coelorum." This combination of texts is a conservative aspect; compare with the motet given in I.10. The integration of the two chants into the texture, however, and the imitative procedures found here are new. For instance, what is the relationship between the lines of measures 1-3 and measures 9-11? The motet is in two parts, the second part in a different meter than the first. The second part contains a good example of one of Josquin's long descending sequences. This motet can also be compared with the texture of Palestrina's motet (I.23).

I.19. Josquin des Prez

"Alma redemptoris Mater/Ave regina coelorum"

Late fifteenth-century motet

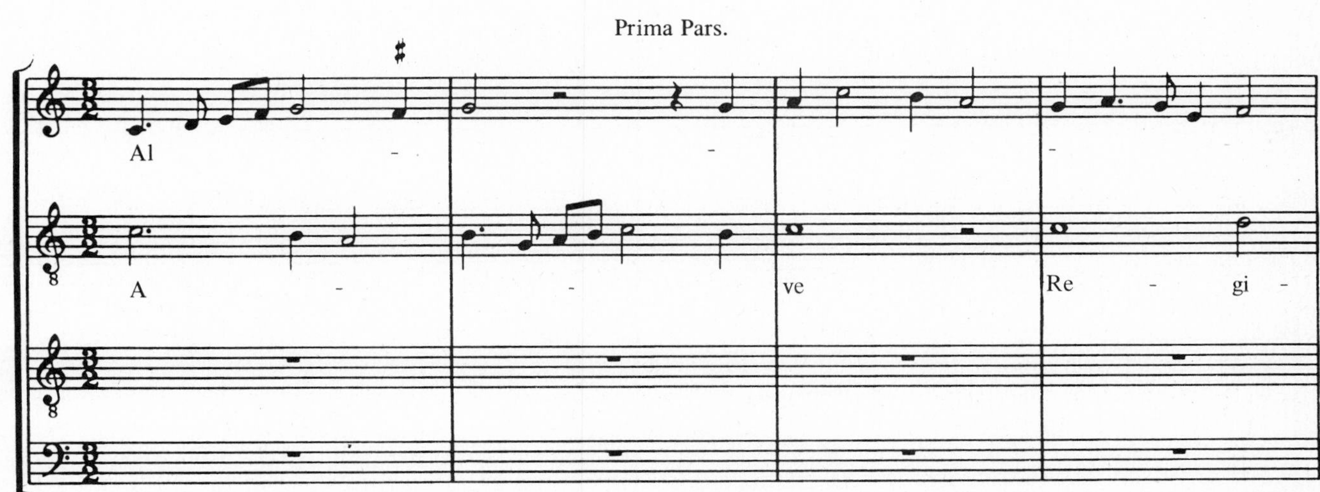

5
ma Re - demp - to - ris ma - - ter,
na coe - lo - - - rum.

9
A - - ve Re - gi - -
Al - - - - -

13
quae per -
na coe - lo - - - rum.
ma Re-demp-to - ris ma - - ter,

17
- vi - a coe - li por - ta ma -
A - - - ve Do - mi - na an - ge - lo -
quae
21
- - - nes, quae
- rum, A - -
A - - ve
per - - vi - a coe - -
25
per - via coe - li por ta ma -
ve Do - mi - na an - ge - lo - rum, A -
Do - mi - na an - ge - lo -
il por - ta ma - - -

29
nes, Et stel -
- ve Do - - -
rum, an - ge - lo - rum
- - - nes

33
- - la ma - ris,
- mi - na an - ge lo - -
Et

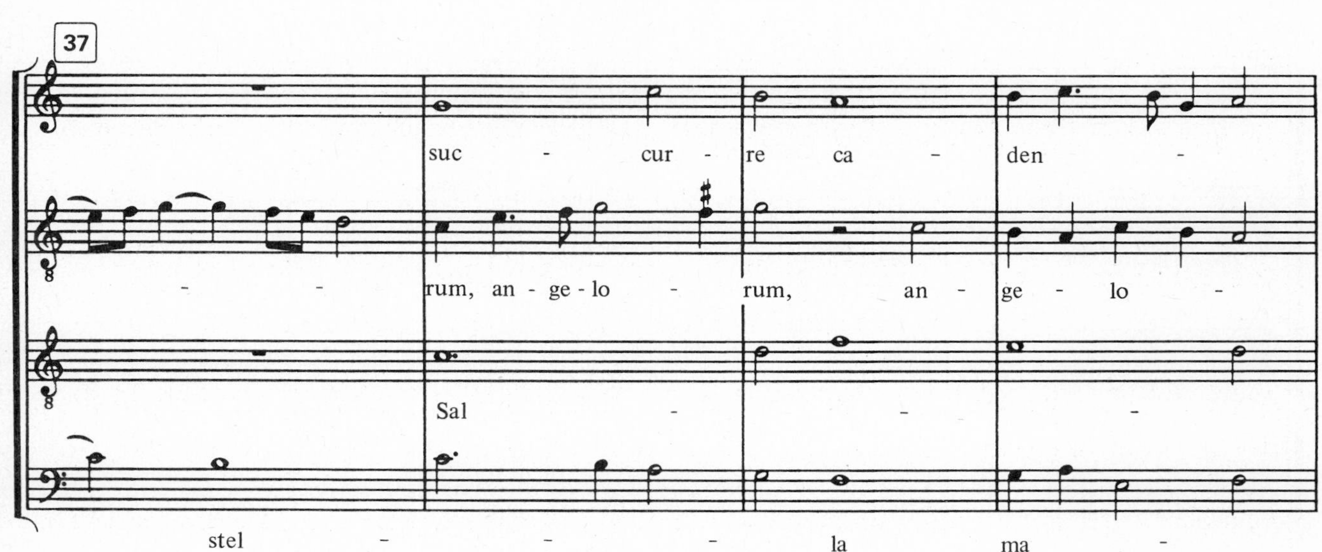
37
suc - cur - re ca - den -
- - rum, an - ge - lo - rum, an - ge - lo -
Sal - - -
stel - - - la ma -

41
- - ti,
rum. Sal - ve ra - - dix sanc -
ve ra - dix sanc -
ris, suc - cur - re ca -
45
sur - ge - re qui cu - rat po - pu -
- - ta, ex qua mun -
- - ta, ex qua mun -
- den - ti
49
lo, po - - - - -
- do lux est - - -
do lux est - or - - -
sur ge - re qui cu - rat

53
- pu - lo.
- or - - ta.
- - ta.
po - pu - lo.
57
Secunda Pars.
Tu,
Gau - de
Gau - de
Tu,
63
quae
Vir - - - go
Vir -
quae ge -

69
ge -
glo - ri - o - sa, glo - ri - o - sa,
- - - go - - -
- - - nu - - -
73
- - nu - -
glo - ri - o - sa, glo - ri - o - sa,
- - - - -
i - - - - -
77
i - - - - sti,
glo - ri - o - - - -
- - - - - sti,

81
na - tu - ra mi - ran -
- - - sa
na - tu - -
85
- - te,
su - - - - - -
su - -
ra mi - ran - te tu -
90
na - tu - ra mi - ran - te, Tu -
- per om - - -
- per
um - - - sanc -

94
um - - sanc - - -
nes spe - ci - o -
om - - - nes spe -
- tum Ge - ni -
99
- tum Ge - ni - to - rem.
- - - sa.
ci - o - - - sa.
to - - - - rem.
104
Vir -
Va - - - - le,
Vir - go

108
go
va
le,
pri

112
pri
va
le,
us

116
us
va
ac
po
ste

120
ac po - ste -
- - - le, va -
Va - - -
- - - ri - us,

124
- ri us, Ga - bri - e -
- - - le va -
le, - - - - -
Ga - bri - e - lis

128
- lis ab
- le, va - - -
ab o - re

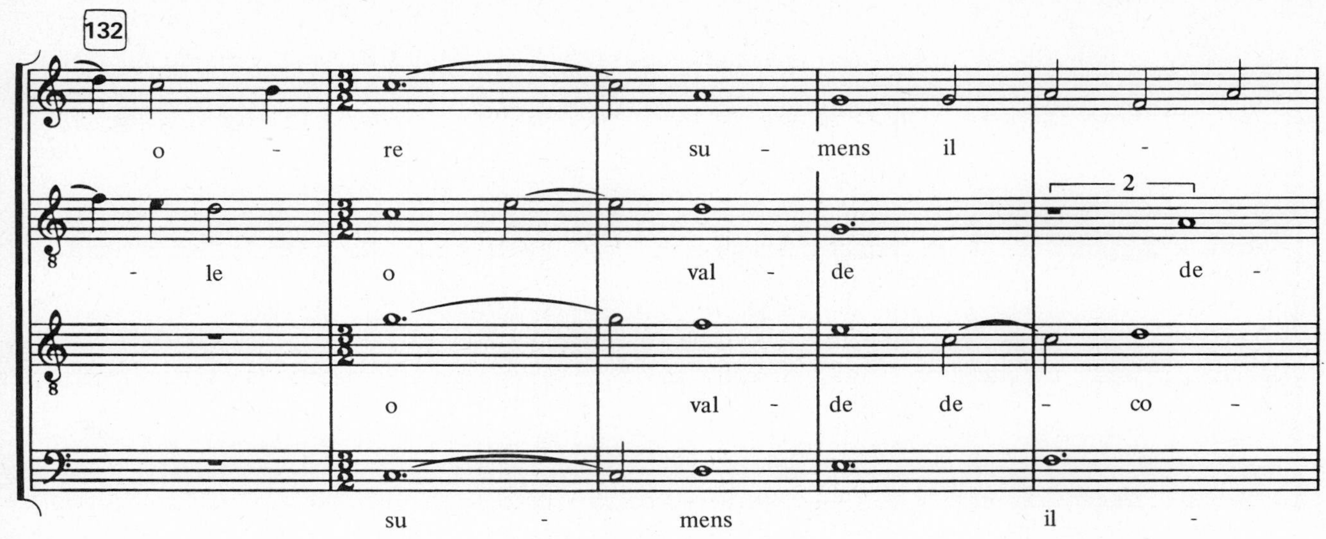
132
o - re su - mens il -
- le o val - de de -
o val - de de - co -
su - mens il -

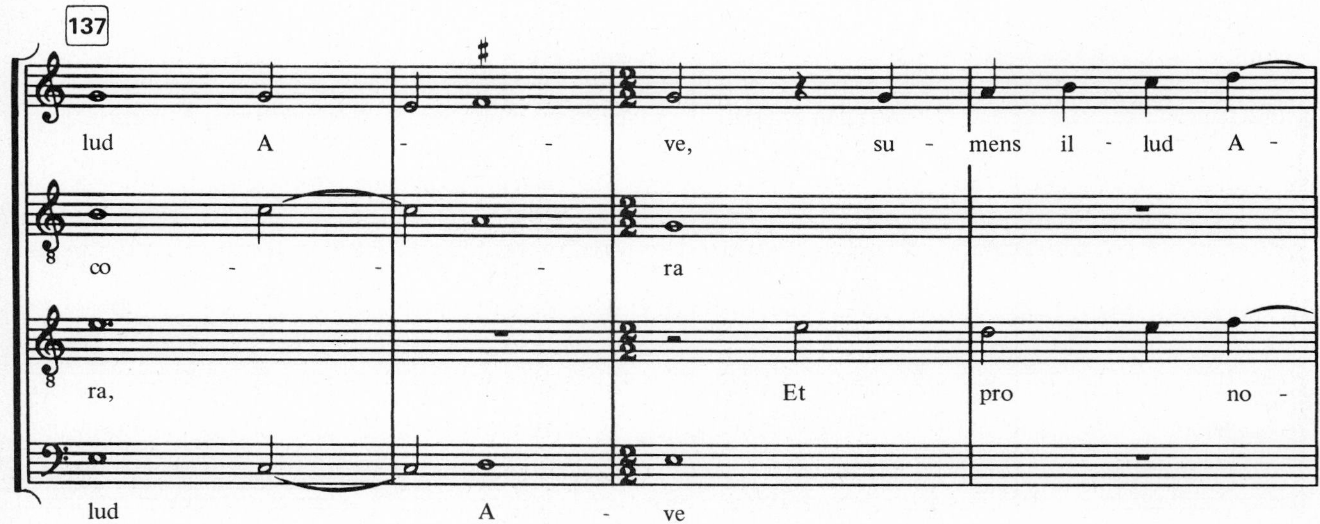
137
lud A - - ve, su - mens il - lud A -
co - - - ra
ra, Et pro no -
lud A - ve

141
- - ve, pec - ca - to rum, pec - ca -
Et pro no - -
- - bis
pec - ca - to -

145
to - - -
bis sem - - per
sem - per Chri - -
rum, pec - ca - to - rum, pec - ca - to -

149
rum mi - se - re - re, mi - se - re -
Chri - stum ex - o - - -
stum ex - o - - -
rum mi - se - re - - -

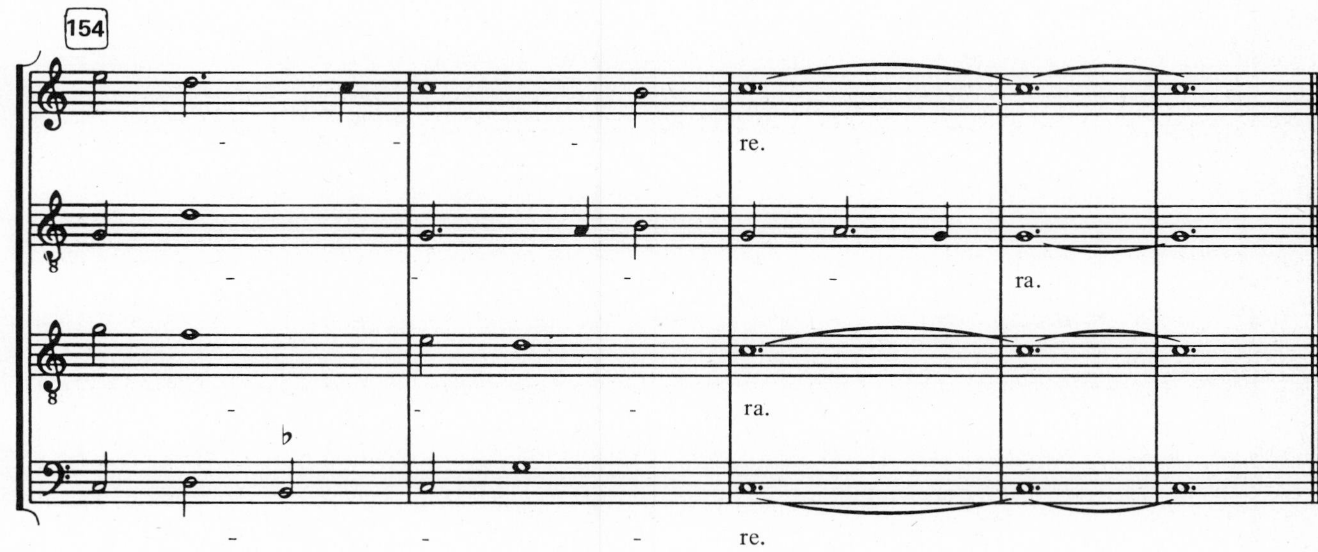
154
- - - re.
- - - - ra.
- - - ra.
- - - re.

I.20 is an instrumental piece by Josquin. It was possibly written for the coronation of Louis XII of France in 1498 as an instrumental fanfare. The tenor line presents a "subject" (*soggetto cavato* or *hidden subject*) derived from the vowels of "Vive le roy" ("Long live the King!"), turned into solfège syllables and thus into notes (*u i u e, e, o i* = ut, mi, ut, re, re, sol, mi or C-E-C-D-D-G-E). This method of deriving a pitch series was common in the Renaissance and has been used by a number of later composers (see, for example Schumann's *Carnaval*, IV.5-IV.7). What is the exact relationship among the three voices which do not have the subject?

I.20. Josquin des Prez

"Vive le roy"

Instrumental canzona (c. 1500)

From *Werken van Josquin des Prez*, Instrumental pieces, ed. M. Antonowycz and W. Elders. Nederlandse Muziekgeschiedenis.

I.21 and I.22 are two examples of late sixteenth-century sacred contrapuntal writing. They are by Orlando di Lasso (Roland de Lassus) (1532-1594) and are from a large collection of works (*Magnum Opus Musicum*) published after Lasso's death; the collection illustrates varying voice combinations. Lasso was an extremely prolific composer and produced over one thousand compositions of all types, sacred and secular.

I.21. Orlando di Lasso

"Justus cor suum"

Cantiones Duarum Vocum. *Magnum Opus Musicum* Volume I.

Late sixteenth-century motet

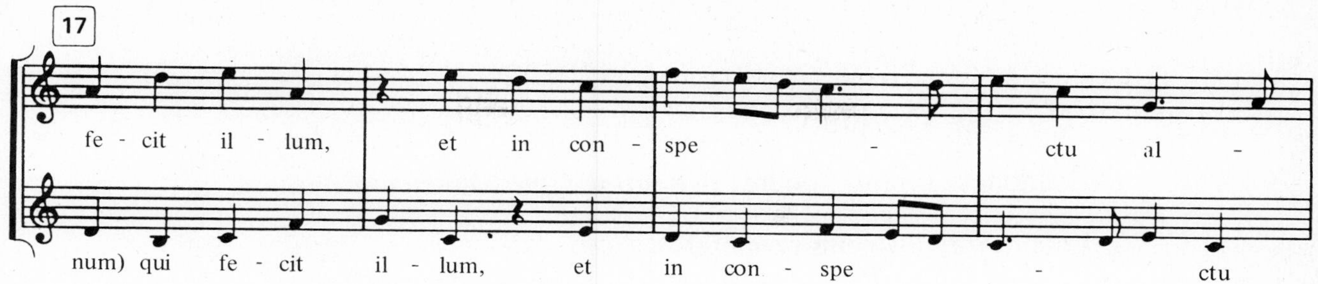

Justum cor suum tradet
ad vigilandum diluculo
ad Dominum, qui fecit illum,
et in conspectu altissimi
deprecabitur.

He will give his heart to resort early
to the Lord that made him, and he
will pray in the sight of the most high.
Eccl. 39:6

I.22. Orlando di Lasso

"Cantate Domino"

Cantiones Trium Vocum. *Magnum Opus Musicum* Volume I.

Late sixteenth-century motet

10
Can - ta - te Do - - mi - no
- vum,) Can - ta - te Do - mi - no can -
- vum, can - ti -
15
can - ti - cum no - -
- ti - cum no - - vum, can -
cum no - - - vum,
- vum, can - ta - te Do - mi -
ta - te Do - - - -
can - . ta - te Do - mi -
20
no can - ti - cum no -
- mi - no can - ti - cum no - - -
no can - ti - cum no - - vum,

- - vum,
- vum, can - ti - cum no -
can - ti - cum no -
25
(can - ti - cum no - vum,)
- - - vum, can - ta - te
- vum, can - ta - te Do - mi -
30
can - ta - te Do - mi - no, can - ta - te Do - mi -
Do - mi - no, (can - ta - te Do - mi - no) o -
no (can - ta - te Do - mi - no)
no o - mnis ter - - ra,
- mnis ter - ra, (o - -
o - mnis ter - ra (o -

Cantate Domino canticum novum omnis terra.

O sing unto the Lord a new song, all the earth.
Psalm 95: 1

I.23 and I.24 are two compositions by Lasso's contemporary, Giovanni Pierluigi da Palestrina (1525-1594). These compositions also illustrate late sixteenth-century sacred contrapuntal writing, and can be compared to Lasso's style (I.21 and I.22) and to that of earlier Renaissance composers (Dufay's mass I.17 and Josquin's mass and motet, I.18 and I.19). Palestrina's motet "Veni sponsa Christi" is based on the Gregorian chant given in I.5. The use of the chant as cantus firmus should be traced carefully through the motet and compared to Josquin's treatment of "Pange lingua" (I.18). The Kyrie of Palestrina's mass *Veni sponsa Christi* is modeled on the motet; this parody procedure is a typical one in the sixteenth century and occurs in a majority of Palestrina's mass settings. Thus the Kyrie should be compared directly with the motet upon which it is based.

I.23. Giovanni Pierluigi da Palestrina

"Veni sponsa Christi"

Late sixteenth-century motet

10
sti, ve - ni spon - sa Chri - sti,
sti, ve - ni
ni spon - sa Chri - - - sti, ve - ni
Ve - ni spon - sa Chri - - sti, ve - ni
15
ve - ni spon - sa Chri - sti, Chri -
spon - sa Chri - sti, ve - ni spon - sa Chri - - sti, ve -
sponsa Christi, ve - ni spon-sa Chri - sti,
sponsa Chri - sti, ve - ni spon -
20
- - sti, ác - ci - pe co - ró - - -
- ni spon - sa Chri - sti, ác - ci - pe co - ró - nam,
ác - ci - pe co - ró - nam, ác - ci - pe co - ró - nam,
sa Chri - sti, ác - ci - pe co - ró - - - -
25
30
- - nam, ác - ci - pe co - ró - nam,
ác - ci - pe co - ró - nam, ác - ci - pe co -
ác - ci - pe co - ró - nam, ác - ci - pe co - ró - -
- nam, ác - ci - pe co - ró - nam, ác - ci - pe

35
ác - ci - pe co - ró - nam, ác - ci - pe co -
ró - nam, ác-ci-pe co - ró -
- nam, ác - ci-pe co-ró - nam,co- - ró -
co - - ró-nam, ác - ci - pe co-ró -
40
- ró - nam, quam ti - bi Dó-mi-nus, Dó -
nam, quam ti - bi Dó-mi-nus, Dó - - mi - nus,
- - nam, quam ti - bi Dó-mi - nus, Dó - mi - nus,
- nam, quam ti - bi
45
- mi - nus, quam ti - bi Dó-mi-nus, quam ti -
quam ti - bi Dó-mi-nus, quam ti - - bi Dó -
Dó - - mi - nus, quam ti - bi Dó-mi-nus,
Dó-mi-nus, Dó - mi - nus, quam
50
- bi Dó - mi-nus præ - pa - rá - vit in æ - tér - num,
- mi - nus præ - pa - rá - vit in æ - tér- - - -
quam ti - bi Dó - mi - nus
ti - bi Dó-mi - nus præ - pá - ra - vit in

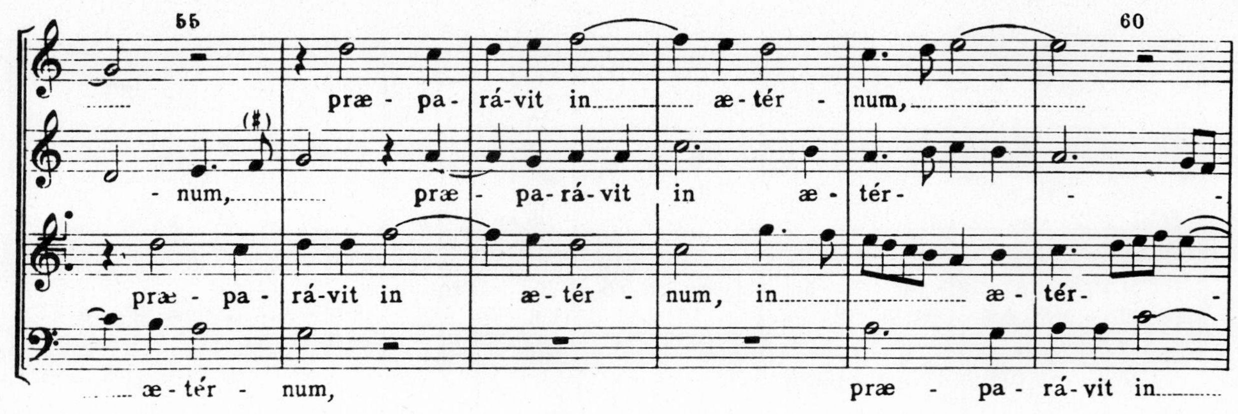

Veni sponsa Christi,	Come, thou bride of Christ,
accipe coronam,	receive the crown
quam tibi Dominus,	which the Lord hath prepared
praeparavit in aeternum.	for thee forever.

I.24. Giovanni Pierluigi da Palestrina

"Missa Veni sponsa Christi"

Kyrie. Late sixteenth-century mass movement

10
son. [Ký-ri-e e - lé- - -i-son.] Ký - ri-e e-lé-
-i - son.
[Ký-ri-e e - léi- - -son.]
Ký - ri - e e- - léi- - - - - - -
Ký- - ri - e e- - lé- - - - -i -
15
-i-son. [Ký - ri-e e - lé- - - - -
[Ký - ri - e e - léi- - - - - -son.] [Ký-ri -
-son. [Ký - ri - e e - lé - i - son.] [Ký-ri -
-son. [Ký - ri-e e-léi - son.] [Ký - ri - e
20
-i - son.] Chri - ste e - léi- - - -
-e e- - -léi - son.] Chri - ste e - lé- - - -
-e e- - -léi - son.]
e - léi - son.]
25
-son. [Chri-ste e - léi- - - - -
-i-son. [Chri-ste e - lé - i-son.] [Chri - ste e - léi- - - - -
Chri - ste e - léi- - -son. [Chri- ste e - lé- - - -i -
Chri - ste e - lé- - -i - son.

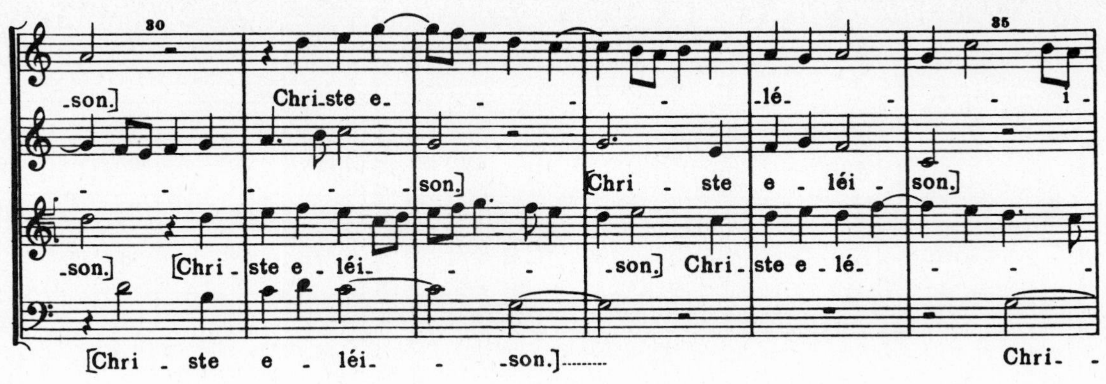
-son.] Chri-ste e- - - - -lé- - - i-
- - - - -son.] [Chri - ste e - léi - son.]
-son.] [Chri - ste e - léi- - - -son.] Chri - ste e - lé- - - -
[Chri - ste e - léi- - -son.] Chri- -

-son. [Chri - ste e-lé- -i - son.] [Chri-ste e - léi- -
[Chri - ste e - léi- - - - - - -son.]
- - -i - son. [Chri - ste e - léi- - -son.] [Chri - ste e - lé -
-ste e - léi- - -son. [Chri - ste e - lé- - -

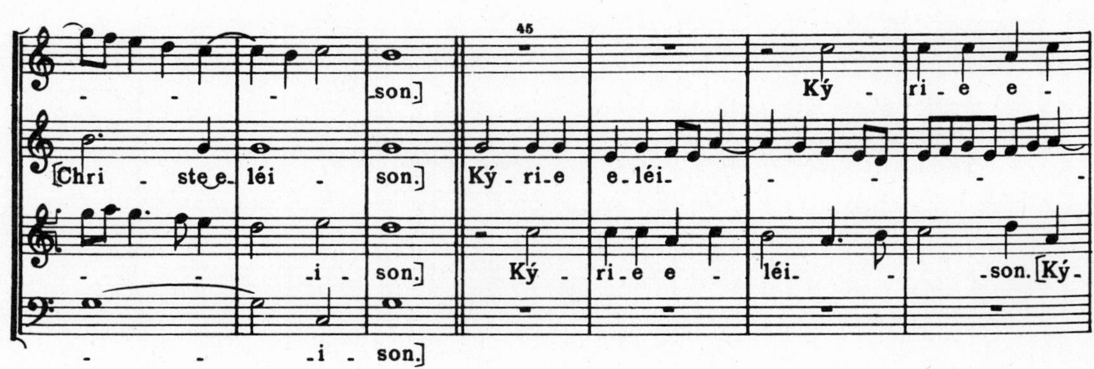
- - - -son.] Ký - ri - e e -
[Chri - ste e - léi - son.] Ký - ri - e e - léi- - - - -
- - -i - son.] Ký - ri - e e - léi- - -son. [Ký-
- - -i - son.]

-léi - son. [Ký - ri - e e - lé- - - -i - son.] [Ký - ri - e e -
- - -son. [Ký - ri - e e - léi - son.] [Ký - ri - e e -
-ri - e e - lé - i - son.] [Ký - ri - e e - lé- - - -
Ký - ri - e e - léi - son. [Ký - ri - e e -

Lord, have mercy upon us.
Christ, have mercy upon us.
Lord, have mercy upon us.

I.25, I.26, and I.27 are three sixteenth-century secular compositions, representing the French homophonic chanson, the English song, and the late Italian madrigal. Gesualdo's madrigal appears in this unit, (although it was written after 1600) because it represents an outgrowth of fifteenth- and sixteenth-century secular style.

I.25. Jacob Arcadelt (c. 1505–1560)

"Le triste cueur que avec vous demeure"

Sixteenth-century French chanson

Compare the harmonic progressions and the phrase structure (including the opening rhythmic motive) in this song with the musical material in Dufay's "Bon jour, bon mois" (I.15).

Le triste cueur avec vous demeure,
Si quelque foys devant voz yeulx souspire,
Prenez pitie a'alleger son martyre,
Et ne souffrez qu'entre voz bras il meure.

If sometimes the sad heart that with you lives,
Sighs before your eyes,
Take pity, cheer its sorrow, and
suffer it to live only in your arms.

I.26. John Dowland (1562–1626)

"Come, heavy sleep"

From *First Booke of Songs or Ayres of foure partes, with Tableture for the Lute (1597)*

This song is a four-part one, accompanied by a lute. It can also be performed as a solo song. Find examples in the song of chromatic-third shifts between chords, a harmonic motion often used by Dowland. Also study the song for functional tonal progressions.

15
eyes, Whose spring of tears doth stop my vi - tal breath And tears my
eyes, Whose spring of tears doth stop my vi - tal breath And tears my
eyes, Whose spring of tears doth stop my vi - tal breath And tears my
eyes, Whose spring of tears doth stop my vi - tal breath And tears, and tears my
20
heart with sor - row's sigh-swoll'n cries. Come, and pos-sess my tir - ed
heart with sor - row's sigh-swoll'n cries. Come, and pos-sess my tir - ed
heart with sor - row's sigh-swoll'n cries. Come, and pos-sess my tir - ed
heart with sor - row's sigh-swoll'n cries. Come, and pos-sess my tir - ed
25
thought - worn soul, That liv - ing dies, that liv - ing dies, that liv - ing
thought - worn soul, That liv - ing dies, that liv - ing
thought - worn soul, That liv - ing dies, that liv - ing
thought - worn soul, That liv-ing dies, that liv-ing dies, that liv-ing

30
dies, till thou on me be stole.
dies, till thou on me, on me be stole.
dies, till thou on me, on me be stole.
dies, till thou, till thou on me, on me be stole.

2 Come, shadow of my end and shape of rest
Allied to death, child to his black-faced night;
Come thou, and charm these rebels in my breast,
Whose waking fancies do my mind affright.
O come, sweet sleep, come, or I die for ever;
Come, ere my last sleep comes, or come never.

I.27 is an Italian madrigal by Don Carlo Gesualdo (c. 1560-1613). It illustrates the chromatic harmonic progressions and the careful attention to the setting of words that are typical of Gesualdo. Does the chromaticism fit into any overall key scheme? The way the vertical sonorities are directed by the smooth linear chromaticism can be compared to chromatic materials of the nineteenth century. This madrigal was one of three chosen by Stravinsky in his *Monumentum pro Gesualdo di Venosa* (1960). Listen to Stravinsky's instrumental version of it and compare how he treats the lines and the vertical sounds with the way Gesualdo treats the same material.

I.27. Carlo Gesualdo

"Beltà, poi che t'assenti"

Madrigals Book VI (1611)

Bel - tà, poi che t'assen-ti, Co-me ne por-ti il cor,
Bel - tà, poi che t'assen-ti, Co-me ne por-ti il cor,
Bel - tà, poi che t'assen-ti, Co-me ne por-ti il cor,
poi che t'assen-ti, Co-me ne por - ti il cor, por-ta i tor-
Bel - tà, poi che t'assen-ti, Co-me ne por-ti il cor, por -

6
por - tai tor - men - ti, por - - tai tormen - ti.
por-tai tor-men - - ti, por-tai tor - -
por - - tai tormen - ti, por - tai tor-men - ti, por-tai tor-
men - ti, por-tai tor - men - ti, por-tai tormen-ti.
tai tormen - ti, por-tai tor - men - ti.
10
Chè tor-men-ta - to cor
men - ti. Chè tor-men-ta - to cor, chè tor-men-
men - ti. Chè tor-men-ta - to cor, chè tor-men-
Chè tor-men - ta- - - - to cor, chè tor-men-
Chè tor-men-ta- - - -
13
può ben sen-ti - re La do - - glia del mo-ri - re,
ta - to cor può ben sen-ti - re La do- - - -glia,
ta - to cor può ben sen-ti - re La do - glia del mo-ri -
ta - to cor può ben sen-ti - re La do - - glia, la
- - to cor può ben sen-ti - re La do- - -

17
la do - glia del mo - ri - re, E un' al - ma
la do- - - -glia del mo - ri - re, E un' al - ma
- re, del mo - ri - re, del mo - ri - re, E un' al - ma
do - glia del mo - ri - re, del mo - ri - re, del mo - ri - re, E un' al - ma
- - - - glia del mo - ri - re, E un'. al - ma
21
sen - za co - re, e un' al - ma sen - za co - - re Non può sen - tir
sen - za co - re, e un' al - ma sen - za co - re Non può sen - tir,
sen - za co - re, e un' al - ma sen - za co - re Non può sen - tir do - lo -
sen - za co - re, e un' al - ma sen - za co - re
sen - za co - re, e un' al - ma sen - za co - re do-
25
do - lo - - re, non può sen - tir, non può sen-
non può sen - tir do - lo- - -
re, non può sen - tir do - lo - - re, do - lo - - re, non
Non può sen - tir do - lo - - re, non può sen - tir do - lo - re, non
lo - - re, do - lo - re,

Beltà, poi che t' assenti,
Come ne porti il cor,
Porta i tormenti.
Chè tormentato cor può ben sentire
La doglia del morire,
E un' alma senza core,
Non può sentir dolore.

Fair one, since you must go,
As you take my heart with you,
Take also its torments.
Such a tortured heart can feel
The pain of dying.
But a soul without a heart
Cannot feel sorrow.

I.28 through I.30 illustrate a procedure that was very common in the sixteenth century: variations over a retained bass line or harmonic pattern. Several familiar patterns were established from their use in dance music and instrumental improvisation; these patterns are given in skeletal form in I.28. The *Romanesca* pattern is given with a melodic line (often known as *Guardame las vacas*) which was commonly associated with it. I.29 and I.30 illustrate the patterns as they occur in a complete composition.

I.28.

Sixteenth-century bass patterns

These patterns are the basis for bass line or harmonic retention throughout a number of variations; the patterns are all similar to one another. What do they have specifically in common?

These patterns and their compositional uses can be studied in: II.1 (Monteverdi), II.3 (Purcell), II.16 (Bach), II.25 (Handel), V.25 (Handy) and V.26 (Brubeck). The sixteenth-century patterns are discussed at some length in Reese's *Music in the Renaissance*, specifically on pages 326 and 524 (revised edition, 1959).

I.29 is a popular sixteenth-century song. It is based on one of the patterns given in I.28. Which one? The melody exists in its modal form, without accidentals, and also with the suggested added E♭'s and F♯'s. The harmonization could be varied in a number of ways; this setting only suggests the harmonic possibilities. How many times is the basic pattern stated in the composition?

I.29.

"Greensleeves"

Traditional sixteenth-century song.

The melody appears in the seventeenth century with Christmas and New Year's texts.

I.30 is a lute composition by Giovanni Terzi, which was published in 1593. It consists of a *Passamezzo* in three parts (three variations on the passamezzo pattern, in a slow quadruple meter), followed by three variations on the passamezzo in the style of a *galliard* (in a typical faster triple meter). This pairing of dances based on the same material carried through into the Baroque dance suite.

The passamezzo pattern in I.30 can be found by looking at the structural chords every two measures. The skeleton pattern has been elaborated by other chords and by a variety of melodic decorations.

I.30. Giovanni Terzi

Pass'e mezzo per b molle in tre modi (1593)

Only the beginnings of the second and third parts are given here.

Trei parti di gagliarde del prescritto pass'e mezzo.

(Three variations in the style of a galliard on the preceding passamezzo.) Complete.

2. parte

From *Lautenspieler des XVI Jahrhunderts*. Oscar Chilesotti, ed. (Leipzig: Breitkopf und Härtel, 1891; facsimile Bologna: Forni, 1969.)

II

1600-1760

This section includes a variety of compositions from the period usually referred to as the Baroque. The end of the sixteenth century was a critical time in the history of music; there were dramatic changes in style from the Renaissance orientation to polyphony and carefully controlled vertical consonances (*prima prattica*) to a newer emphasis on harmonic structures and a freer treatment of dissonance (*seconda prattica*). Claudio Monteverdi was one of the important figures in this musical revolution.

The compositions in this unit illustrate a variety of genres and procedures. Many include a *continuo* part, a bass line played by a low string or wind instrument combined with a keyboard instrument which realized the figured or unfigured bass line with appropriate chords. Since this realization was improvised by the performer, any notation of the keyboard part is only one of many possibilities. Realizations have been mostly eliminated here; the one given in II.1 suggests the process. The student should attempt realizations of other continuo lines, since this element of Baroque music includes both the vertical control and the improvisational element inherent in the style.

Baroque works may better be studied as types of pieces or as compositional processes rather than as abstract formal models. Cantus firmus compositions, suites, variations, and contrapuntal compositions make up the majority of pieces in this unit. The *fugue*, for instance, one type of contrapuntal compostion, is a textural idea that can find many different compositional manifestations. Several fugues, two even using the same subject, are included here for comparison. The emphasis in this unit is on compositions by Bach and, to a lesser extent, Handel, since in Bach's works many Baroque practices and genres are illustrated at the highest level. There is unfortunately not space to include all the important predecessors and contemporaries of Bach, but works by Purcell, Corelli, Couperin, and JKF Fischer suggest the national variety of the late seventeenth and early eighteenth centuries.

A departure from a chronological grouping by composer is a part of this unit, in order to have a separate section on Baroque settings of chorale tunes. Examples II.30-II.41 illustrate settings of 12 different chorale tunes by composers from Scheidt through Bach. These settings can be studied for variances in harmonizations, for different ways of treating a cantus firmus, and for larger compositional types based on the chorale.

Several sources below cover aspects of this period. Of particular difficulty is the problem of ornamentation, one crucial in Baroque music. The books by Dart and Donington and, most recently, by Neumann, give help in this area.

BUKOFZER, MANFRED, *Music in the Baroque Era.* New York: W.W. Norton & Co., Inc., 1947.

DART, THURSTON, *The interpretation of music.* London: Hutchinson University Library, 1954. Includes chapters on the Middle Ages and Renaissance, as well as on the seventeenth and eighteenth centuries.

DAVISON, ARCHIBALD T. and WILLI APEL, *Historical Anthology of Music,* Volume II. Cambridge, Mass.: Harvard University Press, 1959. Anthology of musical examples with commentary; 1600-1780.

DONINGTON, ROBERT, *The interpretation of early music.* New York: St. Martin's Press, Inc., 1974. (new version)

NEUMANN, FREDERICK, *Ornamentation in baroque and post-baroque music:* with special emphasis on J.S. Bach. Princeton: Princeton University Press, 1978.

PALISCA, CLAUDE, *Baroque Music.* Englewood Cliffs, N.J.: Prentice-Hall, Inc., 1968.

II.1 is a composition by Claudio Monteverdi (1567-1643). Monteverdi, in his seven books of madrigals (1587-1619), was instrumental in establishing a new harmonic style; he is also one of the most important composers working in the early seventeenth century in the new genre of opera. Opera was a way of combining expressive word setting, music, and drama; voice lines were often supported by simple instrumental or keyboard accompaniment. Monteverdi's operas span the period from 1607 (*Orfeo*) to 1642 (*L'incoronazione di Poppea*). The end of this last opera is given here, although there is some controversy about the authenticity of this closing duet.

II.1. Claudio Monteverdi

"Pur ti miro"

duet from *L'incoronazione di Poppea* (1642)

Closing duet in the opera. In Nero's royal palace, Poppea is crowned by the Consuls and the Tribunes in the name of the people and the senate of Rome. Poppea and Nero sing a love duet.

20
do, più non pe - - - no, non pe - - no, più non mo - - - ro, non mo -
strin-go, più non mo - - - - - ro, più non mo - - - - - -
25
30
ro. O mia vi-ta, o mio te - so - ro, o mia vi-ta, o mio te-so - ro.
ro. O mia vi-ta, o mio te - so - ro, o mia vi-ta, o mio te-so - ro.
35
40
Io son tua, spe-me mia, dil-lo di
Tuo son io, dil-lo di tu sei
(a tempo)
(rit.)
45
50
spe-me mia, dil-lo di, l'i-dol mio, tu sei pur sì, mio ben,
pur l'i-dol mio, tu sei pur dil-lo di, l'i-dol mio, sì, mio

mia vi_ta sì, sì, sì, sì, sì, mio cor, mia vi_ta sì, sì, sì, sì, sì, sì mio
ben, mia vi_ta sì, sì mio ben, mia vi_ta sì, sì, sì, sì, sì, sì, sì, sì mio
(rit.)
(a tempo)
1.
2.
ben, sì mio ben, mio vi_ta, sì. Io son sì. Pur ti mi_ro, pur ti mi_ro, pur ti
ben, sì mio cor, mia vi_ta, sì. sì. Pur ti go_do, pur ti go_do,
strin - - go, pur ti stringo, pur t'an_no - - - - - - - do, più non
pur t'an_no - - - - - - do, pur ti strin - - - go, pur ti strin_go,
pe - - no, non pe - - no, più non mo - - - - ro, non mo - - ro. O mia vi_ta,
più non mo - - - - ro, più non pe - - - - - no. O mia

I gaze on you, I rejoice in you,
I embrace you, I chain you to me,
I suffer no more, I die no more,
O my life, my treasure.
I am yours, you are mine.
O my hope, say it, say,
you alone are my idol.
Yes my love, my heart, my life.

What process is organizing the bass line? Compare it with the compositional process in I.28-30 and in II.3, II.16 and II.25. Does Monteverdi make any change in the bass pattern?

What overall form does this duet have? This form is found in many Baroque opera excerpts; see, for instance, II.26.

Compositions II.2 and II.3 are by Henry Purcell (1659-1695), an English composer well known for his theatrical compositions as well as his keyboard and chamber music.

II.2. Henry Purcell

Rondo

from *Abdelazer*, incidental music for a play

This rondo was published by Purcell's widow in 1696 as part of *Choice Collection of Lessons for the Harpsichord or Spinnet,* which contains suites as well as individual pieces. The collection contains "Rules for Graces" to explain the markings used; these rules are reproduced here.

RULES FOR GRACES.

A Shake is mark'd thus explain'd thus a beat mark'd

thus explain'd thus a plain note and shake thus explain'd thus a fore fall mark'd thus explain'd thus a back fall mark'd thus explain'd thus a mark for the turn thus explain'd thus the mark for ye shake turn'd thus explain'd thus observe that you allway's shake from the note above and beat from ye note or half note below, according to the key you play in, and for ye plain note and shake if it be a note without a point you are to hold half the quantity of it plain, and that upon ye above that which is mark'd and shake the other half, but if it be a note with a point to it you are to hold all the note plain and shake only the point, a Slur is mark'd thus explain'd thus the mark for ye battery thus explaind thus the bass Clift mark'd thus the Tenner Clift thus the Treble Clift thus a barr is mark'd thus at ye end of every time that it may be the more easy to keep time, a Double bar is mark'd thus and set down at ye end of every Strain, which imports you must play ye strain twice, a repeat is mark'd thus and signifies you must repeat from ye note to ye end of the Strain or lesson, to know what key a tune is in observe ye last note or Close of ye tune, for by that note ye key is nam'd, all Round O end with ye first strain.

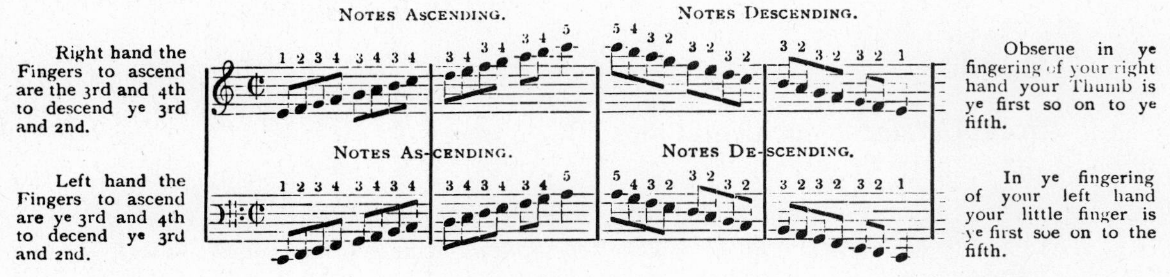

Right hand the Fingers to ascend are the 3rd and 4th to descend ye 3rd and 2nd.
Notes Ascending.
Notes Descending.
Observe in ye fingering of your right hand your Thumb is ye first so on to ye fifth.
Left hand the Fingers to ascend are ye 3rd and 4th to decend ye 3rd and 2nd.
Notes As-cending.
Notes De-scending.
In ye fingering of your left hand your little finger is ye first soe on to the fifth.

What is the tonal plan of this piece? How does it help to delineate the rondo structure?

Compare this work to Couperin's Rigaudon and his table of ornaments (II.6) and to Benjamin Britten's setting of this rondo, which he used as the basis for the variations in "The Young Person's Guide to the Orchestra" (V.21a).

31

II.3. Henry Purcell

Chaconne

from *King Arthur* (produced 1691)

This instrumental excerpt usually occurs in the score of the opera as "First Music." However, it may be performed as an instrumental interlude at various times throughout the production (one recording has it as a closing for the opera).

This composition illustrates Purcell's well known treatment of the *ground bass*, a repeated bass line that serves as the basis for variations above it. How long is the bass pattern here? How many times is it stated? Are there any changes which are applied to the pattern itself? How does Purcell construct an overall form from several statements of the pattern?

The bass pattern here is one of the stock seventeenth- and eighteenth-century patterns. It can be related to the Renaissance patterns given in I.28. A part of this pattern is used in Monteverdi's duet (II.1) and the same pattern is found in Handel's "Chaconne" (II.25) and at the beginning of Bach's *Goldberg Variations* (II.16).

25
30
35
40
45
50
55

II.4 and II.5 are two movements from Sonata V, Op. 2 by Arcangelo Corelli (1653-1713). Corelli was a famous Italian violin virtuoso and established many of the fundamentals of modern violin technique. He also standardized the important Baroque forms of the *concerto grosso*, the *sonata da chiesa*, and the *sonata da camera*. The *concerto grosso* is represented in an example by Handel (II.27 and II.28), who met Corelli and was probably influenced by him. The *sonata da chiesa* ("church sonata") occurs in Corelli's Op. 1 and Op. 3; the four-movement pattern of slow-fast-slow-fast was followed by such composers as Handel.

These two movements, from Corelli's Op.2, follow the *sonata da camera* ("chamber sonata") pattern: a suite with an introduction and three or four dances.

This sonata, in B♭ major, contains a prelude, an allemande, a sarabande, and a gavotte.

What are the rhythmic and metric characteristics of an allemande? a sarabande? a gavotte? (see also II.22 and 23).

What are the formal characteristics of these two movements? They are written for two violins and continuo; how do the three parts interact?

II.4. Arcangelo Corelli

Sonata V, Op. 2

Allemande (1685)

II.5. Arcangelo Corelli

Sonata V, Op.2

Sarabande (1685)

II.6. François Couperin

Pièces de clavecin, Premier livre, deuxième ordre, Rigaudon (1713)

Signs of Ornamentation

II.6 is an excerpt from an *ordre*, or suite, by François Couperin ("le Grand") (1668-1733). Couperin was a famous *claveciniste* at the court of the French kings (Louis XIV and XV) and was the organist at the royal chapel. This composition is from the first book of the *Pièces de clavecin*, published in 1713. Couperin included an *explication* of the signs for ornamentation that he used; this table is reproduced here (compare Purcell's table in II.2). In 1716 Couperin published *L'Art de toucher le clavecin* ("The Art of Keyboard Playing"), which influenced J.S. Bach and may be compared with C.P.E. Bach's treatise on keyboard playing (see III.1).

Couperin's idea of the suite was not the same as the conception of Corelli or J.S. Bach (see II.4-II.5 and II.21-II.23). This *ordre*, in D minor, is the second in the volume; it contains twenty-four separate movements, some of which carry dance names ("courante," "gavotte," "menuet"), some of which are named after people or ideas ("La Garnier," for instance, refers to the wife of one of the chapel organists).

Compare Couperin's treatment of the Rigaudon with Ravel's treatment in the suite *Le Tombeau de Couperin*, a twentieth-century composition which looks back to the suites of Couperin (see V.3 and V.4).

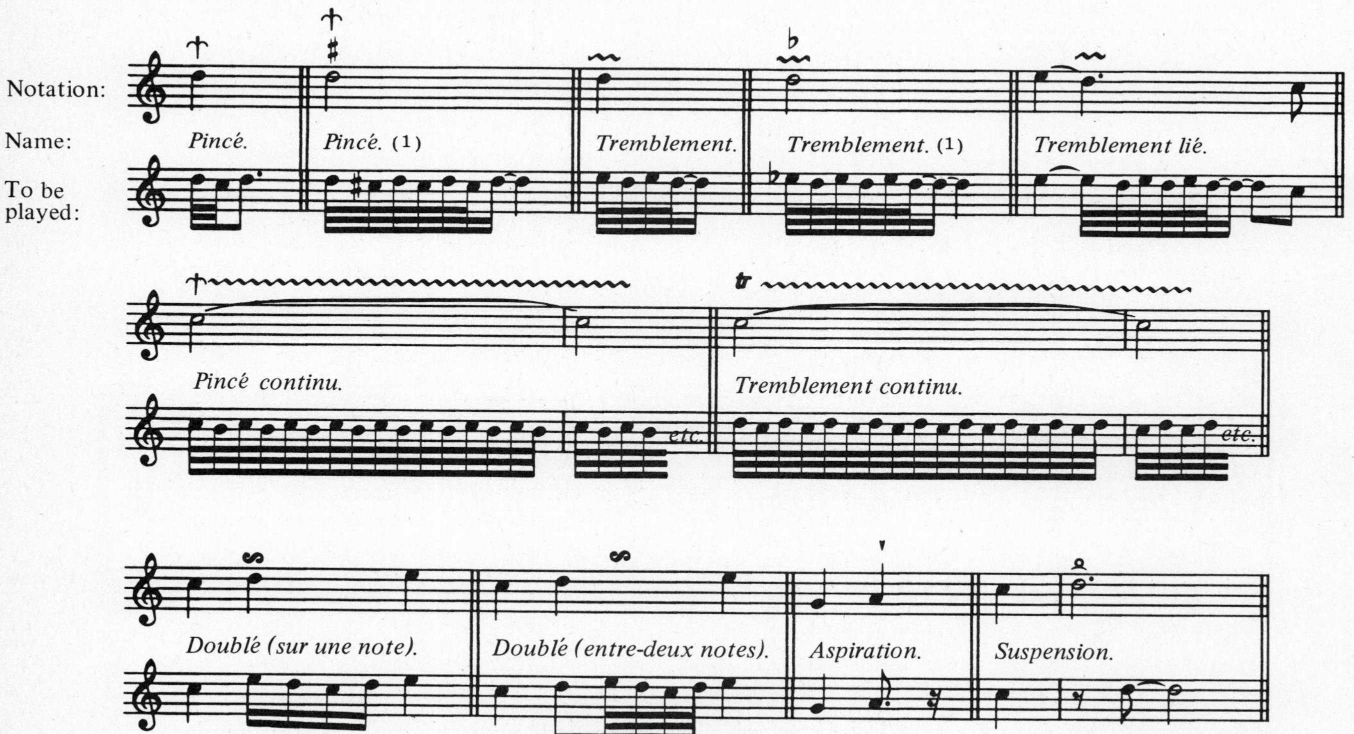

1. "It is the note values which determine the length of the "pincé" and the "treblement"—that is, how many or few strokes or vibrations to include." (Couperin)

Port de voix.
Accent.
Arpègement
en montant.
Arpègement
en descendant.
PREMIERE PARTIE.
5
10
15
20

SECONDE PARTIE.

II.7 is an excerpt from a composition by Johann Kaspar Ferdinand Fischer (c.1665-1746). It is a work for organ entitled *Ariadne musica*, a group of twenty preludes and fugues in nineteen different keys composed to lead organists through the maze of newer major and minor keys (the possibility of writing in so many different keys was made possible by experiments in different tuning systems). The composition given here is the Fugue in E major; it is preceded by a Prelude in E major. All of the compositions in the collection are very short and illustrate a brief working-out of ideas. Bach took the same subject as that in this example and wrote a much more complex fugue on it in the second volume of *The Well-Tempered Clavier* (see II.12).

II.7. J.K.F. Fischer

Fugue in E major

from *Ariadne musica* (published 1702)

Used by permission of European American Music Distributors Corporation, sole U.S. agent for B. Schott's Söhne. From *Liber Organi,* Vol 7, ed. Ernst Kaller ©. B. Schott's Söhne, Mainz 1935, © renewed 1963.

The music of Johann Sebastian Bach (1685-1750) is the best known of any composed during the Baroque era. His music was not well known to the general public, however, until it was revived in the nineteenth century through efforts of musicians like Mendelssohn (see IV.12 for a Mendelssohn composition influenced by Baroque traditions).

The compositions here include excerpts from the two-part inventions and the three-part sinfonias for keyboard (II.8-9), *The Well-Tempered Clavier* (II.10-15), the *Goldberg Variations* (II.16-20), and two of Bach's suites (II.21-23). Additional compositions by Bach are found in II.31-41, which are settings of chorale tunes. The excerpts in this section include four-part harmonizations as well as more extensive organ chorale settings and cantata movements. "S" numbers attached to the compositions refer to the catalogue by Wolfgang Schmieder (also referred to as *Bach-Werke-Verzeichnis* or B.W.V.)

Bach wrote a group of 15 two-part inventions and 15 three-part sinfonias, in 15 different keys, to develop facility in playing a keyboard instrument (a clavichord or a small harpsichord) and to illustrate compositional possibilities of contrapuntal development. It is a fascinating collection to analyze; each composition is built from a very small motive, which is treated to various permutations and contrapuntal combinations. The inventions and sinfonias appeared first in a teaching book (*Klavierbüchlein*) for Bach's son Wilhelm Friedemann (1720).

II.8. J.S. Bach

Two-part Invention in B♭ major No.14 S.785 (c.1720)

What is the basic material of this composition? Find several different ways this material is treated.

II.9. J.S. Bach

Three-part Sinfonia in F minor No.9 S.795 (c.1720)

This composition is a particularly good example of invertible counterpoint in three parts. In addition, it incorporates the standard chromatic descent from the tonic to the dominant. Compare it with the Goldberg Variation No. 15 (II.18.)

5
10
15
20

Examples II.10 through II.15 are a selection of preludes and fugues from *Das Wohltemperierte Klavier (The Well-Tempered Clavier)*, two volumes of preludes and fugues in every major and minor key. *Book I* is from 1722, *Book II* from 1744. This collection has long been regarded as a high point of contrapuntal writing, containing some of the most challenging pieces for keyboard performance. The preludes and fugues of Bach may be compared with J.K.F. Fischer's Fugue in E major from a similar, smaller collection (II.7) and with Hindemith's Interludium and Fugue from his collection of contrapuntal pieces (V.19 and 20).

II.10. J.S. Bach

Fugue XV in G major

from *The Well-Tempered Clavier, Book I* S.860 (1722)

Trace the subject throughout the fugue. What happens to it at measure 20?

II.11. J.S. Bach

Fugue XXI in B♭ major

from *The Well-Tempered Clavier, Book I* S.866 (1722)

This is a classic example of a three-voice fugue, which nearly fits the textbook descriptions. How does the answer in measure 5 relate to the subject?

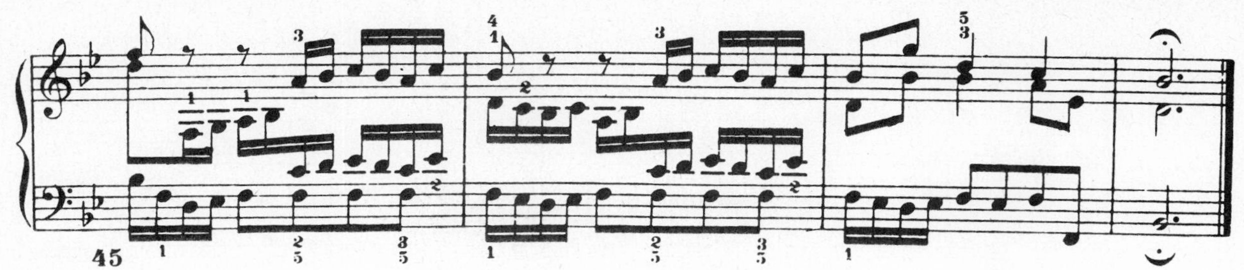

II.12. J.S. Bach

Fugue IX in E major

from *The Well-Tempered Clavier, Book II* S.878 (1744)

This fugue employs the same subject as Fischer's fugue given in II.7. What are the differences between the two fugues? What contrapuntal techniques does Bach use to work out the subject?

II.13. J.S. Bach

Fugue XIV in F♯ minor

from *The Well-Tempered Clavier, Book II* S.883 (1744)

This fugue is a particularly interesting example of a fugue with more than one subject. Study how the subjects are presented and combined throughout the fugue. The combination of contrapuntal ideas can be compared with Handel's use of subjects (II.28) and with Haydn's treatment in a string quartet (III.3).

II.14. J.S. Bach

Prelude XVI in G minor

from *The Well-Tempered Clavier, Book II* S.885 (1744)

The preludes in *The Well-Tempered Clavier* have distinct characters, and often are reminiscent of other pieces by Bach. This prelude is sometimes referred to as the opening of a "French Overture." What characteristics would support such a designation?

oder:

oder:

II.15. J.S. Bach

Fugue XVI in G minor

from *The Well-Tempered Clavier, Book II* S.885 (1744)

oder:
oder:
15
20
oder:
25

oder:
oder:
oder:

Examples II.16 through II.20 are part of one of the most extensive variation sets in the history of music. The theme of the set is a rather simple G major aria, contained in the *Klavierbüchlein* of Anna Magdalena Bach (Bach's second wife). The aria has characteristics of a sarabande and also includes a working-out of one of the traditional *chaconne* patterns. The aria returns at the end of the set.

Thirty variations on the aria appeared in the *Klavierübung*, Volume IV, in 1742. The variations were commissioned by the Russian Count Kayserling and were named after Bach's pupil, Johann Gottlieb Goldberg, who was the count's harpsichordist. The thirty variations follow a complex plan. Every third variation, beginning with Variation 3, is a canon, usually in two voices over a third accompanying voice. The interval of canon moves from the unison in Variation 3 to the ninth (in Variation 27). The other variations alternate regularly between invention-type variations (see Variation 8) and "character" variations, which include many different types of Baroque writing (fugue, French overture, embellished aria, etc.). The few variations here suggest the wide variety of writing found in the set. Amazingly, however, in all the variations Bach retains the phrase structure, the tonal plan, and the basic harmonic structure of the theme, creating what appear to be free contrapuntal voices within a strict formal framework.

II.16. J.S. Bach

Aria

from *Goldberg Variations*, S.988 (1742)

What is the phrase structure of the aria? What is the overall tonal plan? Compare measures 1-8 with the patterns used in Purcell's Chaconne (II.3) and in Handel's Chaconne (II.25). Does this eight-measure pattern recur in the aria?

II.17. J.S. Bach

Variation 8

Goldberg Variations, S.988 (1742)

How are the two lines presented in measures 1-4 used throughout the variation?

15
20
25
30

II.18. J.S. Bach

Variation 15

Goldberg Variations, S.988 (1742)

This is one of the canonic variations. Which voices are in canon? At what interval? What other contrapuntal procedure is being used? How does the harmonic structure of this variation compare with the plan of the theme?

II.19. J.S. Bach

Variation 18

Goldberg Variations, S.988 (1742)

This is another canonic variation. How is the canon operating here? What role does the suspension play in this variation?

II.20. J.S. Bach

Variation 30

Goldberg Variations, S.988 (1742)

This variation is the last in the set. It is labeled a "quodlibet" and is one of the "types" of variations Bach writes on the aria. This quodlibet is a combination of two popular songs; one is presented in the tenor voice in measure 1 and one in the alto voice of measures 2-3 (marked on the music). How are these lines treated in the rest of the variation?

II.21. J.S. Bach

Courante

from Suite for Violoncello No.1 in G major. S.1007.

This is one movement from one of Bach's suites for solo cello. The movements of the suite include Prelude, Allemande, Courante (given here), Sarabande, Menuet I and II, and Gigue. The standard arrangement of movements (Allemande, Courante, Sarabande, optional dances, and Gigue) can be traced back to various seventeenth-century composers, most notably J.J. Froberger (1616-67), who originated this suite arrangement. Compare this arrangement of movements to the Corelli examples (II.4 and II.5) and to Couperin's conception of the suite (II.6).

Although this Courante is notated as a single line, Bach suggests several parts operating polyphonically. How does he create separate "lines"? Can you trace them throughout the movement?

II.22 and II.23 are two movements from Bach's sixth "French" suite for keyboard. The suite contains an Allemande, Courante, Sarabande, Gavotte, Polonaise, Bourrée, Menuet, and Gigue. What is the form of each of the movements given here? How do they compare with the movements given in II.4-5, II.6, and II.21?

II.22. J.S. Bach

Sarabande

from French Suite in E major, No.6, S.817.

II.23. J.S Bach

Gavotte

from French Suite in E major, No.6, S.817.

Compositions II.24 through II.28 are by George Frideric Handel, (Georg Friedrich Händel), (1685-1759). Handel was an exact contemporary of Bach but, in contrast to Bach, traveled from his German birthplace throughout Europe, meeting Italian composers and finally making his home in England. Handel's compositions include works for keyboard and chamber ensembles, but also include large-scale orchestral works, oratorios, and operas. In contrast to Bach's very large output of sacred vocal works, written primarily for his various church positions, Handel produced many secular dramatic works which were produced in London. In addition to keyboard works, the excerpts here illustrate the opera and the concerto grosso, two important types of Baroque music.

II.24. G.F. Handel

Aria con Variazioni

from Suite in B♭ major (c.1733)

This keyboard suite includes a prelude, sonata, aria con variazioni, and a minuet. It thus represents a different sort of keyboard suite from Bach's "French" suites (see II.22-23) and from Couperin's *ordres* (see II.6). The aria of this movement is the theme that Brahms chose for one of his sets of variations (see IV.25). Only the first of Handel's five rather simple variations is given here. Compare it in harmony and texture to the way Brahms varied the same theme.

Aria con Variazioni

4

7

1. 2.

Var. 1

9

11

II.25. G.F. Handel

Chaconne in G major.

Variations 1, 4, 62.

Handel wrote several chaconnes in G major and G minor, all based on the standard ground or chaconne pattern. This pattern, which opens with a descent from tonic to dominant, can be traced back to Renaissance models (see I.28-30). This particular chaconne is exactly like the pattern used by Purcell (II.3) and is the opening of the Aria of the *Goldberg Variations* by Bach (II.16). In this composition, Handel wrote sixty-two variations on the chaconne pattern. These particular three represent several different textural presentations of the pattern. The process of writing many variations which do not necessarily group into a larger pattern is different from the compositional idea behind a long set such as Bach's *Goldberg Variations*.

Serse (Xerxes) is one of Handel's operas which was produced in London in 1738. The aria from that opera given here shows Handel's mastery of the style of Italian opera, and is in a typical form of Recitative-Da capo aria. The repeat of the first section was undoubtedly embellished by the performer.

How does this opera excerpt compare with Mozart's recitative and aria (III.6)? Try realizing the figured bass of the recitative.

The plot of *Serse* is a comedy involving four people: King Xerxes, Romilda, her sister Atalanta, and the King's brother Arsamene. In this aria, from Scene V of Act II, Romilda is tormented by the fact that Arsamene, whom she loves, seemingly has betrayed her and reciprocates the attention of Atalanta. However, the opera ends happily, with Romilda and Arsamene reunited.

(Accompanied recitative)
Shall I love him? It can't be true. Deceitful lover, false sister, you rejoice in my unhappiness! Wicked girl! Lying man! Shall I love him? It can't be true. But you who hear me in this delirious state, do you wish to know what it is that leads me to merciless fury?
(Aria)
It is that tyrant jealousy that afflicts my soul. Its poison has infected my heart and condemns me to bitter pain.

II.26. G.F. Handel

"L'amerò?....È gelosia"

from *Serse* (1738)

Andante
Violino I
Violino II
Viola
ROMILDA
Bassi
(Violoncello, Violone, Cembalo)
È ge-lo-si-a quel-la ti-ran-na, che tan-to af-fan-na l'a-ni-ma mi-a,
Was in mir auf-glüht, ste-tig sich meh-rend, mich ganz ver-zeh-rend, o wie zer-quält's mich,
l'a- -ni-ma mi- -a; è ge-lo-si-a
o wie zer-quält's mich! Was in mir aufglüht,
quel-la ti-ran-na, è ge-lo-si-a quel-la ti-ran-na, che tan-to af-fan-na, tan-to af-fan-na
ste-tig sich mehrend, was in mir aufglüht, ste-tig sich meh-rend, mich ganz ver-zeh-rend, ganz ver-zeh-rend,
l'a- -ni-ma mi-a, è ge-lo-sia quel-la ti-ran-na, che tan-to af-fan-na,
o wie zer-quält's mich! Was in mir auf-glüht, ste-tig sich mehrend, mich ganz ver-zeh-rend,

a tempo
Adagio
a tempo
tan - to af-fan-na l'a - - ni-ma mi - a, l'a - ni-ma mi - a.
ganz ver-zeh-rend, o wie zer - quält's mich, das Gift der Ei - fersucht.
1.
2.
Del
Mit
Fine
(parte)
(ab)
suo ve-le - no m'a-sper - se il se - no, e mi con-dan-na a pe-na ri - a, a
tau - send Schmerzen mir raubt's die Sin-ne, mir brennt's im Herzen, das Gift der Ei-fer-sucht, mir brennt's
a tempo
Adagio
a tempo
pe-na ri - a, e mi con-dan-na a pe-na ri - a.
im Herzen, mir brennt's im Her-zen, das Gift der Ei - fer-sucht!
Da Capo

II.27 and II.28 are two movements from one of Handel's concerti grossi. This one, Op.6 No.2 in F major, is one of a group of twelve in Op.6, dating from 1739-40. It is in four movements (Andante larghetto, Allegro, Largo, and Allegro, ma non troppo), following the model of the Italian *sonata da chiesa* (see the discussion before II.4). Vivaldi and Bach, in their concerti grossi written somewhat earlier than Handel's, follow a three-movement pattern (fast-slow-fast).

The two movements given here illustrate the timbral and dynamic contrasts inherent in the concerto grosso, characterized by the concertino (small group of solo instruments) and the ripieni (the full ensemble). This score is taken from a 1906 edition. A more recent version presents a concertino of two oboes, two violins, and continuo (violoncello and cembalo I), contrasted with a full ensemble which adds two other violin parts, viola, and bassi (violoncello, violone, bassoon, and cembalo II).

II.27. G.F. Handel

Largo

from Concerto Grosso Op. 6 No.2 in F major. (1739-40)

Adagio.
Larghetto andante, e piano.
Adagio.

II.28. G.F. Handel

Allegro, ma non troppo

from Concerto Grosso Op.6 No.2 in F major. (1739-40)

One melodic idea is presented in measures 1-4. A second idea occurs in measures 28-31. Trace what happens to these two ideas throughout the movement. Compare Handel's treatment of more than one melodic idea with Bach's treatment (II.13) and with Haydn's treatment (III.3).

25
30
Solo.
40
45
35
Tutti.
50
Solo.

Tutti.
Tutti.
Solo.
Solo.
Solo.
Solo.
Solo.
Solo.
Tutti.
Tutti.
Tutti.
Tutti.

Tutti.
Solo.
Adagio.

Domenico Scarlatti (1685-1757) is another important contemporary of Bach and Handel. (All three composers were born in the same year.) Scarlatti met Handel in Italy and, like Handel, had at least one opera premiered in London. However, Scarlatti spent most of his life in Spain, in the royal court, and is best known for his harpsichord "essercizi," or sonatas, which he composed there. The sonatas, published in several volumes from 1738 to 1757, are one-movement compositions which explore various possibilities of harpsichord writing and establish many of the techniques of modern piano playing. They are also interesting from the point of view of form, as many of them suggest the classical sonata-allegro form.

There are at least 555 of these sonatas; they have been the object of much study and have been catalogued by Alessandro Longo and more recently by Ralph Kirkpatrick. L. and K. numbers are both given for this example. Kirkpatrick's book, *Domenico Scarlatti* (Princeton Univerity Press, 1953; reprint New York 1968), is the source of much information about these works.

II.29. Domenico Scarlatti

Sonata K.412 (L.182) in G major.

Study the large-scale form and tonal movement in this sonata. How is it similar to the plan of C.P.E. Bach's sonata movement (III.1)? to Mozart's sonata in D major (III.8)?

15
20
25
tr
30
tr
36

42
47
52
57
62
67

73
tr
[⩫]
79
tr
84
tr
[⩫]
90
[⩫]
96
101
tr

II.30 through II.41 illustrate a number of Baroque settings of the German Protestant chorale tune. This collection of chorale settings gives some idea of the variety of harmonizations and textures possible, merely suggesting, however, the wide range of possibilities for cantus firmus compositions. Some tunes are given in several different settings, some in only one harmonization. The sources of the chorale tune, the text of the hymn, the translation, and the harmonization or setting of the tune are listed for most of the compositions. The musical sources for some of these chorale tunes can be traced back to Gregorian chant; the last two tunes given here ("Nun komm, der Heiden Heiland" and "Christ lag in Todesbaden") are both similar to existing chants.

The differences in harmonic choice and voice leading between settings of the same tune should be closely studied. In some cases, various harmonizations of the same tune by J.S. Bach himself may be compared. Also included in these examples are a few of the sixty-nine chorale melodies that Bach wrote out with only figured bass underneath. In one case Bach's own realization is given; the student should try to realize the other examples, following the figures indicated. The last two chorale tunes are examples of Bach's treatment of a cantus firmus in more complicated textures (see II.40b and II.41c-d).

Although each chorale melody has many stanzas of text, only one or two stanzas of text are given. An attempt has been made to associate the specific stanza of text with a particular harmonization, since word painting or religious symbolism in a certain stanza is often reflected in the musical treatment. The clearest examples are found in II.41, the excerpts from Bach's Cantata No.4.

J.S. Bach's son, Carl Philipp Emanuel (see III.1), published a collection of 371 chorale harmonizations by his father in a series of four volumes (1784-1787). The number in this collection of "371" is given for each of the Bach chorale harmonizations included here. Several publications have revised this chorale collection and added various sorts of commentary, while retaining the traditional numbering (a mistake in numbering was changed in 1831, so that the final collection numbers 371, not 370). In addition to the number in the "371," the source of the chorale from Bach's compositional output is given, if known. "No source" indicates that the particular place of the chorale in Bach's larger works is not known.[1]

The sixty-nine melodies with figured bass were added to the collection of 371 chorales in 1832. These melodies come from a publication of 1736; some of the figured basses may not be by Bach himself, but in the case of at least two of the examples given here we have Bach's own realizations of the figured bass.

II.30, II.31, and II.32 compare a Baroque harmonization of a tune with a standard hymnbook version. The three versions are taken from *The Chorale Book for England*, edited by William Sterndale Bennett and Otto Goldschmidt (London: Longman, Green, et al., 1863-1865). This book is a compilation of earlier harmonizations of the chorales and contains useful commentary on the sources of the tunes and the harmonizations. It is one of the publications which includes the translations of Catherine Winkworth, now standard texts for many hymns.

[1]A standard collection of the "371" chorales is edited by Albert Riemenschneider (New York: G. Schirmer, 1941). The Riemenschneider edition also includes the sixty-nine figured melodies and has useful commentary.

II.30a.

"Vom Himmel hoch" ("From Heaven above")

Melody: Martin Luther, 1539. Text: Martin Luther, 1535. Translation: Catherine Winkworth, 1863. Harmonization: Bennett/Goldschmidt *Chorale Book.*

II.30b.

"Vom Himmel hoch" ("From Heaven above").

Harmonization by Samuel Scheidt (1587-1654), from *Das Görlitzer Tabulaturbuch* (1650).

Bach includes several settings of this tune in the *Christmas Oratorio* (see 371, #46, 344); he also wrote a set of five canonic variations on the tune for organ.

A.
tid - ings of great joy I bring, Where -
lit - tle child, of low - ly birth, Shall
gu - ten Mär bring ich so viel, da-
B.
10
A.
of I now will say and sing:
be the joy of all your earth.
10
von ich singn und sa - gen will.
B.

II.31a.

"Wachet auf!" ("Wake, awake").

Melody: Philipp Nicolai, 1599. Text: Philipp Nicolai, 1599. Translation: Catherine Winkworth, 1863. Harmonization: Bennett/Goldschmidt *Chorale Book.*

II.31b.

"Wachet auf!" ("Wake, awake").

Harmonization by J.S. Bach; 371 #179.

This chorale closes Cantata No.140 ("Wachet auf, ruft uns die Stimme") with the third stanza of the hymn given here ("Gloria sei dir").

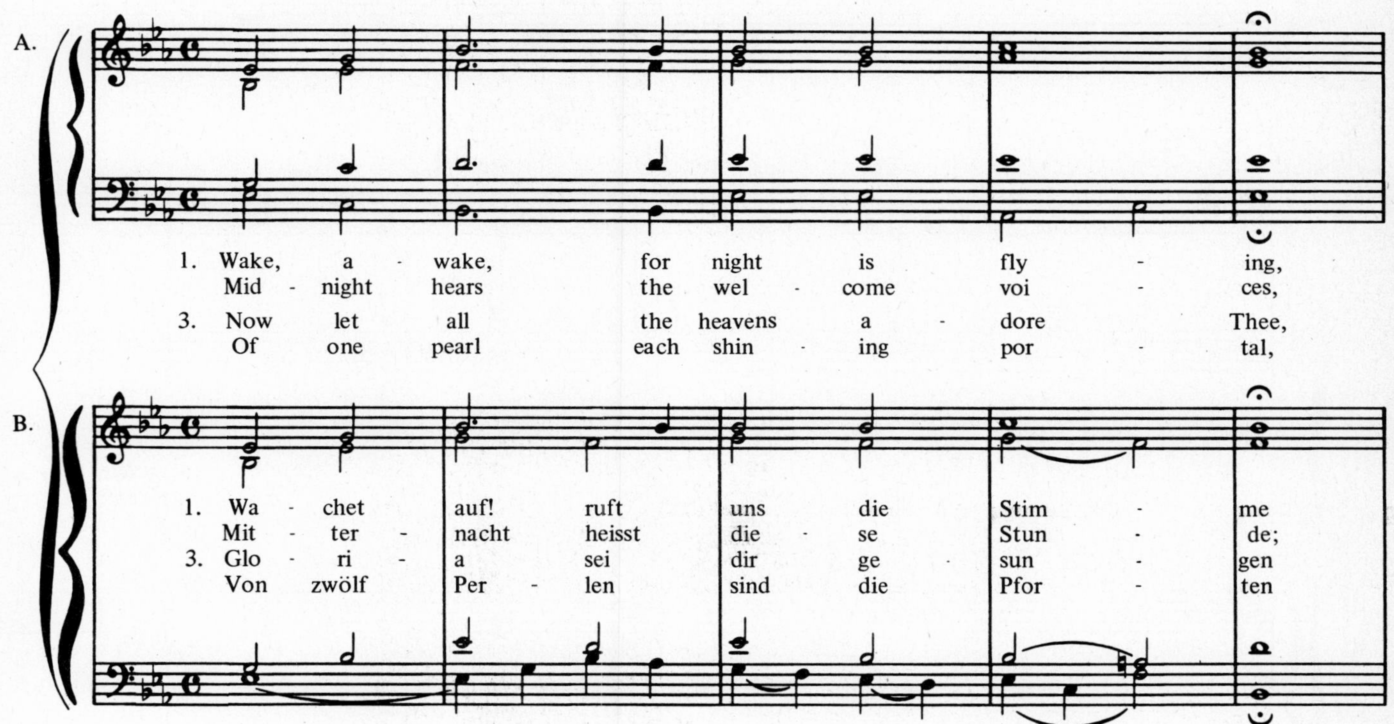

A.
1. Wake, a - wake, for night is fly - ing,
Mid - night hears the wel - come voi - ces,
3. Now let all the heavens a - dore Thee,
Of one pearl each shin - ing por - tal,
B.
1. Wa - chet auf! ruft uns die Stim - me
Mit - ter - nacht heisst die - se Stun - de;
3. Glo - ri - a sei dir ge - sun - gen
Von zwölf Per - len sind die Pfor - ten

6
A.
The watch - men on the heights are cry - ing;
And at the thrill - ing cry re - joi - ces:
And men and an - gels sing be - fore Thee,
Where we are with the choir im - mor - tal
6
B.
der Wäch - ter sehr hoch auf der Zin - ne:
sie ru - fen uns mit hel - lem Mun - de:
mit Men - schen und eng - li - schen Zun - gen,
an dei - ner Stadt: wir sind Con - sor - ten
12
A.
A - wake, Je - ru - sa - lem at last!
Come forth, ye vir - gins, night is past!
With harp and cym - bal's clear - est tone;
Of an - gels round Thy daz - zling throne;
12
B.
wach auf, du Stadt Je - ru - sa - lem!
wo seid ihr klu - gen Jung - frau - en?
mit Har - fen und mit Cym - beln schon.
der En - gel hoch um dei - nen Thron.

17
A.
The Bride - groom comes, a - wake,
Nor eye hath seen, nor ear
17
B.
Wohl auf! der Bräut - gam kommt.
Kein Aug' hat je ge - spürt,
21
A.
Your lamps with glad - ness take;
hath yet at - tain'd to hear
21
B.
steht auf! die Lam - pen nehmt.
kein Ohr hat je ge - hört

25
A.
Hal - le - lu - jah! And
What there is ours, But
25
B.
Al - le - lu - ja! macht
sol - che Freu - de. Dess
29
A.
for His mar - riage feast pre - pare, For
we re - joice, and sing to Thee Our
29
B.
euch be - reit zu der Hoch - zeit, ihr
sind wir froh, i - o! i - o! e -

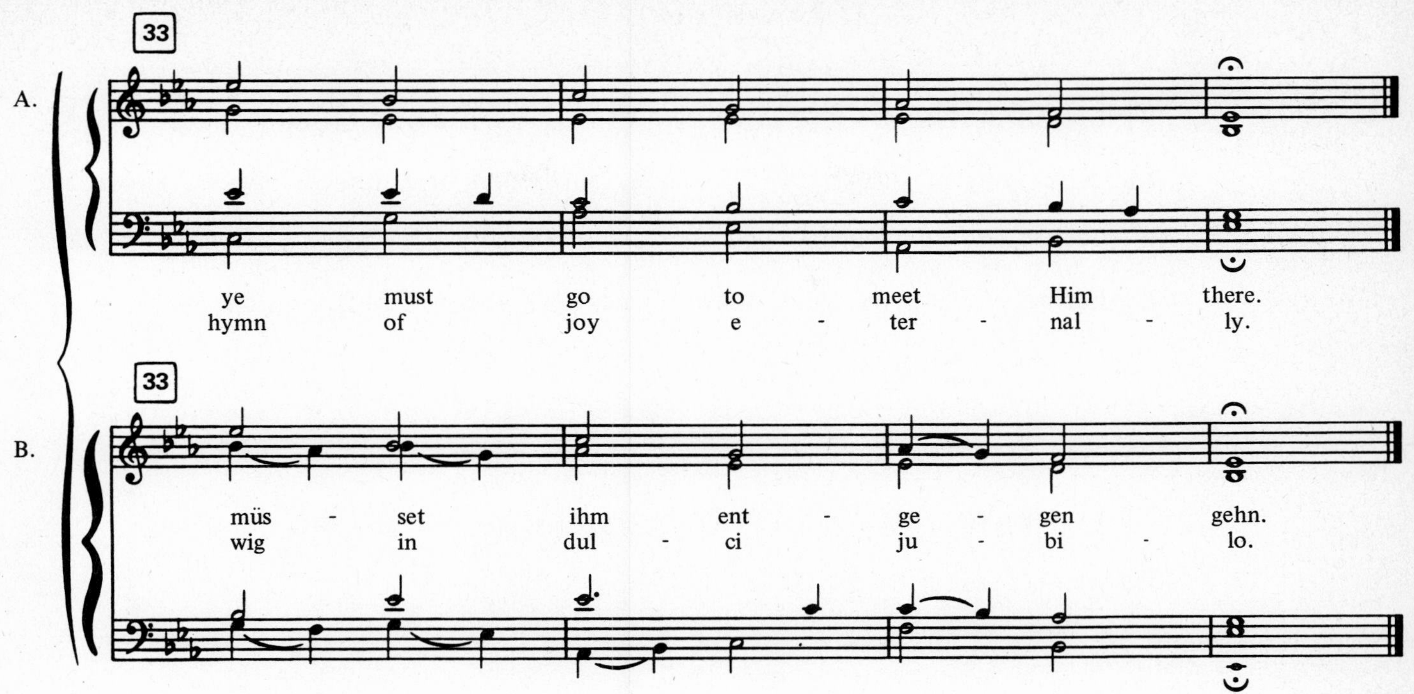
33
A.
ye must go to meet Him there.
hymn of joy e - ter - nal - ly.
33
B.
müs - set ihm ent - ge - gen gehn.
wig in dul - ci ju - bi - lo.

II.32a.

"Nun danket alle Gott" ("Now thank we all our God").

Melody: Johann Crüger (1598-1662), published in Johann Crüger's *Geistliche Kirchenmelodien* (Berlin, 1649). Text: Martin Rinkart, 1636. Translation: Catherine Winkworth, 1863. Harmonization: Bennett/Goldschmidt *Chorale Book*.

II.32b.

"Nun danket alle Gott" ("Now thank we all our God").

Harmonization: J.S. Bach, 371 #32. No source.

5
A
Who from our mo - ther's arms Hath bless'd us on our way With
5
B
der uns von Mut - ter - leib und Kin - des - bei - nen an un -
9
A
count - less gifts of love, And still is ours to - day.
9
B
zäh - lig viel zu gut und noch jetz - und ge - than.

II.33 compares two settings of the same tune, one by Pachelbel and one by Bach.

II.33a.

"Jesu, meine Freude" ("Jesu, priceless treasure")

Melody: Johann Crüger, 1653. Text: Johann Franck, 1653. Translation: Catherine Winkworth. Harmonization: Johann Pachelbel (1653-1706).

Jesu, meine Freude,
Meines Herzens Weide,
Jesu, meine Zier,
Ach, wie lang, ach lange
Ist dem Herzen bange
Und verlangt nach dir!
Gottes Lamm, mein Bräutigam,
Ausser dir soll mir auf Erden
Nichts sonst liebers werden.

Jesu, priceless treasure,
Source of purest pleasure,
Truest friend to me,
Ah, how long I've panted,
And my heart hath fainted,
Thirsting, Lord, for Thee!
Thine I am, O spotless Lamb,
I will suffer naught to hide Thee;
Naught I ask beside Thee.

II.33b.

"Jesu, meine Freude" ("Jesu, priceless treasure")

Harmonization by J.S. Bach in Motet No.3 ("Jesu, meine Freude").

Translation: Catherine Winkworth, 1869.

This harmonization opens the motet with verse 1 of the text and closes it with verse 6 of the text (371, #263). Bach has other harmonizations of this chorale in the "371."

1. Je-su, price-less treas-ure, Source of pur-est pleas-ure,
Long my heart hath pant-ed 'Till it well-nigh faint-ed,

6. Hence all thoughts of sad-ness! For the Lord of gladness,
Those who love the Father, Though the storms many gather,

Tru-est Friend to me! Thine I am, O spotless Lamb!
Thirsting after Thee.

Jesus, enters in. Yea, whate'er I here must bear,
Still have peace within;

10
au - sser dir soll mir auf Er - - den nichts sonst Lie-bers wer - - den.
den-noch bleibst du auch im Lei - - de, Je - su, mei-ne Freu - - de.

I will suffer nought to hide Thee, Ask for nought beside Thee.
Thou art still my purest pleasure, Jesu, price-less treas-ure!

II.34-II.36 are three harmonizations from the "371" collection.

II.34.

"Wie schön leuchtet der Morgenstern" ("How lovely shines the morning star!")

Melody: P. Nicolai, 1599? Text: Philipp Nicolai, 1599. Translation: anonymous (Moravian hymn book, 1890). Harmonization: J.S. Bach, 371 #278. No source.

Wie schön leuchtet der Morgen-stern voll Gnad' und Wahrheit von dem Herrn, die
du Sohn Da-vids aus Jakobs Stamm, mein Kö - nig und mein Bräuti - gam, hast

How love-ly shines the morning star! The nations see and hail a-far Thee
Thou David's Son of Jacob's race, My bridegroom and my king of grace, For

5
sü - sse Wur-zel Jes - se;
mir mein Herz be - ses - sen.
Lieb-lich, freundlich, schön und herrlich,

light in Ju-dah shining; Lowly, holy, great and glorious,
Thee my heart is pining!

Thou victorious, Prince of graces, Fill-ing all the heav'nly places.

II.35.

"Ach, bleib bei uns, Herr Jesu Christ." ("Lord Jesus Christ, with us abide").

Melody: anonymous, 1589. Hymn text: Nikolaus Selnecker, 1611. Translation: Benjamin Hall Kennedy, 1863. Harmonization: J.S. Bach, 371 #177. No source.

Lord Jesus Christ, with us a-bide, For now, behold, 'tis e-ven-

tide: And bring, to cheer us through the night, Thy Word, our true and only light.

II.36.

"In dulci jubilo"

Melody: anonymous, 1535. Hymn text: anonymous, 14th or 15th century. Translation: Catherine Winkworth, 1869? Harmonization: J.S. Bach, 371, #143. No source.

In dul-ci ju-bi-lo sin-get und seid froh,
In dul-ci ju-bi-lo Sing and shout be-low,
un-sers Her-zens Won-ne liegt in prae-se-pi-o
He for whom we're pin-ing Lies in prae-se-pi-o
leuch-tet als die Son-ne ma-tris in pre-mi-o
Like the sun is shin-ing Ma-tris in pre-mi-o.
Al-pha es et O, Al-pha es et O.
Al-pha es et O, Al-pha es et O.

II.37-II.39 are three melodies with figured bass from the collection of sixty-nine published in Schemelli's *Gesangbuch* of 1736. They also appear (in alphabetical order) in a collection entitled *Geistliche Lieder und Arien.* II.37 and II.38 also appear in the "371" collection.

II.37a.

"Sei gegrüsset" ("Hear my pleading")

Melody: Gottfried Vopelius, 1682. Figured bass: J.S. Bach.

Compare this unrealized version with II.37b, Bach's own realization of the figures. How does Bach interpret the figures "9 8"? Compare measure 12 of the realization to the figured version; what are the differences?

II.37b.

"Sei gegrüsset, Jesu gütig" ("Hear my pleading, Jesu, Treasure")

Melody: Gottfried Vopelius, 1682. Text: Christian Keimann, 1663. Translation: Robert W. Ottman, 1963. Harmonization: J.S. Bach, 371 #172. No source.

Sei ge-grü - sset, Je - su gü-tig, ü - ber al - les Mass sanftmü -

Hear my pleading, Je-su, Treasure, Gentle, kind, beyond all meas-

5
thig! Ach wie bist du so zer - schmissen, und dein gan-zer Leib zer - ris - sen!

ure, Ah, how wert Thou made to languish, As Thy body hung in an-guish,

10
Lass mich dei - ne Lieb' er - er - ben und da - rin - nen se - lig ster - ben!

May I all Thy love in-her-it And in death Thy bless-ing merit.

II.38.

"So gibst du nun, mein Jesu, gute Nacht" ("O must Thou, my Jesus, say good night")

Melody: anonymous, 1694. Figured bass: J.S. Bach.

Compare your realization with Bach's version in the "371," # 206.

II.39.

"O Jesulein süss" ("O sweet Child Jesus")

Figured bass: J.S. Bach.

This chorale does not appear in the "371" collection.

II.40 a.

"Nun komm, der Heiden Heiland." ("Now come, Thy Saviour of the Race")

Melody: anonymous? 1524. Text: Martin Luther, 1524. (Enchiridion, Erfurt, 1524).

Harmonization: Samuel Scheidt (1587-1654) from *Das Görlitzer Tabulaturbuch* (1650).

Compare Scheidt's harmonization of the tune with the harmonization implied by Bach's setting in II.40b.

The tune, "Nun komm der Heiden Heiland," is related to the fourth century hymn, "Veni redemptor gentium."

Bach's harmonization of the tune can also be studied in the "371" collection, Nos.28 and 170 (from Bach's cantatas No.36 and 62).

Gott solch Ge - burt ihm be - stellt.
That the Lord had such a birth.

II.40b.

"Nun komm, der Heiden Heiland"

J.S. Bach, organ chorale prelude S.659

This composition is one of three based on the same chorale tune from a collection of organ chorales ("Eighteen Chorales of various sorts"). In what voice or voices does the chorale tune appear? What has happened to the tune? Trace the tune carefully through the work; do the voices which do not have the cantus have any relationship to the melody?

Compare Bach's compositional process in this work to Dunstable's treatment of a chant melody (I.14) and to Josquin's treatment (I.18).

5
10

15
20
25

The next group of examples presents several versions of a tune known as "Christ ist erstanden" ("Christ has arisen") and, in a slightly different form, as "Christ lag in Todesbanden" ("Christ lay in the bonds of death"). The tunes are similar, particularly at the beginning, to the Gregorian sequence "Victimae paschali laudes" (see I.2); in fact, Luther's text follows closely the Latin verses of the sequence.

II.41 a.

"Christ ist erstanden."

II.41 b.

"Christ lag in Todesbanden."

(Luther, 1524.)

First verse of Luther's text given.

Christ lag in To - des - ban - den, für un - ser Sünd ge - ge - ben,
Der ist wi - der er - stan - den, und hat uns bracht das Le - ben,
Des wir sol - len frö - lich sein, Gott lo - ben und dank - bar sein,

und sing - en Ha - le - lu - ia, Ha - le - lu - ia.

One of the most complex settings of "Christ lag in Todesbaden" is J.S. Bach's *Cantata No.4*. This cantata is a series of variations on the tune, much in the manner of seventeenth-century compositions. Bach's cantata consists of an opening instrumental Sinfonia, followed by seven verses, each using the cantus firmus and each setting one verse of Luther's seven-stanza text. All of these settings are very interesting; the whole cantata should be studied in detail. Furthermore, the form of the entire work is somewhat symmetrical, in that verses 1, 4, and 7 are for chorus, verses 2 and 6 are duets, and verses 3 and 5, both given here, are solos.

The German and English texts for verses 1, 3, 5 and 7 are given below. The English translation is by Gerhard Herz, who has edited a useful score with much helpful commentary on the cantata (Norton Critical Scores, New York, 1967).

Verse I.

Christ lag in Todesbanden
Für unsre Sund gegeben,
Er ist wieder erstanden
Und hat uns bracht das Leben;
Des wir sollen fröhlich sein,
Gott loben und ihm dankbar sein
Und singen Hallelujah,
Hallelujah!

Christ lay in bonds of death
sacrificed for our sins,
He is again arisen
and has brought life to us;
therefore we shall be joyful,
praise God and be thankful to him
and sing hallelujah,
hallelujah!

Verse III.

Jesus Christus, Gottes Sohn,
An unser Statt ist kommen
Und die Sünde wegettan,
Damit den Tod genommen
All sein Recht und sein Gewalt,
Da bleibet nichts denn Tods Gestalt,
Den Stach'l hat er verloren.
Hallelujah!

Jesus Christ, Son of God,
has come in our stead
and has done away with sin,
thereby from death has taken
all its rights and its power,
hence nothing remains but death's image,
death has lost its sting.
Hallelujah!

Verse V.

Hier ist das rechte Osterlamm,
Davon Gott hat geboten,
Das ist hoch an des Kreuzes Stamm
In heisser Lieb gebraten,
Das Blut zeichnet unsre Tür,
Das hält der Glaub dem Tode für,
Der Würger kann uns nicht mehr schaden.
Hallelujah!

Here is the true Easter Lamb,
that God has offered us,
which high on the tree of the cross
is roasted in burning love;
its blood marks our door,
Faith holds this up to death,
the strangler can no longer harm us.
Hallelujah!

Verse VII.

Wir essen und leben wohl
In rechten Osterfladen,
Der alte Sauerteig nicht soll
Sein bei dem Wort der Gnaden,
Christus will die Koste sein
Und speisen die Seel allein,
Der Glaub will keins andern leben.
Hallelujah!

We eat and live well
on the true Passover bread,
the old leaven shall not exist
beside the word of grace;
Christ will be the food
and feed the soul alone,
faith will live on no other.
Hallelujah!

II.41c. J.S. Bach

"Christ lag in Todesbanden"

Cantata No.4, Verse 3

Where is the chorale tune? What is the relationship of the other voices? How does the harmonization implied in this verse compare with the four-part harmonization in Verse 7? One example of Bach's powerful musical treatment of certain words occurs in this verse at "Tod's Gestalt" ("Death's image"). What musical means does Bach use to set off this text?

20
da - mit dem Tod ge - nom - - men
all' sein Recht und sein' Ge - walt,
25
Adagio.
Allegro.
forte
da blei - bet nichts denn Tod's - - - - ge - stalt,
f
30
tr
den Stach'l hat er ver - - lo - - ren.
35
Hal - le - lu - jah, hal - le - lu - jah, hal - le - lu - jah, hal - le - lu - jah, hal - - - -

II.41d. J.S. Bach

"Christ lag in Todesbanden,"

Cantata No. 4, Verse 5.

In which voice or voices does the tune appear in this verse? Study carefully the orchestra parts before answering! The setting of words is again a dramatic feature of this verse. For instance, what musical ideas are coupled with "Kreuzes" ("cross," measures 27-29), with "Tode" ("death," measures 65-67), and with "Würger" ("strangler," measures 71-74)?

10
15
— O_ster_lamm, da_von Gott hat___ ge_bo_ten, da_von Gott hat_ ge_bo_ -
20
25
ten, das ist hoch an des Kreu_zes Stamm, hoch an___ des___ Kreu_
30
35
_ _zes, des Kreuzes Stamm in hei_sser Lieb'___ ge_bra_ten, in hei_sser Lieb' ge_bra_ _

40
45
ten, das Blut zeich_net, das Blut zeich_net, zeich - - net unser Thür,
50
55
das Blut zeich - - net unser Thür, das hält der Glaub'
60
65
dem To - - de für, das hält der Glaub' dem To - - - - - -
tasto

70
tr
- de für, der Wür - - - - - - - - - - - - - - - ger
piano
75
80
kann uns nicht, nicht, nicht, nicht mehr scha - den. Halle-lujah,
85
halle-lujah, hal le-lujah, halle-lu jah, halle - lujah, halle - lujah, halle - lujah, halle -

90
tr
95
- - lujah, hal - le-, hallelu - jah, halle - lujah, hal - lelu - jah!

II.41e. J.S. Bach

"Christ lag in Todesbanden,"

Cantata No. 4, Verse 7.

This straightforward, four-voice harmonization closes the cantata. What tonal implications are there in the tune as Bach is using it that makes the overall key structure somewhat ambiguous? How does Bach harmonize the end of each phrase?

III

1760-1830

This group of compositions includes a selection of the most important forms and genres of the Classical and early Romantic period. The changes in the first movement sonata form can be traced from C.P.E. Bach's concise example through Beethoven's much expanded Op. 57 ("Appassionata") piano sonata and Op. 130 string quartet. Formal models such as the minuet and trio, theme and variations, and rondo are represented by straightforward Mozart and Haydn examples and by more complex examples, such as Beethoven's personal and highly interesting compositions. Schubert is included in this time period, since he was a contemporary of Beethoven. There is no attempt to settle the argument of when early Romantic style begins; rather the emphasis is on the major composers (Mozart, Haydn, Beethoven, Schubert) within a given time period.

In the study of these compositions a grasp of basic materials (melodic lines, rhythmic patterns, harmonic and tonal structure, etc.) should be combined with an understanding of the larger architectural design. The study guide should be consulted for a grouping of compositions by formal design and for a suggested order of study. Starting from ideas of balance and formal logic, each composer developed a different realization of what we now call a "formal type." Remember that the sonata-allegro form was codified by theorists into a textbook model only in the nineteenth century and that theorists of the late eighteenth century spoke of a flexible design that emphasized key contrast and reconciliation but not necessarily thematic contrast. Enough examples are provided here to see in a certain formal type both similarities and the more important differences—the compositional variances from the pattern. The example of the concerto first-movement form is closest to the standard textbook model. It should be compared with other of Mozart's concerto movements, which deviate considerably from the model.

There has been an attempt to represent here as many different genres as possible. The period produced many important examples of the keyboard sonata, the string quartet, and the symphony. Other types of writing are represented by a few examples of the concerto, the short piano piece, and the art song. Unfortunately, space limitations restrict an adequate representation of opera, but the excerpt from Mozart's *Don Giovanni* provides a comparison with earlier and later opera excerpts in the anthology.

This period of prolific composition deserves serious study because of the perfection and ingenious variety of musical structure achieved by a group of composers acknowledged as one of the most important in the history of music.

A selection of general books and anthologies that cover this period is given below. There are also, of course, many books on individual composers and on specific types of compositions.

JANDER, OWEN, *Music of the Classical Era.* New York: Thomas Y. Crowell, 1967. Twenty examples for analysis plus text.

KIRBY, F.E., *Music in the Classic Period.* New York: Schirmer, 1979. Anthology with commentary.

PAULY, REINHARD G., *Music in the Classic Period.* Englewood Cliffs: Prentice-Hall, 1973.

ROSEN, CHARLES, *The Classical Style* (Haydn, Mozart, Beethoven). New York: W.W. Norton & Co. Inc., 1971. A stimulating discussion of classical language and form as expressed in the works of the three most famous composers.

ROSEN, CHARLES, *Sonata Forms*. New York: W.W. Norton and Co. Inc., 1980. The patterns of the sonata form in the eighteenth century and later changes in the form. (Examples range from Scarlatti to Bartók.)

Carl Philipp Emanuel Bach (1714-1788) was the third son of Johann Sebastian Bach. He was a chamber musician for Frederick the Great in Berlin and later was a music director in a church in Hamburg. He was a well-known keyboard performer of his day, and his "Essay on the True Art of Playing Keyboard Instruments" (1753-62) is a useful source of performance practices.[1] This sonata movement is from the third of six collections of sonatas, free fantasias, and rondos "für Kenner und Liebhaber" ("for connoisseurs and amateurs"). It is the third sonata in the collection; only the first movement is given here. A second movement (Andante in F major) is followed by the last movement in F minor (Andantino grazioso). The key scheme, melodic ideas, and rhythmic materials of this movement should be compared with those of Scarlatti's sonata movement (II.29), Mozart's sonata movement (III.8), and at least one of Beethoven's sonata movements (III.11, III.16, or III.17). The ascending arpeggiated opening of this movement is a favorite melodic idea of the time; this movement can be directly compared with the first movement of Beethoven's sonata in F minor, Op. 2 No.1.

III.1. C.P.E. Bach

Sonata III in F minor (1781)

first movement, Allegro assai

[1]"A Contribution to the Study of Ornamentation" by Heinrich Schenker, tr. by Hedi Siegel in *The Music Forum* Volume IV (1976: Columbia University Press) is an interesting document on ornamentation, on form and on C.P.E. Bach's keyboard style. Schenker intended his work as an introduction to his edition of C.P.E. Bach's keyboard works.

15
p
20
ff
25
30
pp
f
1.
2.
35
40

p
ff
p
mf
f
p
f

70
75
80
85
90
1.
2.
p
ff
pp
f

III.2 through III.5 are compositions by Franz Joseph Haydn (1732-1809). Haydn spent much of his life as Kapellmeister for Prince Esterhazy; the two string quartet movements given here date from these years. III.2 is a movement from an early piano sonata or divertimento; III.5 is a movement from one of Haydn's late symphonies, performed during his second visit to London at the end of the eighteenth century.

III.2. F.J. Haydn

Menuet and Trio

from Divertimento (Partita) in C major, Hoboken XVI, 1 (c.1760)

This movement, the last, is preceded by an Allegro and an Andante movement.

III.3 is the fourth movement (Finale) from a Haydn string quartet. This movement is entitled "Fuga a due Soggetti" ("Fugue with two subjects") and is one of a group of quartets that have contrapuntal last movements. The opening second violin line is one of the stock seventeenth- and eighteenth-century patterns. For two other eighteenth-century uses, see Handel's "And with His stripes we are healed" from *The Messiah* and Mozart's Kyrie, from the *Requiem*.

What happens to the basic material at measure 92? at measure 112? at measure 145? Compare the use of two subjects in this movement to the use of multiple melodic ideas in II.13 and II.28.

III.3. F.J. Haydn

String Quartet in F minor, Op. 20 No. 5

fourth movement (Finale) (1772)

55
60
65
70
75
80
85
90
al rovescio
95
100
105
110
115
m.v.

120
125
130
135
140
145
ff in Canone
150
155
160
165
170
175
180

III.4 is the fourth movement (Finale) of a string quartet, illustrating a much different idea of closure than the movement given in III.3. What melodic and rhythmic ideas unify the movement? What factors create sectional contrast and delineation?

III.4. F.J. Haydn

String Quartet in G major, Op. 54 No. 1

fourth movement (Finale) (1788)

50
60
dimin.
dimin.
dimin.
dimin.
70
80
90

100
110
cresc.
cresc.
cresc.
cresc.
120
130
140

150
cresc.
cresc.
160
170
180
190

III.5 is the first movement of Haydn's Symphony No. 100 ("The Military"), one of the second series of "London Symphonies," performed in London in 1794. The "Military" nickname is suggested by the percussion section in the second movement (an Allegretto movement in C major) and in the fourth movement (a finale in G major).

The first movement is a large-scale example of the sonata movement form. Where does the exposition begin? Where is the second key area established in the exposition? How does the material in the second key area relate to the beginning of the exposition? Tonal shifts such as those between measures 124-27 and measures 238-39 are especially striking. What function do they have in the overall tonal scheme of the movement?

III.5. F.J. Haydn

Symphony No.100 in G major ("Military")

first movement (1794)

1.
Fg.
p dolce
Vl. I
Vl. II
Vla.
Vlc. e Cb.
10
Fl.
Ob.
Cor.
Tr.
Timp.
a 2
cresc.
dim.
15
20

Allegro
Fl.
Ob.
Vl. I
Vl. II
Vla.
Vlc.
A
Fg.
Cor.
Tr.
Timp.
Cb.
a 2
tr
Vlc. e Cb.

Fl.
Ob.
Fg.
Cor.
Tr.
Timp.
Vl. I
Vl. II
Vla.
Vlc. e Cb.
a 2
60
65
70
B
sf dim.
dim.
p
tr
75

Fl.
Ob.
Fg.
Vl.I
Vl.II
Vla.
Vlc. e Cb.
dim.
p
pp
1.
80
85
C
pizz.
95
Cor.
Tr.
Timp.
ff
a 2
sf
90
100
arco

Fl.
Ob.
Fg.
Cor.
Tr.
Timp.
Vl.I
Vl.II
Vla.
Vlc. e Cb.
a 2
f
p
pizz.
105
110
115
120
125

Fg.
Vl.I
Vl.II
Vla.
Vlc.
Cb.
dim.
arco
130
135
Fl.
Ob.
Cor.
Tr.
Timp.
a 2
140
D
145
150

2

Fl.
Ob.
Fg.
Cor.
Tr.
Timp.
Vl. I
Vl. II
Vla.
Vlc.
Cb.
Vlc. e Cb.
a 2
1.
E
155
160
165
170
175

Fl.
Ob.
Fg.
Cor.
Tr.
Timp.
Vl.I
Vl.II
Vla.
Vlc.
Cb.
Vlc. e Cb.
180
185
190
195
200
p dolce
a 2
dim.
tr

Fl.
Ob.
Fg.
Cor.
Tr.
Timp.
Vl. I
Vl. II
Vla.
Vlc. e Cb.
205
F
210
215
220
225
230
a 2
dim.
pizz.

Fl.
Ob.
Fg.
Vl.I
Vl.II
Vla.
Vlc. e Cb.
pp
1.
p
arco
235
G
Cor.
Tr.
Timp.
ff
a 2
240
245
250

H
Fl.
Ob.
Fg.
Cor.
Tr.
Timp.
Vl. I
Vl. II
Vla.
Vlc. e Cb.
a 2
cresc.
ff
255
260
H
265
270
275

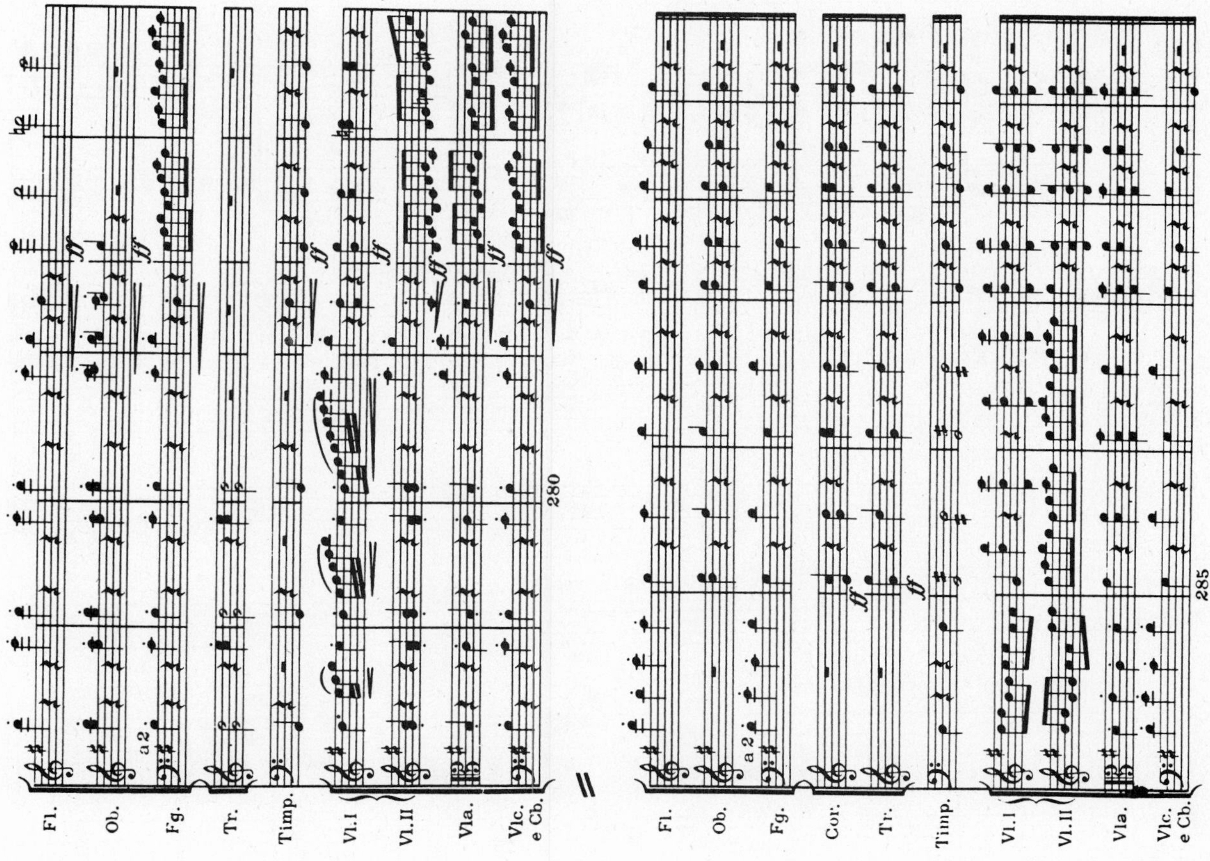
Fl.
Ob.
Fg.
a 2
Tr.
Timp.
Vl.I
Vl.II
Vla.
Vlc. e Cb.
ff
280
Fl.
Ob.
Fg.
a 2
Cor.
Tr.
Timp.
Vl.I
Vl.II
Vla.
Vlc. e Cb.
ff
285

III.6 through III.10 are compositions by Wolfgang Amadeus Mozart (1756-1791). The examples range from earlier works through examples of his mature writing for keyboard, orchestra, and chamber ensemble. Mozart spent his life in Salzburg and Vienna, in service at various churches and courts; he also had close ties with Prague and other European cities.

K. numbers, from the Köchel catalogue, are given here, together with the newer E. numbers (from the revised Einstein catalogue).

III.6 is a recitative and aria from Mozart's opera *Don Giovanni.* The opera was written in 1787 to a libretto by Lorenzo da Ponte and was premiered at Prague. This aria was added in later performances of the work. The aria is sung by Donna Elvira in Act II, near the end of the opera, and expresses her conflicting emotions: joy because Don Giovanni will soon be punished, sorrow because she still loves him, even though he has betrayed her.

Is Mozart employing a standard instrumental form in this aria? Compare this excerpt with Handel's recitative and aria (II.26) and with Verdi's excerpt (IV.21).

III.6. W.A. Mozart

"In quali eccessi, o Numi.....Mi tradì quell' alma ingrata." (1787)

Recitative and Aria from *Don Giovanni*

puo-te tar-dar l'i-ra del cie-lo, la giu-sti-zia tar-dar.
heaven will surely over-whelm thee, it is swift to de-stroy.
(with energy)
Sen-tir già par-mi la fa-ta-le sa-et-ta,
The lightning flash of re-tri-bu-tion im-pendeth,
che gli piomba sul ca-po!
it will soon be up-on thee!
A-per-to veg-gio il ba-ra-tro mortal!
E-ter-nal ru-in at last will be thy doom.
Mi-se-ra Elvi-ra! che con-tra-sto d'af-fet-ti,
Wretched El-vi-ra! What a tem-pest within thee
in sen ti nasce!
thy heart di videth!
Per-chè que-sti so-spi-ri?
Ah wherefore is this longing?

35
Aria.
E.
e quest' am-ba-scie? Mi tra-dì quell' al-ma in-
These pangs of sor-row? Cru-el heart, thou hast be-
p
40
gra-ta, quell' al-ma in-gra-ta, in-fe-li-ce, o
tray'd me, thou hast be-tray'd me, Grief un-end-ing up-
Cl.
Fag.
cresc.
p cresc.
45
Di-o! mi fa, in-fe-li-ce, o Di-o! mi fa, in-fe-
on me he cast, grief un-end-ing on me he cast, grief, ah
Vlns.
mfp
sfp
Fag.
Cl.
50
li-ce, o Di-o! o Dio! mi fa.
grief un-end-ing up-on me he cast.
sfp
Fl.
Fag.
55
Ma tra-di-ta, e ab-ban-do-na-ta,
Pity yet lin-gers, I'll not up-braid thee,
Vlns.
Fl.

E.
pro - vo an-cor per lui pie - tà, pro - vo an-cor per
Ne'er can I for-get the past, ne'er can I for-
Cl.
Vlns.
Fag.
lui pie - tà, pro - - vo an-cor per lui, per
get the past, ne'er can I, can I for-
Str.
Fag.
Cello
mfp
mf
lui, per lui pie - tà.
get the hap - py past.
Mi tra - di quell' al - ma in-gra-ta, quell'
Cru-el heart, thou hast be-tray'd me, thou
Cl.
Fag.
al - ma in - gra - ta, in - fe - li - ce, o Di - o! mi fa, in - fe - li - ce, o
hast be - tray'd me, Grief un - end-ing up-on me he cast, Grief un-end - ing
Cl.
Fag.
cresc.
p cresc.
mfp
sfp
Di - o! mi fa, in - fe - li - ce, o Di - o! o Dio! mi fa!
on me he cast, Grief, ah, grief un-ending on me he cast!
mfp
sfp
Cl.
Cor.

E.
Quan - do sen-to il mio tor - mento, il mio tor-mento, di ven-det - ta il
When my wrongs a - rise be - fore me, a-rise be-fore me, Thoughts of ven - geance
95
Vln.
Cello.
Fl.
Vln.
100
cor fa - vel-la, ma se guar - do il suo ci - men - to,
stir my bo-som, But the love that at first he bore me
Str.
105
pal - pi - tan - do il cor mi va, pal - pi - tan -
Binds my heart to him at last, Binds my heart
Fl.
Fag.
110
do il cor, il cor mi va, il
to him, to him at last, binds
Fag. & Cello.
115
120
cor mi va. Mi tra - dì quell'al - ma ingra - ta, quell' al - ma in -
it to him! Cru - el heart, thou hast be - tray'd me, thou hast be -
Fl.
Fl.
Cl.

E.
gra-ta, in-fe-li-ce, o Di-o! mi fa, in-fe-li-ce,o Di-o! mi
tray'd me, Grief un-end-ing up-on me he cast, Grief un-end-ing on me he
cresc.
p cresc.
mfp
sfp
fa, in-fe-li-ce,o Di-o, o Dio! mi fa!
cast, Grief, ah grief un-ending up-on me he cast.
Vlns
Cello & Wood.
Ma tra-di-ta, e ab-ban-do-na-ta, pro-vo an-
Pi-ty yet lin-gers, I'll not up-braid thee, Ne'er can
sf
p
cor per lui pie-ta, per lu-i
I for-get the past, ah, nev-er
Fl.
Cl.
Fag.
Cello
Str.
pie-tà, pro-vo an-cor per lui pie-tà,
for-get, ne'er can I for-get the past,

III.7 and III.8 are movements from two of Mozart's keyboard sonatas (probably written for the pianoforte). How are the movements similar in their formal design? The chromaticism of III.7, measures 43-57, is especially worth careful study.

III.7. W.A. Mozart

Sonata in F major, K.280 (E.189e)

second movement (1774)

15
20
25
30
35
40

III.8. W.A. Mozart

Sonata in D major, K.284 (E.205b)

first movement (1775)

65
70
cresc.
75
80

85
90
95
100
105
110
p
tr
f

III.9 is the last movement of a four-movement string quartet in D minor (K.421, E.417b) written by Mozart in June, 1783. It is one of a set of quartets dedicated to Haydn; this finale could be compared to the two last movements of Haydn's quartets given in III.3 and III.4. Mozart's movement is an interesting set of variations on a twenty-four-measure theme.

1. What is the phrase structure and the harmonic plan of the theme?
2. Where does each variation begin? What variational procedures are used for each section?
3. How does Mozart organize the variations into an overall form? Are there contrasts and returns?

This set of variations may be compared to others in the anthology (see study guide).

III.9. W.A. Mozart

String Quartet in D minor, K.421 (E.417b)

fourth movement (1783)

40
45
50
55
60

65
70
75
80
85
90

95
100
105
110
Più Allegro.
115
120
125

III.10 is the first movement of one of three horn concertos that Mozart wrote in E♭ major. It follows "normal concerto form" very closely. Compare the orchestral exposition with the exposition of material by the horn and orchestra. Where would a cadenza be inserted in this movement?

III.10. W.A. Mozart

Concerto for Horn and Orchestra in E♭ major, K.447 (E.447)

first movement (1783)

Cl.
Fg.
Vni
Vla
Vc. e Cb
25
Cl.
Fg.
Vnl
Vla
Vc. e Cb
p
30
Cl.
Fg.
Cr.
Vnl
Vla
Vc. e Cb
p
35
Cl.
Fg.
Cr.
Vnl
Vla
Vc. e Cb
p

40
Cl.
Fg.
Cr.
Vni
Vla
Vc. e Cb
45
Cr.
Vni
Vla
Vc. e Cb.
50
Cr.
Vni
Vla
Vc. e Cb
55
Cr.
Vni
Vla
Vc. e Cb.
60
Cr.
Vni
Vla
Vc. e Cb

65
Cl.
Fg.
Cr
Vni
Vla
Vc. e Cb
Cl.
Fg.
Cr.
Vnl
Vla
Vc. e Cb
cresc.
cresc
cresc
cresc
70
Cl.
Fg.
Vni
Vla
Vc. e Cb
75
Cl
Fg.
Vni
Vla
Vc. e Cb

80
Cl.
Fg.
Vni
Vla
Vc. e Cb
85
Cl.
Fg.
Cr.
Vni
Vla
Vc. e Cb
90
Cr.
Vni
Vla
Vc. e Cb
95
Cr.
Vni
Vla
Vc. e Cb
Cr.
Vni
Vla
Vc. e Cb

100
Cl.
Vni
Vla
Vc. e Cb
105
Cl.
p
Fg.
p
Cr.
Vni
Vla
Vc. e Cb
110
Cl.
Fg.
Cr.
Vni
Vla
Vc. e Cb
115
Cl.
f
Fg.
f
Vni
f
Vla
f
Vc. e Cb
f

120
Cl.
Fg.
Cr.
Vni
Vla
Vc. e Cb
p
130
Cl.
Fg
Cr
Vni
Vla
Vc. e Cb
p
125
Cr.
Vni
Vla
Vc. e Cb
135
Cr.
Vni
Vla
Vc. e Cb

140
Cr.
Vni
Vla
Vc. e Cb
145
Cr.
Vni
Vla
Vc. e Cb
150
Cl.
Fg
Cr.
Vni
Vla
Vc. e Cb
155
Cl.
Fg.
Cr.
Vni
Vla
Vc. e Cb
160
Cl.
Fg.
Cr.
Vni
Vla
Vc. e Cb

Cl
Fg
Cl
Vni
Vla
Vc. e Cb
165
Cl.
Fg.
Cr.
Vni
Va
Vc. e Cb
cresc.
f
170
Cl.
Fg.
Cr.
Vni
Vla
Vc. e Cb
175
Cl
Fg.
Vni
Vla
Vc. e Cb

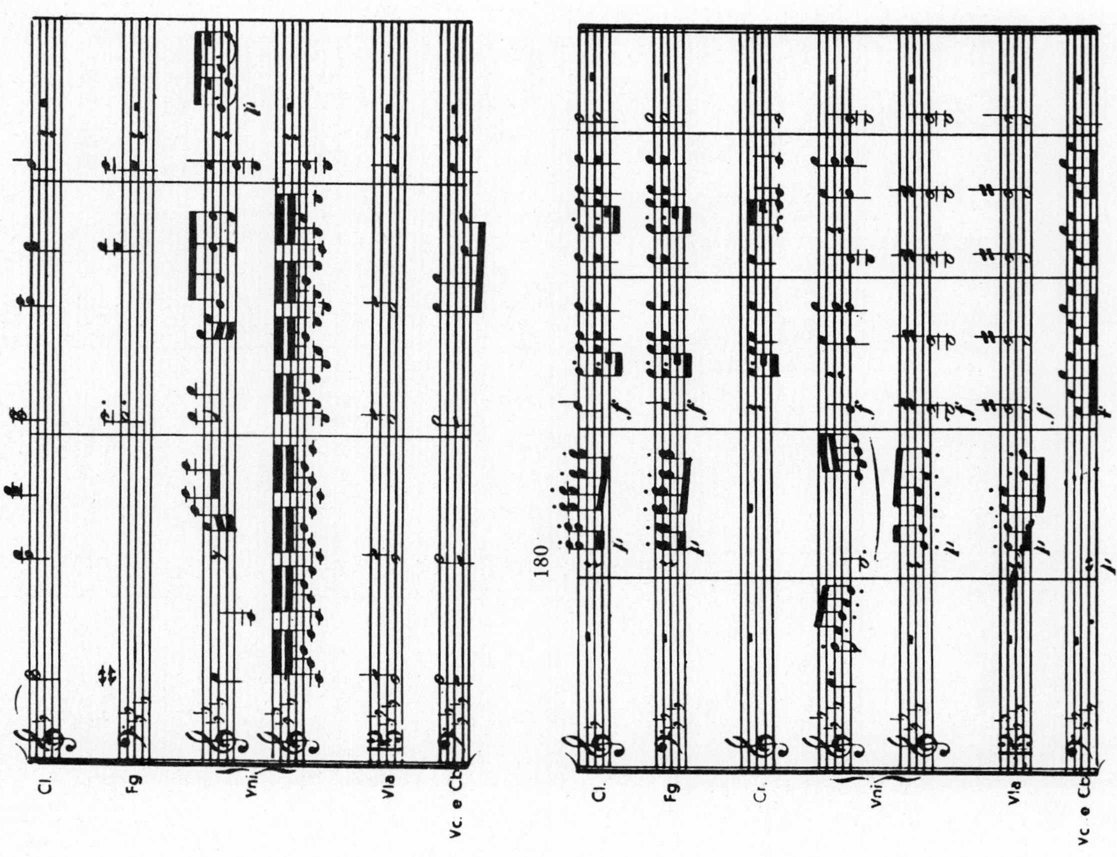
Cl.
Fg
Vni
Vla
Vc. e Cb
180
Cl.
Fg
Cr.
Vni
Vla
Vc. e Cb

III.11 through III.19 present part of a variation set as well as several movements from the piano sonatas and string quartets of Ludwig van Beethoven (1770-1827). Representative works from the three periods of Beethoven's compositional style are included. Each movement suggests detailed study of form and of treatment of the basic material, since Beethoven is a master of construction of large architectural shapes from the smallest amount of musical material.

Examples III.11, 12, and 13 are the complete early piano sonata Op. 14 No.1 in E major. Study each movement in detail, and observe any similarities among the movements in key scheme, melodic material, etc. What roles do E major, E minor, B major, and C major have in the whole sonata?

Movement I could be compared to the first movement of Mozart's piano sonata (III.8) and to other Beethoven first movements (III.16 and 17).

How does the second movement compare with a standard minuet-trio form (like, for example III.2)? What things are similar and what different?

Does the rondo form of the third movement have any similarities to a sonata-movement form? Compare this movement with other rondo movements in the anthology (see study guide).

III.11. Ludwig van Beethoven

Piano Sonata in E major, Op.14 No.1

first movement (c.1799)

20
25
30
35
40
45
50
cresc.

55
sf
ff
sf
p
pp
60
1.
2.
cresc.
65
cresc.
70
p
cresc.
rf
75
p

pp
80
cresc.
sf
p
85
90
decresc.
f
sf
95
p
100

decresc.
pp
105
cresc.
f
f
p
110
f
p
sf
f
[p]
115
120
p
p
p
125
p
130
135

140
145
cresc.
150
155
160
decresc.

III.12. Ludwig van Beethoven

Piano Sonata in E major, Op.14 No.1

second movement (c.1799)

p
cresc.
sf
p
pp
cresc.
Maggiore
p
p
p cresc.
decresc.
p decresc. pp
D. c. Allegretto e poi la Coda.
Coda.
[p]
p decresc.
pp

III.13. Ludwig van Beethoven

Piano Sonata in E major, Op.14 No.1

third movement (c.1799)

30
decresc.
pp
cresc.
p
35
sf
40
cresc.
sf
45
sf
f
50
p

55
f
60
65
p
70
decresc.
75
80
cresc.
decresc.

85
p
cresc.
p
90
95
cresc.
tr
tr
[f]
[p]
100
pp
105
pp
110
p
cresc.
ff
115
sf

120
sf
sf
decresc.
p
pp
125
p
cresc.
130
tr.
f

III.14. Ludwig van Beethoven

String Quartet in G major, Op.18 No.2

second movement (1798-1800)

This is the slow movement from one of a group of six of Beethoven's early string quartets. The movement has a middle section which contrasts in tempo and key with the first section. How does Beethoven connect these two sections? (Study measures 23-29.) What later ramifications does this connection have? Find measures where a similar process of connection or closure is used.

Tempo I.
cresc.

70
cresc.
p
75
fp
f
80

III.15, 16, and 17 are from the middle years of Beethoven's compositional career.

III.15 is the beginning of one of Beethoven's most famous variational compositions. The set contains an introduction, in which the bass line of the theme is presented successively in octaves and in two, three, and four parts; the theme, in which a prominent melodic line is added to the bass; fifteen variations with coda; a large fugue; and a final section which contains two more complete variations. The basic material of the work was evidently very interesting to Beethoven, since it occurs in three of his other works: No.7 of the twelve contradances for orchestra and the finale of the ballet music for *Die Geschöpfe des Prometheus* (both from around 1801) and in the last movement of Symphony No. 3 in E♭ major ("Eroica") of 1803. The symphonic movement is also a large variation set and is structured in a similar way; the bass line is presented first and varied, before the melodic line is introduced. However, the two compositions, one for orchestra, one for piano, are completely different in overall structure and could be compared for similarities and differences in form.

This set of Beethoven's may be compared to other variation works in the anthology (see study guide).

1. What are the interesting features of the bass line? Compare it to the Renaissance and Baroque ground formulas (see, e.g. I.28 and II.3).
2. How does the melodic line presented in the theme relate to the bass line already stated?
3. In Variation 6, how is the harmonization of the melodic line different from the other variations?
4. Variation 8 is the end of a section of variations. How are Variations 1-8 grouped together or contrasted with each other?

III.15. Ludwig van Beethoven

Fifteen variations (with Fugue) in E♭ major, Op. 35 ("Eroica")

Introduction, Theme, and Variations I-VIII (1802–3)

A QUATTRO.
decresc.
TEMA.
dolce
cresc.
decresc.
decresc.
dolce
VAR. I.

VAR. II.
Presto.
Tempo I.
f
p
sf
ff

VAR. III.
f
f
sf
sf
ff
p
cresc.
sf
ff
p
VAR. IV.
p
1.
2.
cresc.
cresc.
f
sf
p
p
1.
2.
cresc.

VAR. V.
pp
cresc.
sf
p
VAR. VI.
p
f
cresc.
p
pp
tr

Canone all' ottava.
VAR. VII.
1.
2.
VAR. VIII.
1.
2.
1.
2.

III.16 is one of the most famous Beethoven sonata movements.

1. How has Beethoven expanded the traditional sonata movement form in this sonata?
2. How is the beginning of the recapitulation different from the beginning of the exposition?
3. The half steps F-G♭ and C-D♭ are extremely important in the stucture of this movement. Find several specific places where Beethoven emphasizes this relationship by harmonic motion, by key relationships, and by melodic motives.
4. How does the key area at the end of the exposition relate to F minor? Compare this key relationship to the key structure of C.P.E. Bach's F minor sonata (III.1).

III.16. Ludwig van Beethoven

Piano Sonata in F minor ("Appassionata"), Op.57

first movement (1804)

p
pp
ff
f
p
ff
p
ff
p
sfp
sfp
dimin.
pp
pp
dolce

40
cresc.
45
p
f
sf
p
[pp]
50
f
ff
55
f
sf
ff
sf
sf
sf
60
8
ff

[p]
sfp
diminuendo
pp

sf
sf
[sf]
sf
sf
fp
sfp
sfp
dim.
pp
cresc.
f

p
cresc.
f
p
cresc.
f
sempre più forte
ff
Ped.
sempre Ped.

sempre Ped.
130
ff
135
p dimin.
pp
140

145
cresc.
150
f
f
f
p
pp
ff
p
155
p
ff
p
ff
160
p
ff
f
sf
p
165
sfp
sf[p]
170
dim.

pp
dolce
175
cresc.
180
p
f
p
185
pp
190
f
ff
sf

195
sf
sf
sf
200
p
fp
fp
sf
f
p diminuendo
pp
205
cresc.

210
p
cresc.
sf
215
sf
sf
ff
Ped.
220
sempre fortissimo
Ped.
Ped.
Ped.
Ped.
Ped.
ff

225
230
235
Ped.
sempre Pedale
p dimi - nu - en - do
ritar - dan - - do
Adagio.
Più Allegro.
pp
ff
p

cresc.
sf

255
ff
ff
p dimin.
Ped.
260
pp
più piano
ppp

III.17 is the first movement of a three-movement sonata. The titles of the movements are "The Farewell," "The Absence," and "The Return" (movements two and three are joined together). The opening "Lebe wohl!" ("Farewell" or "Adieux") motive provides material that Beethoven works with extensively later in the movement. Trace this motive throughout the movement. (Consider the descending three-note melodic line as well as its associated intervals and harmonic progression.)

III.17. Ludwig van Beethoven

Piano Sonata in E major, Op. 81a

first movement (1809)

sf
sfp
25
cresc.
sf
sfp
30
8
cresc.
f
35
sf
sf
sf
sf
40
p
45
50
espressivo

55
espressivo
60
p
65
1.
2.
70
p
f
75
p
p
80
85

90
cresc.
f
p
95
sempre dimin.
100
105
pp
cresc.
110
f
ten.
sf
p
cresc.
115
sf
sfp
cresc.
120
sf
sfp
cresc.
125
f
sf
130
sf
p
135

8
140
espressivo
145
espressivo
150
155
p
160
p
f
165
p
cresc.
sf
sfp
170
[cresc.]
sf
sfp
175
cresc.
sf
sfp
f
180
8
p
185
190

195
200
cresc
sf
dolce
205
cresc.
210
p dolce
215
220
cresc.
225
230
235
dim.
p
240
245
cresc.
p
pp
250
255
pp
pp
cresc.
f

III.18 and III.19 are the first two movements of Beethoven's late string quartet, Opus 130. The quartet contains six movements, the last one of which was intended to be the "Grosse Fuge" ("Great Fugue"). However, Beethoven withdrew that overwhelming fugue and wrote a new finale for the quartet, making the fugue an independent composition. All of the late quartets, including the "Grosse Fuge," are related by their use of short melodic motives (in many cases variants of exactly the same set of intervals), by their use of counterpoint, by their quick changes of tempo and key, and by a profundity of expression and structure that is revealed only after careful study.

The first movement of Opus 130 depends on the melodic ideas presented in measures 1-2 and measures 15-16. How does Beethoven create a sonata movement from these ideas? Where does he establish a "contrasting key area"? Can you see a design in the key changes throughout the movement?

Compare sonata form in this movement to Beethoven's earlier use of the form and to Bartók's use of the form in his string quartet No.4 (V.18).

III.18. Ludwig van Beethoven

String Quartet in B♭ major, Op.130

first movement (1825)

cresc.
p cresc.
non ligato
p cresc.
non ligato
p cresc.
non ligato
20
f
p
cresc.
Allegro.
f non ligato
25
non ligato
f non ligato
30
cresc.
sf

35
dim.
40
cresc.
45
50
una corda
55
Corda C
sotto voce

60
65
pp ben marcato
ben marc.
pp ben marcato
pp ben marcato
poco cresc.
poco cresc.
poco cresc.
poco cresc.
70
pp
pp
pp
pp
cresc.
cresc.
cresc.
cresc.
75
p
cresc.

80
cresc.
85
sf
ff
90
più p
pp
1.
2.
Tempo I.
95
Allegro.
pp non ligato
p cresc.

Adagio ma non troppo.
100 Allegro.
Adagio ma non troppo.
p
cresc.
pp
pp non ligato
espressivo
Allegro.
105
sempre p
non ligato
110
115
120
125

130
dim.
pp
cresc.
non ligato
f
p
135
cresc.
ten.
ben marcato
140
non ligato
f non ligato
cresc.
ten.
145

dim.
dim.
dim.
150
cresc.
cresc.
cresc.
cresc.
155
dim.
dim.
dim.
dim.
160
sotto voce
165

170
175
cresc.
180
pp ben marcato
185
poco cresc.
190
non ligato

195
cresc.
p
200
205
ff
sf

210
dim.
Adagio ma non troppo.
215
cresc.
Allegro.
f non ligato
pp
Adagio ma non troppo.
Allegro.
220
Adagio ma non troppo.
Allegro.
225
cresc.
230

III.19. Ludwig van Beethoven

String Quartet in B♭ major, Op.130

second movement (1825)

What has happened to the traditional minuet and trio movement in this quartet? Which elements are still present? Which have changed?

Presto.

L'istesso tempo.

1.
2.
25
sf
p
cresc.
30
f
pp
35
40
45
ff
dim.
50
55
L'istesso tempo.
ritar - dan - do

60
65
70
75
80
85
90
pp sempre
pp sempre
pp sempre
pp sempre

III.20 through III.24 are compositions by Franz Schubert (1797-1828). Schubert spent his life in Vienna and is best known for his piano music, his chamber music, and his incredible outpouring of *Lieder* (art songs), some of which are grouped into song cycles. The few examples here can only suggest Schubert's compositional procedures and his ability to set texts. Particularly worthy of note is his fondness for the chromatic third relationship and for modal mixtures.

III.20 and III.21 are two short waltzes from a collection for piano. What key areas are established in No. 14? How are these keys related? What is the first chord of No. 29? These two examples illustrate the simple textures and phrase structure, combined with harmonic and tonal innovations, which are the basis for much nineteenth-century piano music. (See, for example, the Chopin Mazurkas IV.16-IV.17).

III.20. Franz Schubert

Waltz, Op.9 No.14

(1816-21)

III.21. Franz Schubert

Waltz, Op.9 No.29

(1816-21)

III.22 and III.23 are two of the twenty songs in Schubert's song cycle, *Die schöne Müllerin* (text by Wilhelm Müller). Note the contrast between the turbulence of No. 5 ("Am Feierabend") and the sorrow and resignation of No.19 ("Der Müller und der Bach"). The brook is a continuing image throughout the cycle.

1. How does Schubert fit his accompaniment to the text?
2. How do modal mixtures play a part in these songs?
3. Schubert provides good examples of many of the standard types of chromatic chords (augmented sixths, Neapolitans, embellishing diminished 7ths). Find an example of each type of chord and study its use in the larger context of voice leading and tonal structure.

III.22. Franz Schubert

"Am Feierabend" ("Evening Leisure")

from *Die schöne Müllerin* (1823)

dre - hen al - le Stei - ne, dass die schö - ne Mül - le-rin
merk - te mei - nen treu - en Sinn, dass die schö - ne Mül - - - le-rin
merk - te mei - nen treu - - en Sinn!
decresc.
Ach, wie ist mein Arm so schwach! was ich he - be, was ich tra - ge, was ich
schneide, was ich schla - ge, je - der Knap - pe thut mir's nach, je - der Knap - pe thut mir's

40
nach. Und da sitz' ich in_der gro_ssen Run_de, in der
45
stil_len, küh_len Fei_er_stun_de, und der Mei_ster sagt zu
50
al_len: eu_er Werk hat mir ge_fal_len, eu_er Werk hat mir ge_fal_len; und das
55
lie_be Mäd_chen sagt_ al_len ei_ne gu_te Nacht, al_len ei_ne gu_te
60
Etwas geschwinder.
Nacht. Hätt' ich tau_send Ar_me zu rüh_ren, könnt' ich
pp
sf
p
f

65
brau - send die Rä - der füh - ren, könnt' ich we - hen durch al - le Hai - ne, könnt' ich
70
dre - hen al - le Stei - ne, dass die schö - ne Mül - le - rin merk - te
mei - nen, mei - nen treu - - en Sinn, dass die schö - ne Mül - le -
75
rin merk - te mei - nen, mei - nen treu - - en Sinn,
80
dass die schö - ne Mül - le - rin merk -
p
f
p

No. 5 Am Feierabend

Hätt'ich tausend Arme zu rühren!
könnt' ich brausend die Räder führen!
könnt' ich wehen durch alle Haine!
könnt' ich drehen alle Steine!
dass die schöne Müllerin
merkte meinen treuen Sinn.

Ach, wie ist mein Arm so schwach!
Was ich hebe, was ich trage,
was ich schneide, was ich schlage,
jeder Knappe thut mir's nach
Und da sitz' ich in der grossen Runde,
in der stillen, kühlen Feierstunde,
und der Meister sagt zu Allen:
euer Werk hat mir gefallen;
und das liebe Mädchen sagt:
Allen eine gute Nacht.

W. Müller

Evening Leisure

With a thousand arms as their master!
Could I turn the wheel even faster!
Could I waken all trees with blowing,
Could I keep the millstone going,
That the lovely millermaid can
See how faithful I can be!

Ah! but I am so frail, in the
lifting and the holding, in the
cutting and the molding,
Any boy can do as well.
And I sit in a large circle
In the quiet evening hour of leisure,
And the master speaks to all:
Your work has pleased me.

And the maiden, my delight,
Wishes all a good night.

III.23. Franz Schubert

"Der Müller und der Bach" ("The Miller and the Brook")

from *Die schöne Müllerin* (1823)

wel - ken die Li - lien auf je - - dem Beet; da muss in die Wolken der Voll - mond
geh'n, da - mit seine Thränen die Menschen nicht seh'n; — da hal - ten die Englein die
(Der Bach.)
Au - gen sich zu und schluchzen und sin - gen die See - le zur Ruh. Und
wenn sich die Lie - be dem Schmerz ent - ringt, ein Sternlein, ein neu - es, am
Him - mel er - blinkt, ein Sternlein, ein neu - es, am Him - mel er - blinkt; da

springen drei Ro-sen halb roth und halb weiss, die wel-ken nicht wie-der, aus
Dor- - nen - reis; — und die En - gelein schneiden die Flü-gel sich ab und
geh'n al - le Morgen zur Er - de her - ab, und geh'n al - le Mor-gen zur
(Der Müller.)
Er - - de her-ab. Ach, Bäch - lein, liebes Bächlein, du meinst- es so
gut, ach, Bäch - lein, a-ber weisst du wie Lie - - be thut? — Ach,

un - - ten, da un - ten die küh - le_ Ruh, ___ ach, Bäch - lein, liebes Bächlein, so
sin - ge_ nur zu, ach, Bäch - lein, liebes Bächlein, so sin - ge_ nur zu!

No. 19 Der Müller und der Bach

(Der Müller)

Wo ein treues Herze in Liebe vergeht,
da welken die Lilien auf jedem Beet;
da muss in die Wolken der Vollmond geh'n
damit seine Thränen die Menschen nicht seh'n
da halten die Englein die Augen sich zu,
und schluchzen und singen die Seele zur Ruh.

(Der Bach)

Und wenn sich die Liebe dem Schmerz entringt,
ein Sternlein, ein neues, am Himmel erblinkt;
da springen drei Rosen, halb roth und halb weiss,
die welken nicht wieder, aus Dornenreis;
und die Engelein schneiden die Flügel sich ab
und geh'n alle Morgen zur Erde herab.

(Der Müller)

Ach Bächlein, liebes Bächlein
du meinst es so gut;
ach Bächlein, aber weisst du,
wie Liebe thut?
Ach unten, da unten die kühle Ruh'
ach Bächlein, liebes Bächlein,
so singe nur zu.

The Miller and the Brook

(The Miller)

When a heart is faithful and dies true,
the lilies all wither, the roses too;
the moon in the heaven no longer appears,
but hides in the clouds so that none see its tears;
the angels are silent, their songs will cease,
they cry in their sorrow: "Now rest ye in peace."

(The Brook)

When love is triumphant in grief and pain
A new star arises in Heaven again;
Three red and white roses now spring from the thorn,
And never to wither shall greet the new morn;
And the Angels will cut off their wings and will walk
On earth every morning to visit and talk.

(The Miller)

Ah brook, my dear companion, so tender and true,
Ah brook, do you know then what love can do?
Below, ah below there, how cool, how blest!
Ah, brook, my dear companion, now sing me to rest.

III.24 is an entr'acte from the incidental music Schubert wrote for the play *Rosamunde* in 1823. The play is in four acts; this music appeared after the third act. Schubert used the opening section of this music as the beginning of the second movement of his String Quartet in A minor, Op. 29 (1824) and as the theme for a theme and variations set in his Impromptu in B♭ major, Op. 142 No. 3 for piano (1827).

What is the overall form of the movement? What is the form of measures 1-32? Compare and contrast this section with measures 33-66 and measures 67-95. What are the relationships between important key areas in the work? Study carefully the harmony in places such as measures 17-28.

III.24. Franz Schubert

Entr'acte

from Incidental Music for the play *Rosamunde* (1823)

20
Fl.
Ob
Cl
Fg.
Cor. (B)
Vl.
Vla.
Vlc. e Cb.
cresc.
25
30
Minore I.
35
Ob.
Cl.
Vl.
Vla.
Vlc. e Cb.
40
Fl.
Ob.
Cl.
Fg.
espress.

Fl.
Ob
Cl.
Fg.
Vl.
Vla
Vc. Cb.
Cor. (B)
decresc.
Minore II.
simili
pizz.
Maggiore da capo

Fl.
Ob.
Cl.
Fg.
Cor. (B)
Vl.
Vla.
Vc. Cb.
75
80
85
90
95
Maggiore da capo

IV

1830-1900

The nineteenth century was a time of expansion of both the traditional formal patterns and the major-minor tonal system of the eighteenth century. This section includes many examples of the short piano piece and the art song, two important genres in the century, where chromatic harmony and key relationships can be studied most easily. Although it was impossible to include as lengthy a composition as a Bruckner or Mahler symphony movement, a longer sonata movement by Brahms illustrates the nineteenth-century use of first movement sonata form. In addition, two orchestral works (Berlioz's *Symphonie Fantastique* and Wagner's Prelude to Act I of *Tristan und Isolde*) illustrate the new use of the orchestra and can also be studied, as can other examples in this unit, for motivic development and character change which occur in many nineteenth-century compositions.

A choral excerpt by Mendelssohn illustrates the Baroque influence that is apparent in some nineteenth-century works. The excerpt from Verdi's *Aida* may be compared with the Baroque and Classical operatic excerpts elsewhere in the anthology. Finally, the expanded tertian system and the revival of older scale bases are represented in compositions by Mussorgsky and Wolf at the end of the section.

Beethoven and Schubert are usually included in a study of the development of nineteenth-century music. Their compositions at the end of the previous section should be viewed as the basis for many of the harmonic and tonal ideas of the composers in this section. In addition, Schubert is usually credited with establishing the art song as an important nineteenth-century genre.

Nineteenth-century music is only now receiving a significant amount of historical and analytical study. A periodical entitled *Nineteenth-Century Music* (Berkeley: University of California Press, first published July, 1977) contains many articles of interest. Other sources include:

EINSTEIN, ALFRED, *Music in the Romantic Era*. New York: W.W. Norton & Co., Inc., 1947.

LONGYEAR, REY M., *Nineteenth-Century Romanticism in Music* (2nd ed.). Englewood Cliffs, N.J.: Prentice-Hall, 1973.

Since nineteenth-century musical romanticism was so closely connected to romanticism in the other arts, particularly literature, books providing a broader view should also be consulted.

Examples IV.1-IV.2 are from one of the best-known compositions of the nineteenth century, Hector Berlioz's *Symphonie Fantastique*. Berlioz (1803-1869) was a French composer and critic who wrote important books on orchestration as well as musical criticism during his years as a Paris music critic. His compositions include operas and works for orchestra and for voice(s) and orchestra.

Symphonie Fantastique is a five-movement work for orchestra, written in 1830 and revised in 1831. The work follows a program which was distributed to the audience at the first performance, although Berlioz later changed his mind about how literally the music should be understood in the light of the story. The story concerns an ideal woman (Harriet Smithson, an actress whom Berlioz did not meet until after the symphony was completed), who is represented musically by a recurring melodic line (*idée fixe*). The five movements ("Dreams-Passions," "A Ball," "Scene in the Country," "March to the Scaffold," and "Dream of a Witches' Sabbath") present the artist and his ideal love in different situations. Although Berlioz follows some of the classical formal traditions, the symphony is filled with innovative uses of the orchestra, formal ambiguities, and what were regarded as crude harmonic progressions.

The instrumentation of the work is given below. The ophicleide line is now usually played by a tuba. Just a glance at the list of instruments reveals a new emphasis on the winds, the percussion section, and the harp.

Instrumentation

Flutes (*Fl.*)
II doubles on Piccolo (*Fl. picc.*)
Oboes (*Ob.*)
II doubles on English horn (*C. ingl.*)
Clarinets (*Clar.*) in B♭, (*B*), A, C, E♭ (*Es*)
Bassoons (*Fag.*)

Horns (*Cor.*) in E♭ (*Es*), E, F, B♭ (*B*), C
Cornets (*Ctti.*) in B♭ (*B*), A, G
Trumpets (*Tr.*) in C, B♭, (*B*), E♭ *Es*)
Trombones (*Tromb.*)
Ophicleides (*Oph.*)

Timpani (*Timp.*)
Bass drum (*Gr. Tamb.*)
Snare drum (*Tamburo*)
Cymbals (*Cinelli*)
Bells (*Campane*)
2 Harps (*Arpa*)

Violin I (*Viol. I*)
Violin II (*Viol. II*)
Viola
Cello (*Vcello., Vcllo.*)
Double Bass (*C.B.*)

A book helpful in studying this piece is the Norton Critical Score, *Berlioz: Fantastic Symphony*, edited by Edward T. Cone (New York: W.W. Norton & Co., Inc., 1971). In addition to a score of the symphony (some of which has been reproduced here), the book contains useful critical commentary.

IV.1. Hector Berlioz

Symphonie Fantastique

first movement ("Dreams-Passions"), opening (1830)

After a slow introduction, the *idée fixe* is first presented in measures 72-111. What are the characteristics of this melodic line? How can you describe the accompaniment to this line? Listen to the complete movement to determine what happens to this material.

poco rallent.
2
Retenu jusqu'au premier mouvement
Fl.
Ob.
Clar.
Cor.
Fag.
Viol.
Solo
cresc. poco a poco
dim.
div.
unis.
pizz.
Un poco ritard
Tempo I
p dolce
arco
cresc. molto

a 2.
III.
I. Solo
sans rallentir
I.
Soli
unis.
pizz.
prenez les sourdines
arco
Solo I.
III. Solo
arco
legg.
ôtez les sourdines
cresc. poco a poco

59
cresc. poco a poco
I.
p cresc. poco a poco
(cresc. poco a poco)
5
dim.
cresc.
div.
arco
pizz.
cresc.
64
Allegro agitato e appassionato assai (𝅗𝅥 = 132)
Une mesure de ce mouvement équivaut au quart de la précédente.
One bar of this tempo is equal to a quarter-bar of the preceding.
I. Solo
Fl.
Ob.
Clar.
Cor.
Fag.
Timp.
Viol.
canto espressivo
Allegro agitato e appassionato assai. (𝅗𝅥 = 132.)
72
poco
84
dolce
cresc. poco a poco
Vcello. e C.B. unis.
(segue)
94
animez
retenu
dim.
102
a tempo
Vcello.
C.B.
un peu retenu

111
a tempo con fuoco
6
un peu retenu
Fl.
Ob.
Clar.
Cor. I.II.
Cor. III.IV.
Fag.
Timp.
Viol.
Solo
a 2.
cresc.
arco
121
un peu plus animé
Cor.
pizz.
132
7
dim.
142
unis.
div.

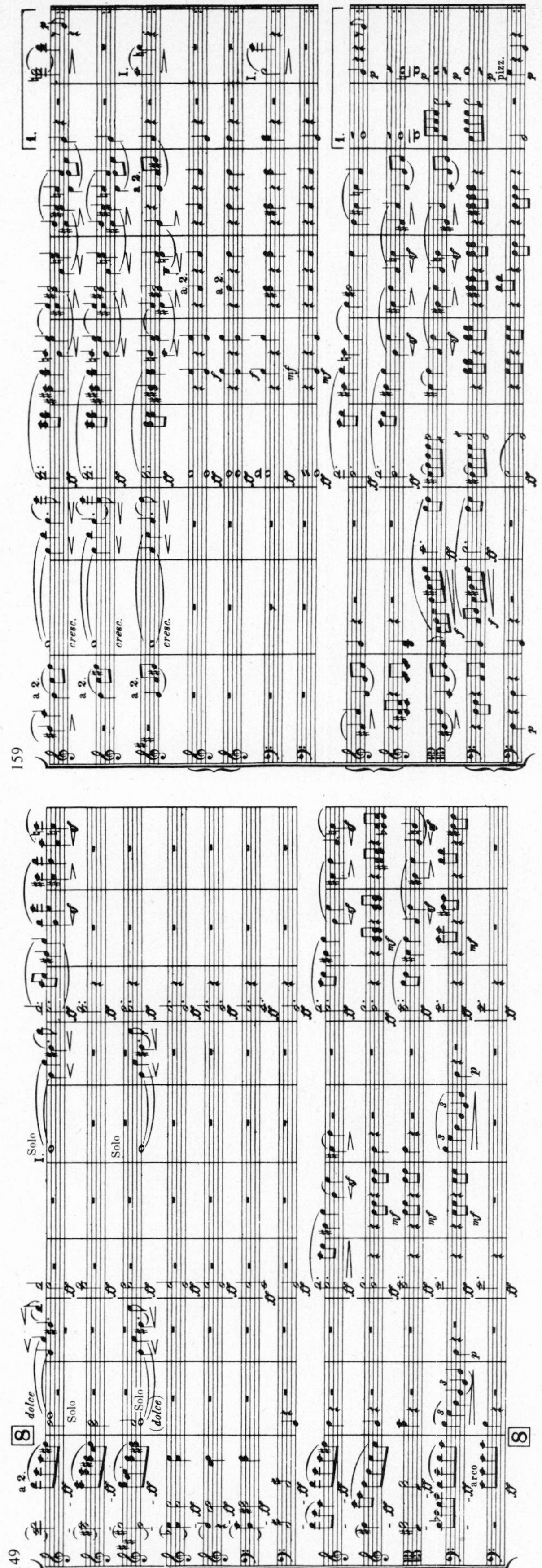

149
a 2.
8
dolce
Solo
(dolce)
I.
arco
159
cresc.
pizz.

IV.2. Hector Berlioz

Symphonie Fantastique

second movement ("A Ball"), opening (1830)

The artist now finds his beloved in the midst of the tumult of a party. Where does the *idée fixe* occur? What changes have been made as compared to the first movement? (Consider meter, tempo, dynamics, instrumentation, etc.) This sort of "character transformation" of a melodic idea is common in nineteenth-century music.

This movement has a rather standard Introduction-A-B-A′-Coda form. Measure 176 represents the return to the first main material.

19
Fl.
Ob.
p cresc.
Arpa I.
Arpa II.
Viol.
cresc. sempre
29
21
Fl.
Ob.
Clar.
in E.
Cor. in C.
Arpa I.
Arpa II.
Viol.
Vcllo. e C.B.
22
38
Viol.
p dolce e tenero
Viola.
Vcllo. e C.B.
49
rallent.. - - Tempo I
Solo
Arpa I.
Viol.
Vcllo.
pizz.
C.B.
59
Fl.
Clar.
Cor. in E
p cresc.
Arpa I.
Arpa II.
Viol.
23

68
Fl.
Clar.
Cor.
Solo
Arpa I.
Solo
Arpa II.
Viol.
arco
arco
78
24
Fl.
Clar. a 2.
Cor.
Arpa I.
Arpa II.
Viol.
cresc.
pizz.
pizz.
pizz.
24
87
25
Soli
Fl.
Ob.
Clar.
Cor.
Arpa I.
Arpa II.
Viol.
sempre pizz.
sempre pizz.
arco
arco
arco
25
sans retenir
98
Soli I.
Fl.
Ob.
Clar.
Cor.
Ctto
cresc. poco
Arpa I.
Arpa II.
Viol.
Vello e C.B.
poco f
sans retenir

109
26
Fl.
Ob.
Clar.
Cor.
Ctto
Viol.
Vello.
C.B.
presque rien
poco f
119
I.
Solo espressivo
Solo espressivo
128
I. Solo
Vello. e C.B.
138
cresc - - - en - - da - poco - - - - a - - poco
147
cresc.
poco f
157
27
Solo
dimin.
cresc. poco a poco
(dimin.)

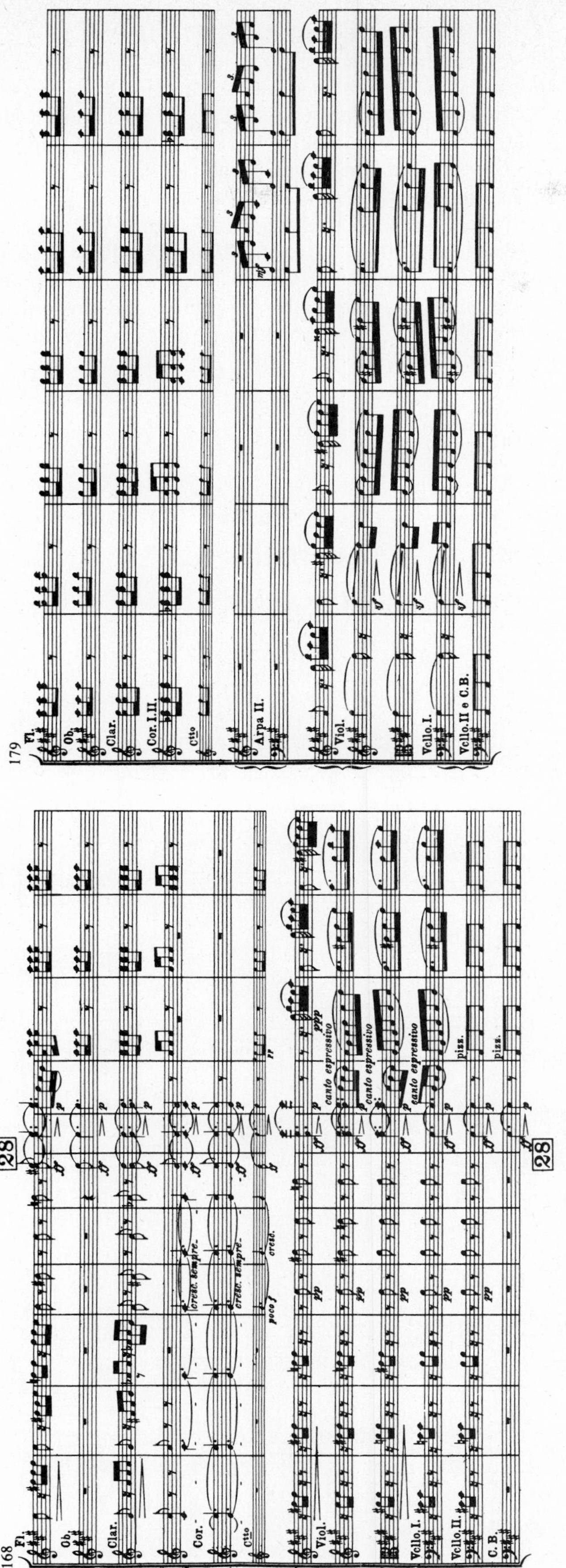
168
Fl.
Ob.
Clar.
Cor.
C^tto
Viol.
Vello. I.
Vello. II.
C. B.
cresc. sempre
cresc. sempre
poco f
cresc.
pp
ff
p
28
canto espressivo
canto espressivo
canto espressivo
ppp
pizz.
pizz.
pp
179
Fl.
Ob.
Clar.
Cor. I. II.
C^tto
Arpa II.
mf
Viol.
Vello. I.
Vello. II e C.B.

Compositions IV.3-IV.11 are by Robert Schumann (1810-1856), one of the major figures in musical romanticism. He is also known for his literary activities, since he founded the *Neue Zeitschrift fur Musik,* an important German musical periodical, in 1834. Schumann wrote many articles for the journal, including a detailed analysis of Berlioz's *Symphonie Fantastique* (see IV.1-2).

The two genres represented here (solo piano pieces and art songs) are the two areas in which Schumann produced most prolifically. IV.3 and IV.4 are two of thirteen pieces found in *Kinderscenen* ("Scenes from Childhood"). They present a contrast of character: one is regular in phrase structure, illustrating Schumann's fondness for repeated rhythmic patterns, one is more irregular and presents the "dreamy" side of Schumann's work. Both present clear examples of diatonic triads combined with various sorts of embellishing dominants.

IV.3. Robert Schumann

"Wichtige Begebenheit" ("An important event")

No.6 from *Scenes from Childhood*, Op.15 (1838)

IV.4. Robert Schumann

"Der Dichter spricht" ("The poet speaks")

No.13 from *Scenes from Childhood*, Op.15 (1838)

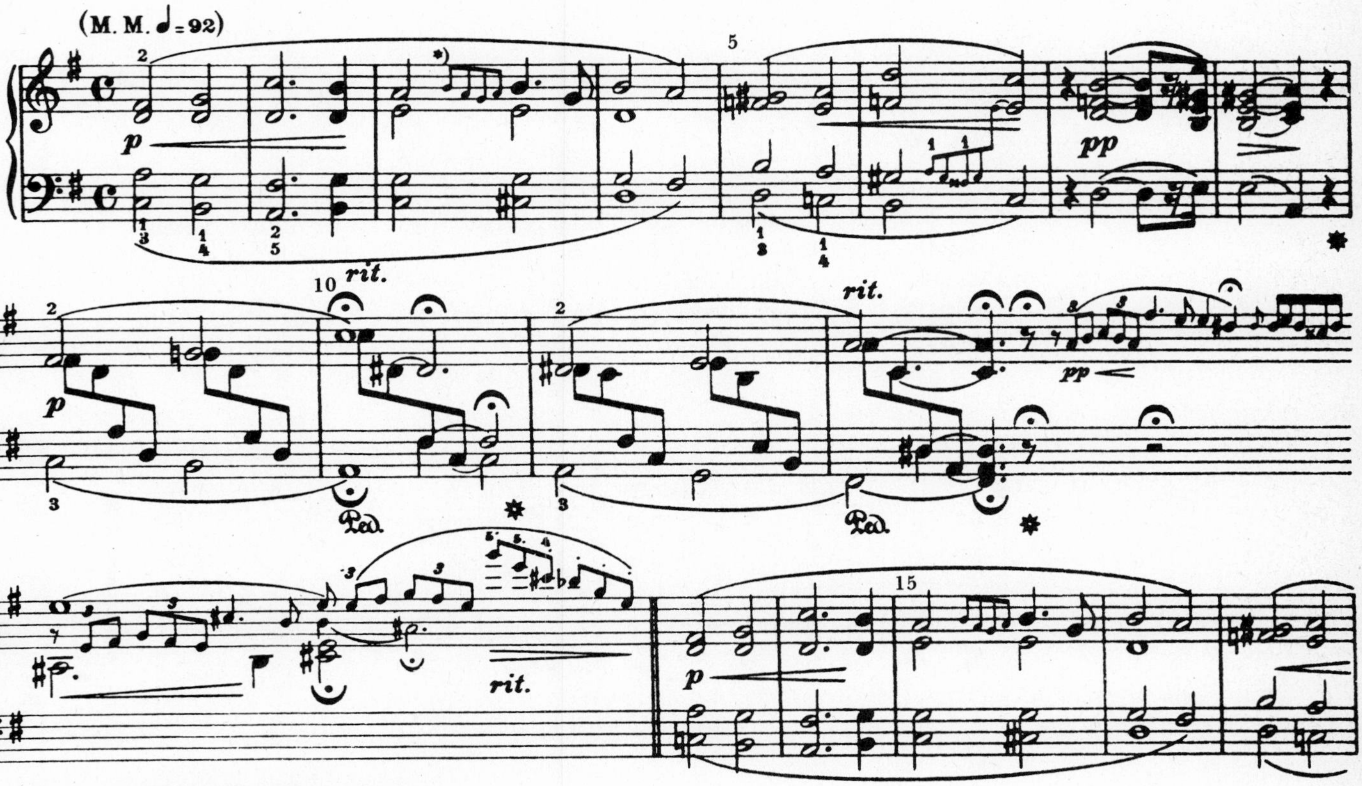

(M. M. ♩ = 92)

rit.

rit.

rit.

*) This turn should be played very tranquilly

IV.5 through IV.7 are from one of Schumann's cycles for piano, *Carnaval* (1834-35). The cycle consists of twenty scenes, most of which are based on the same four notes. Schumann took the name of a town, ASCH, which at the time had a romantic connection for him, and turned the letters into the equivalent notes. Using German note names, he obtained A, E♭, C, B or A♭, C, B. (AS in German can mean A, E♭, or A♭; H is the letter for B natural.) This melodic motive is indicated at the beginning of the three excerpts given here; notice how the same set of notes can be used to generate contrasting movements. (This process of transfer from letters into notes can be compared with Josquin's *soggetto cavato* in I.20.)

The three excerpts given here immediately follow the opening "Préambule." Other scenes in the set represent Schumann's dreamy side ("Eusebius") and his impetuous side ("Florestan"), as well as other carnival characters ("Pantalon et Colombine") and portraits of friends ("Chopin"). The cycle ends with a return to much of the material of the opening Préambule, now in the form of a "March of the *Davidsbündler* against the Philistines."

IV.5. Robert Schumann

"Pierrot"

No.2 from *Carnaval*, Op.9 (1834-35)

Who is "Pierrot"? How is the character represented here? Study this piece for the interaction of meter, rhythmic patterns, and phrase structure. What are the regular elements? What creates ambiguity?

For a very different characterization of Pierrot, see the excerpts from Schoenberg's *Pierrot Lunaire* (V.5-6).

sempre cresc.
Ped.

IV.6. Robert Schumann

"Arlequin"

No.3 from *Carnaval*, Op.9 (1834-35)

IV.7. Robert Schumann

"Valse noble"

No.4 from *Carnaval*, Op.9 (1834-35)

How is a tonal center established at the beginning of this waltz? Compare this with Schubert's waltzes, III.20 and 21, for harmonic and tonal procedures.

Schumann's songs number over 250 and include individual songs as well as important song cycles. Many of the songs were composed in 1840, the year of Schumann's marriage to Clara Wieck, a famous pianist. In fact, some of the songs of this year were composed by Clara herself.

"Widmung" is a song on a text by Friedrich Rückert. It is from a group of songs known as *Myrthen*, which, however, is not a song cycle, since the texts are by several different poets and there is no particular unifying idea. It is a good song in which to observe Schumann's modulatory procedures and his use of chromatic chords.

Does the logic of chromatic voice leading suggest a note mistake in measure 40? How are the two main key areas of this song related? How does Schumann approach and leave the second key area?

IV.8. Robert Schumann

"Widmung" ("Dedication")

from *Myrthen*, Op.25 No.1 (1840)

Schmerz, du mei-ne Welt, in der ich le-be, mein Him-mel
du, dar-ein ich schwe-be, o du mein Grab, in das hinab ich e-wig mei-nen Kum-mer gab!
ritard.
p
Du bist die Ruh', du bist der
Ped.

Frie - den, du bist vom Him - - - - mel
mir beschie - den. Daß du mich liebst, macht mich mir
wert, dein Blick hat mich vor mir ver - klärt, du hebst mich
ritard.
lie - - bend ü - ber mich, mein gu - ter Geist, mein bess'res
ritard.
p
Ped. * Ped. * Ped. *

Ich!
Du mei_ne See _ le, du mein Herz, du meine
Wonn', o du mein Schmerz, du mei_ne Welt, in der ich
le _ be, mein Him _ mel du, dar _ ein ich schwe _ be, mein gu _ ter
Geist, mein bess _ res Ich!
ritard.
steigend und eilend
ritard.
ritard.

Du meine Seele, du mein Herz,
Du meine Wonn', o du mein Schmerz,
Du meine Welt, in der ich lebe,
Mein Himmel du, darein ich schwebe,
O du mein Grab, in das hinab
Ich ewig meinen Kummer gab!
Du bist die Ruh', du bist der Frieden;
Du bist vom Himmel mir beschieden.
Dass du mich liebst, macht mich mir wert,
Dein Blick hat mich vor mir verklärt,
Du hebst mich liebend über mich,
Mein guter Geist, mein bess'res Ich!

Du meine Seele, du mein Herz,
Du meine Wonn', o du mein Schmerz,
Du meine Welt, in der ich lebe,
Mein Himmel du, darein ich schwebe,
Mein guter Geist, mein bessres Ich!

Friedrich Rückert

You, my soul, you my heart,
You, my delight, you, my grief,
You, my world, in which I live,
You my heaven, into which I soar,
O you my grave, in which forever
I have laid my sorrow!
You are the rest, you are the peace,
You are sent from heaven to me.
That you love me makes me worthy,
Your glance has transfigured me,
Your love lifts me above myself,
My good spirit, my better self!

You, my soul, you my heart,
You, my delight, you, my grief,
You, my world, in which I live,
You my heaven, into which I soar,
My good spirit, my better self!

Dichterliebe ("A Poet's Love") is a cycle of sixteen songs on poems by Heinrich Heine. The songs selected here illustrate the sensitive way in which Schumann sets the text as well as some of the musical procedures which unify the cycle. For instance, the first song, ambiguous in its tonal center, leads directly into the second song and only there finds a clear resolution of key. (Schumann often alternates between a major key and its relative minor.) Song No.12 is followed by a rather extended piano postlude; this postlude returns again at the end of the whole cycle (after Song No.16, not given here). Songs No.1 and 12 are especially appropriate examples of Schumann's "Eusebius" character, and illustrate an expressive use of chromatic harmony and accented non-chord tones.

An edition of the songs in the Norton Critical Score series (New York: W.W. Norton & Co., Inc., 1971) edited by Arthur Komar, may be helpful in studying the cycle. This book includes a reprint of an article by Allen Forte, who explains Schenker's conception of musical structure by discussing Schenker's sketch of Song No.2.

IV.9. Robert Schumann

"Im wunderschönen Monat Mai" ("In the beautiful month of May")

No. 1 from *Dichterliebe*, Op.48 (1840)

How does Schumann create an ambiguity of key center?

15
p
Im wun - derschönen Mo - nat
Mai, als al - le Vö - gel san - gen, da
20
hab' ich ihr ge - stan - den mein Seh - nen und Ver -
lan - gen.
25
ritard.
Ped.
*

No. 1. "Im wunderschönen Monat Mai"

Im wunderschönen Monat Mai,
Als alle Knospen sprangen,
Da ist in meinem Herzen
Die Liebe aufgegangen.

Im wunderschönen Monat Mai,
Als alle Vögel sangen,
Da hab' ich ihr gestanden
Mein Sehnen und Verlangen.

"In the beautiful month of May"

In the beautiful month of May
When all the buds were bursting,
Then within my heart
Love unfolded too.

In the beautiful month of May,
When all the birds were singing,
Then I confessed to her
My longing and desire.

IV.10. Robert Schumann

"Aus meinen Tränen spriessen" ("From my tears spring forth")

No.2 from *Dichterliebe*, Op.48 (1840)

How does this song continue or complete the tonal direction of Song No.1?

10
wenn du mich lieb hast, Kind - chen, schenk' ich dir die Blu - men all, und vor
pp
Ped.
15
ritard.
3
dei - nem Fen - ster soll klin - gen das Lied der Nach - ti - gall.
pp
*

No. 2. "Aus meinen Tränen spriessen"

Aus meinen Tränen spriessen
Viel blühende Blumen hervor,
Und meine Seufzer werden
Ein Nachtigallenchor.

Und wenn du mich lieb hast, Kindchen,
Schenk' ich dir die Blûmen all',
Und vor deinem Fenster soll klingen
Das Lied der Nachtigall.

"From my tears spring forth"

From my tears spring forth
many blooming flowers,
And my sighs become
A choir of nightingales.

And if you love me, my child,
I will give you all the flowers,
And shall sound before your window
The song of the nightingale.

IV.11. Robert Schumann

"Am leuchtenden Sommermorgen" ("On a bright summer morning")

No.12 from *Dichterliebe*, Op.48 (1840)

What is the harmonic function of the first chord in the song? How is this function changed in measure 8? What is the harmonic function of measures 17-19? Of measures 20-28?

10
Blu - men, ich a - ber wand - le stumm.
p
Es flü - stern und spre - chen die Blu - men, und
15
Langsamer.
pp
schau'n mit - lei - dig mich an: Sei uns - rer Schwe - ster nicht
pp
ritard.
20
bö - se, du trau - riger, blas - ser Mann.
p

No. 12. "Am leuchtenden Sommermorgen"	**"On a bright summer morning"**
Am leuchtenden Sommermorgen *Geh' ich im Garten herum.* *Es flüstern und sprechen die Blumen,* *Ich aber wandle stumm.*	On a bright summer morning I walk around the garden. The flowers are whispering and speaking, But I walk in silence.
Es flüstern und sprechen die Blumen, *Und schau'n mitleidig mich an:* *Sei unserer Schwester nicht böse,* *Du trauriger blasser Mann!*	The flowers are whispering and speaking, and they look with pity on me: Be not angry with our sister, You sorrowful, pale man.

Felix Mendelssohn (1809-1847) was a German composer who spent much of the end of his life in England. Mendelssohn, in addition to his compositional activities, was well known as the music director of the Gewandhaus orchestra in Leipzig and as the founder of the Leipzig Conservatory of Music. He is one of the musicians who furthered the nineteenth-century revival of the music of Bach and Handel, and he sometimes consciously modeled his works on Baroque compositions.

Elijah is one of Mendelssohn's oratorios and follows a Baroque outline of choruses, recitatives, and arias. The work opens with a brief comment by Elijah the prophet (sung by a baritone), followed by an overture for the orchestra. The opening chorus, given here, is joined to the end of that overture. The chorus ends on the dominant and connects with a modulatory recitative. The oratorio was received enthusiastically at its premiere in Birmingham, England in 1846.

IV.12. Felix Mendelssohn

"Help, Lord!"

from *Elijah* (1846)

Analyze the harmonic progression in measures 1-9.

How does Mendelssohn treat the melodic line stated in the tenor in measures 10-13? What happens at measure 41 and following? Compare this chorus with Handel's contrapuntal writing, found in II.28, and Bach's writing for voice and orchestra, found in II.41.

10
har-vest now is o - ver, the summer days are gone;
And yet no pow-er cometh to
p
15
And yet no power com-eth to help us!
The har-vest now is o - ver, the summer days are gone,
help us, And yet no pow - er com - eth, com-eth to
And yet no power com-eth to help us,
The har-vest now is o - ver, the
And yet no pow - er
help us, no pow- er com - eth to help us, The har-vest now is o -
And yet no power com-eth to help us!
cresc.

20
summer days are gone, And yet no power com-eth to help us,
com - eth, com - eth to help us, no power com - eth to help us! The
ver, the har-vest now is o - - ver, And yet no power cometh, And
The
cresc.
And yet no pow - er com - - - eth, com-eth to help us, no pow-er
har-vest now is o - ver, the sum - - - mer days are gone,
yet no power com-eth, yet no pow - er com - - eth,
har-vest now is o - ver, the summer days are gone, And yet no power cometh to
25
com - - eth to help us, The har - vest now is o - - -
And yet no pow - er com - eth to help us, And yet no
And yet no pow - er com - eth to help us,
help us, no pow - er, com - eth to help us, yet no

ver, And yet no power cometh to help us, no power cometh to help us!
power cometh to help us, no pow-er com-eth to help us! The
The har-vest now is o-ver, the summer days are gone; And yet no
power cometh to help us, And yet no pow-er com-eth to help us!
30
The har-vest now is o-ver, the summer days are gone,
har-vest now is o-ver, the summer days are gone, And yet no power cometh to
pow-er cometh to help us, no pow-er com-eth, And yet no power cometh to
The har- -vest now is o-ver, the harvest now is o-ver, And yet no
più f
35
And yet no pow-er cometh to help us, the har-vest now is o-ver! Will then the
help us! The har-vest now is o-ver, the har-vest now is o-ver! Will then the
help us, And yet no pow-er, no pow-er cometh to help us! Will then the
pow er, no pow-er, yet no pow-er cometh to help us! Will then the
f
pp

Lord be no more God in Zi - - on? Will then the
Lord be no more God in Zi - - on? Will then the
Lord be no more God in Zi - - on? Will then the
Lord be no more God in Zi - - on? Will then the
f
cresc.
Lord be no more God in Zi - - on? Will then the
Lord be no more God in Zi - - on? Will then the
Lord be no more God in Zi - - on? Will then the
Lord be no more God in Zi - - on? Will then the
cresc.
f
40
Lord be no more God in Zi - - on? Will then the
Lord be no more God in Zi - - on? in
Lord be no more God in Zi - - on? The har - vest now is
Lord be no more God in Zi - - on?
f

Lord be no more God in Zi - - on?
Zi - - - on? The har - vest now is
o - - ver, The sum mer days are gone, And yet no
Will then the Lord be no more God, Will then the
45
The har - vest now is
o - - ver, the sum-mer days are gone, And yet no
pow - er com - eth to help us, to help us! Will then the
Lord be no more God in Zi - - on, no more God in
o - - ver, the sum - mer days are gone, The sum - mer days are
pow - er com - eth to help us! Will then the Lord be no
Lord be no more God in Zi - - on, no more God in
Zi - - on? The har - vest now is o - - ver, The har - vest now is
più f

gone, The har - vest now is o - ver, the summer days are gone! Help,
more God, no more God in Zi - on? The harvest now is o -
Zi - on, no more God in Zi - on? The harvest now is
o - ver, The har - vest now is o - ver; Help,
Lord! Help! The har-vest now is o - ver, is
ver, Lord, the har-vest now is o - ver, is
o-ver, the summer days are gone, The har-vest now is
Lord! The har-vest now is o - ver, The har-vest now is
o - ver, The summer days are gone, and yet no pow - er cometh to help us!
o - ver, The summer days are gone, and yet no pow - er cometh to help us!
o - ver, The summer days are gone, and yet no pow - er cometh to help us!
o - ver, The summer days are gone, and yet no pow - er cometh to help us!
dim.
p

IV.13-IV.18 are several compositions by Frédéric Chopin (1810-1849), a Polish pianist and composer who spent much of his life in Paris. Chopin is best known for his compositions for piano; the ones here range from short dances to a more extended nocturne. Each suggests a careful study of harmony, voice leading, and tonal relationships, as well as a study of piano texture.

IV.13-15 are three preludes from Chopin's set of 24 Preludes Op.28. Chopin's set moves from C major and its relative minor through the circle of fifths, thus ending with preludes in F major and D minor. How does this plan contrast with Bach's arrangement of the *Well-Tempered Clavier*?

Information about the Preludes is given in the Norton Critical Score (New York: W.W. Norton & Co., Inc., 1973), edited by Thomas Higgins.

IV.13. Frédéric Chopin

Prelude No. 20 in C minor

from *Preludes* Op.28 (1836-39)

IV.14. Frédéric Chopin

Prelude No.21 in B♭ major

from *Preludes* Op. 28 (1836-39)

What is the harmonic function of measures 17-32? Compare the harmonic and tonal structure of this prelude with Schumann's song, IV.11.

25
pp
30
cresc.
35
ff
40
dimin.
45
50
55
cresc.
f

IV.15. Frédéric Chopin

Prelude No.22 in G minor

from *Preludes* Op.28 (1836-39)

IV.16-IV.17 are two of Chopin's many mazurkas. In these Polish dances Chopin, within a regular phrase structure, explores various pianistic effects and harmonic relationships.

IV.16. Frédéric Chopin

Mazurka in A minor

Op.7 No.2 (1830-31)

How does the opening of the piece relate to A minor? What is the relationship of the chords in measures 17-23? What is the harmonic and tonal goal of this section?

35
scherz.
40
Ped.
45
riten.
a tempo
50
dolce
legato
55
scherz.
1.
2.
D. C. al Fine

IV.17. Frédéric Chopin

Mazurka in G major

Op.67 No.1 (1835)

30 scherzando
35
marcato
40
45 a tempo
riten.
50
55
leggiero
60
cresc.

IV.18. Frédéric Chopin

Nocturne in C♯ minor

Op.27 No.1 (1834-35)

This example illustrates some of the pianistic textures that are usually associated with Chopin's nocturne writing. In addition, it is a fascinating study of form and of chromatic harmonic and tonal relationships. A detailed discussion of those elements may be found in Felix Salzer's article, "Chopin's Nocturne in C♯ minor, Op. 27 No. 1" in *The Music Forum*, Volume II (1970), pages 283-97.

25
ritenuto
Più mosso. 𝅗𝅥. = 54.
30
ten.
p
poco a poco
cresc.
35
f
sf
40
sempre più stretto
cresc.
45
appassionato
ff
Ped.

sostenuto
fff
50
ritenuto
dim.
Agitato.
sotto voce
poco
55
a
poco
cresc.
ed
60
accelerando
ritenuto
65
con anima
f
ten.
stretto
tr
70
ten.
tr
pp
ten.
75
tr
cresc.
ed
80
acceler.

fff
con forza
Tempo primo.
sotto voce
Ped. p
sf legato
ritenuto
con duolo
calando
p
sf
rallentando
Adagio.
p
sf
sf > pp

Richard Wagner (1813-1883) was and is one of the most discussed composers of the nineteenth century. Wagner's concept of a *Gesamtkunstwerk* ("total art work") where the music, dramatic structure, stage setting, etc. are all under the control of one person, led finally to the construction of a special building (the *Festspielhaus* in Bayreuth, Germany) for the performance of his music dramas. His largest works, four operas which comprise a cycle known as *Der Ring des Nibelungen* (1853-1874), are perhaps the longest and most complex compositions in the history of music. They have been analyzed in terms of their psychological and philosophical as well as their musical content.

Wagner's ideas of "non-absolute" music, or music that depends on the representation of ideas, characters, and events (often by a system of identifying musical motives, or leitmotifs) were opposed to the "absolute" music of composers like Brahms. The different aesthetic positions were debated extensively; no composer escaped serious examination of Wagner's musical and aesthetic ideas.

The excerpts given here are related to Wagner's opera *Tristan und Isolde*, one of the milestones of nineteenth-century music. The Prelude to Act I of the opera has often been analyzed in terms of its "atonality." It is useful to remember, however, that Wagner's music was still based on the major/minor tonal system, and that he himself wrote a "concert ending" to the Prelude in A major. Many of Wagner's other compositions reveal a much more traditional approach to tonality.

Wagner wrote extensively about his literary and musical ideas, as well as about many other subjects. There is also a very large bibliography of writings about Wagner: a few helpful sources for *Tristan* are

MITCHELL, WILLIAM T., "The Tristan Prelude: Techniques and Structure," *The Music Forum* I, 1967, 162-203. Detailed analysis of the tonal structure.

NEWMAN, ERNEST, *The Life of Richard Wagner*. 4 volumes. New York, Alfred A. Knopf, 1933-46.

——— *The Wagner Operas*. New York, Alfred A. Knopf, 1949.

WOLZOGEN, HANS VON, *Guide through the Musical Motives of Richard Wagner's Tristan and Isolde*. Tr. Neuhaus. Reinboth, Leipzig, 1889. An early guide to the story and the main musical material. Wolzogen and Gustav Kobbe published guides to the Wagner operas, which presented the leitmotifs and gave them names.

ZUCKERMAN, ELLIOTT, *The First Hundred Years of Wagner's Tristan.* Columbia University Press, New York, 1964. An interesting discussion of the influence of Wagner's *Tristan* on other artists and other fields (e.g. Nietzsche, Thomas Mann).

Tristan und Isolde was written from 1857 to 1859, but was not premiered until 1865. *Tristan* is a three-act opera; the beginnings of the first and third acts are very similar and are both given here. The material from the Prelude to Act I is transformed melodically and harmonically into the Prelude to Act III (a much shorter orchestral piece). Both Preludes connect directly with Scene I of the act, and both acts open with a monophonic line (in Act I, the voice of a sailor; in Act III a shepherd's melody played on the English horn). Both of these lines are given here for comparison.

IV.19. Richard Wagner

Prelude to and opening of Act I

from *Tristan und Isolde* (1857-59)

The Prelude to Act I is based on several small musical ideas which are transformed and returned within a large arched structure created by orchestration, dynamics, and texture. The Prelude reaches a climax in measures 81-84, recedes, and connects directly with Act I, Scene I. Measures 1-3, one of the most famous passages in music, present three separable components: 1) a leap up, followed by chromatic descent, 2) a chromatic ascent, and 3) a succession of two chords in which the tense "Tristan" chord of measure 2 resolves to a major-minor seventh in measure 3. (The G♯ of measure 2 may also be considered a non-chord tone, moving to the sonority of F-B-D♯-A, which suggests a French augmented sixth resolving to a dominant chord.)

Other important melodic ideas, many related to each other, are stated in measure 17ff (cello line), measure 25ff (cello line), and measure 63ff (violins). See also the line in the basses (measures 28-29) and the melodic fragment in measures 36-37, which both are derived from previously stated material.

The Prelude to *Tristan* is given here in a full orchestral score for the first 25 measures, as well as in piano reduction. It may be studied for the development of basic material, for its overall shape, for its use of the orchestra, and for its underlying tonal structure. For instance, how do measures 1-4, 5-7, and 8-11 relate to each other? What happens in measures 12-16? Where does the succession of cadential chords in measures 3, 7, and 11 return later in the Prelude? Where does the chord of measure 2 return? Does it ever move to something different than an E major-minor seventh?

Einleitung.
Langsam und schmachtend.
5
10
3 Flöten.
(kl. Flöte)
2 Hoboen.
2 Klarinetten. in A.
Englisch Horn.
in F.
4 Hörner.
in E.
3 Fagotte.
Baßklarinette. in A.
3 Trompeten. in F.
3 Posaunen.
Baßtuba.
Pauken.
Triangel u. Becken.
Harfe.
Langsam und schmachtend.
I.
Violinen.
II.
Bratschen.
Violoncelli.
Kontrabässe.
pp
cresc.
dim.
cresc.
sf
p

zu 2
15
Gr.Fl.I.
Hob.
Klar. I in A.
Engl.H.
in F.
Hr.
in E.
Fag.
Baßkl. in A.
I.
Viol.
II.
Br.
Vcl.
K.B.
cresc.
più f
pizz.
Bog.
20
poco rall.
(auf dem G)
riten.
a tempo
25
Hr. III. IV in E.
dim.
zart

Lento e languido.
Langsam und schmachtend.
pp
dim.
p
cresc.
sf
più f
ff
f
poco rall.
riten.
a tempo
dolce
zart
espress.
ten.
animato
belebt
Animando.
Belebend.
molto cresc.

rallent.
a tempo
45
dolce
ff
dim.
zart
dim.
p
p
50
sf
p
cresc.
f
f
p
55
cresc.
60
f
più f
ff
Ped.
meno f
espress.
65
sempre più f
marcato
f
70
f
più f

più f
molto espress.
75
ff
sempre f
più f
80
più f

Il tempo poco a poco ritenuto.
Allmählich im Zeitmass etwas zurückhaltend.

(The Curtain rises.)
(Der Vorhang geht auf.)

Scene I.

(A pavilion erected on the deck of a ship richly hung with tapestry, quite closed in at back at first. A narrow hatchway at one side leads below into the cabin.
Isolda on a couch, her face buried in the cushions. — Brangæna, holding open a curtain, looks over the side of the vessel.)

Mässig langsam.
THE VOICE OF A YOUNG SAILOR (from above, as if from the mast-head).

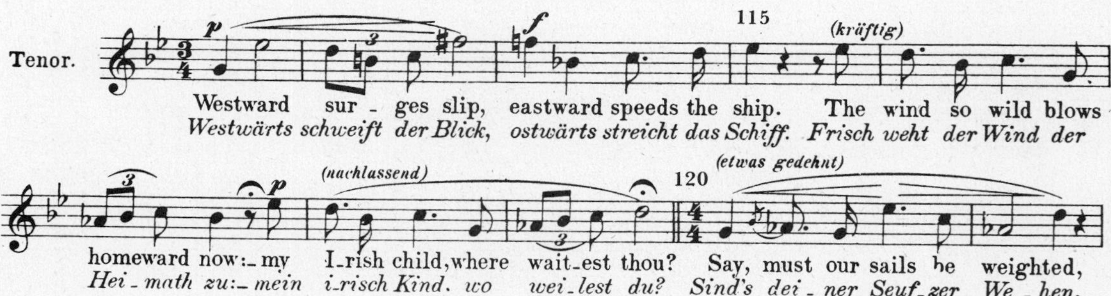

Tenor.
(kräftig)
Westward sur - ges slip, eastward speeds the ship. The wind so wild blows
Westwärts schweift der Blick, ostwärts streicht das Schiff. Frisch weht der Wind der
(nachlassend)
(etwas gedehnt)
homeward now:— my I - rish child, where wait - est thou? Say, must our sails be weighted,
Hei - math zu:— mein i - risch Kind. wo wei - lest du? Sind's dei - ner Seuf - zer We - hen,

IV.20. Richard Wagner

Prelude to and opening of Act III

from *Tristan und Isolde* (1857-59)

Compare this Prelude to the Prelude to Act I. What material is the same? How has the material been changed? Is this Prelude in a "key"? What elements of functional harmony is Wagner using? Compare the monophonic line here with the one in Act I for tonal structure, melodic motives, contour, etc. This section of the opera is very similar to Wagner's "Wesendonk" song, "Im Treibhaus." In fact, two of this set of five songs are studies for *Tristan*, written while Wagner was in exile in Switzerland to texts by Mathilde Wesendonk, the wife of one of his patrons.

Scene I.

(The garden of a castle. At one side high castellated buildings, on the other a low breastwork broken by a watchtower; at back the castle-gate. The situation is supposed to be on rocky cliffs; trough openings the view extends over a wide sea horizon. The whole scene gives an impression of being deserted by the owner, badly kept, here and there delapidated and overgrown.

In the foreground inside lies Tristan under the shade of a great lime-tree sleeping on a couch, extended as if lifeless. At his head sits Kurvenal, bending over him in grief, and anxiously listening to his breathing. From without comes the sound of a Shepherd's air.)

(The Shepherd shows the upper half of his body over the breastwork and looks in with interest.)

Giuseppe Verdi (1813-1901) is best known for his amazing output of operas, spanning the entire time period of this unit. Verdi's last opera, *Falstaff*, was produced in 1893, when he was eighty years old. *Aida* dates from 1871 and illustrates some of the characteristics of Verdi's later style. The repeated-chord accompaniments, regular phrase structures, and predictable forms of some of the earlier operas have given way to a more subtle use of the orchestra and a greater variety of harmonic and tonal relationships. However, Verdi retains clearly delineated sections and continues to emphasize the expressive qualities of the voice.

The following excerpt occurs at the beginning of the first scene of Act I of the opera. Radames, an Egyptian general, expresses his desire to be chosen to lead his country to war against the Ethiopians. He then muses on his love for Aida, a captive Ethiopian.

How does Verdi establish key areas in this aria?

How does this excerpt compare in form, in the use of the voice, and in text setting to the excerpts by Handel (II.26) and Mozart (III.6)?

IV.21. Giuseppe Verdi

"Celeste Aida"

from *Aida* (1871)

20
cin - to dir - ti: per te ho pu - gna - to, per te ho
splen - dor, say - ing: For you I con - quered. See your de -
f
vin - to!
fend - er!
ff
25
pp
Andantino. (♪ = 116.)
con espress.
Ce - le - ste A - i - da, for - ma di -
Fair - est A - i - da, star of my
p
m.s.
30
dolce
pp
vi - na, mi - sti - co ser - to di lu - ce e
dream - ing, Born of the sun - light bathed by the
m.s.

35
fior,
dew,
del mio pen-
Rul - ing my
8
portate la voce
sie - ro tu sei re - gi - na, tu di mia
heart, so taunt - - ing, re - deem - ing I on - ly
24
ten.
m.s.
40
vi - ta sei lo splen - dor.
live in my love for you.
p espress.
m.s.
sempre dolciss.
Il tuo bel cie - lo vor - rei ri - dar - ti, le dol - ci
Un - to your peo - ple I shall re - store you, Un - to the
m.d.
m.s.
m.d.
m.s.

45
animando un poco
brez-ze del pa-trio suol: un re-gal ser - to sul crin po -
breez-es that fanned your brow! Greet-ing their prin - cess, They'll come be -
ten.
m.d.
con entusiasmo
f
sar - ti, er - ger-ti un tro - no vi - ci - no al
fore you, While at your throne I shall worship and
f
col canto
50
sol, ah! Ce - le - ste A -
bow. Ah! Fair - est A -
p
leggerissime
espress.
i - da, for - ma di - vi - na,
i - da, star of my dream - ing,

55
mi - sti - co rag - gio di lu - ce e
Born of the sun - light, bathed by the
pp
fior, del mio pen - sie - ro
dew, Rul - ing my heart, so
p
60
tu sei re - gi - na, tu di mia
taunt - ing, re - deem - ing, I on - ly
vi - ta sei lo splen - dor.
live in my love for you.
p

parlante ppp
Il tuo bel cie - lo vor-rei ri-dar - ti, le dol - ci brez - ze del pa-trio
Un - to your peo - ple I shall re-store you, Un - to the breez-es that fanned your
ancora p
animando
f
suol; un re - gal ser - to sul crin po - sar - ti, er - ger - ti un
brow! Greet - ing their prin - cess They'll come be - fore you, I at your
ancora p
pppp
ppp
dim.
tro - no vi - ci - no al sol, un tro - no vi - ci - no al
throne will wor-ship and bow. A throne, to - ken of my
tr
pp leggermente
morendo
pp
sol, un tro - no vi - ci - no al sol.
vow! A throne, to - ken of my vow!
p
ppp
allarg. e morendo

IV.22 through IV.26 are several compositions by Johannes Brahms (1833-1897). Brahms represents the more conservative side of nineteenth-century music in his formal procedures, which were solidly grounded in the traditional forms of the Classical period, or in contrapuntal models of Renaissance and Baroque composers. He also opposed the idea expressed by Liszt and Wagner that music could follow some sort of "program." However, in his harmonic and tonal procedures Brahms is clearly in the mainstream of nineteenth-century composition, and in his subtle development of motives he influenced many of the German composers at the beginning of the twentieth century. His Fourth Symphony, last movement, for instance, is a sort of model for Webern's *Passacaglia* Op. 1.

IV.22. Johannes Brahms

Intermezzo in A major

Op.76 No.6 (c.1878)

This piece illustrates several typical features of Brahms' rhythmic style. What are they?

15
rit.
Ped.
Ped. simile
20
espressivo
25
p grazioso
col Ped.
30
Ped. sempre
35
40
45
p

50
Ped.
Ped simile
55
60
p
Ped. come prima
65
dolce
70
ben legato
rit.
75
Ped. simile
80
espressivo

IV.23. Johannes Brahms

Intermezzo in A minor

Op.76 No.7 (c.1878)

Moderato semplice.

15
1.
2.
p
dolce
Ped. sempre
20
p
25
p
poco cresc.
30
p

dimin. e poco rit.

IV.24. Johannes Brahms

Romance in F major

Op.118 No.5 (1893)

In some of his compositions Brahms seems to be influenced by the modal progressions of the Renaissance. What evidence of modality do you see in this piece? (Compare also m.1 with the opening of the Romanesca, I.28.) What is the textural relationship between measures 1-2 and 5-6? Between measures 1-2 and 9-10? What happens harmonically and tonally from measure 17 on?

rit.
p
più espressivo
p dolce
rit.
dim.
Allegretto grazioso.
molto p e dolce sempre
Ped.

p dolce
p leggiero
pp
dim.
tr
Ped.

IV.25 is the beginning of a very large set of variations that Brahms wrote on a theme by Handel (see Handel's theme and variations in II.24). Brahms' set includes twenty-five variations and a large-scale fugue.

How does Brahms vary the theme harmonically and tonally? What sorts of textures does he create? Study Variations 6, 7, and 8 especially for texture, and Variations 2 and 3 for rhythmic structure. How does Brahms make a progression from one variation to the other?

IV.25. Johannes Brahms

Theme and Variations 1-8

from *Variations and Fugue on a Theme by Handel,* Op.24 (1861)

Var. 2
animato
p
legato
20
1.
2.
cresc.
Var. 3
25
p dolce
30
1.
2.

Var. 4
risoluto
stacc.
sf
35
8
f
40
1.
2.
Var. 5
espress.
p
45
cresc.

Var. 6
legato
p sempre
50
1.
2.
p
55
Var. 7
con vivacità
p
60
cresc.
f
sf
cresc.
f

Var. 8
65
70
cresc.
75
dim.
8

IV.26 is the first movement of the second of three sonatas for violin and piano by Brahms. The second movement alternates *Andante tranquillo* and *Vivace* sections; the third movement is *Allegretto grazioso*.

The first movement follows models by Beethoven and thus should be analyzed for its large-scale tonal structure, its developmental techniques, and the proportional relationships of different parts of the movement.

IV.26. Johannes Brahms

Violin Sonata in A major

Op.100, first movement (1886)

cresc.
24
cresc.
f
30
f
f
37
mp cresc.
f
dim.
45
dim.
p
teneramente
p
p dolce
52

56
60
cresc.
f
p
64
dim.
molto dolce
espress.
68
72
cresc.
cresc.
f
f

77
dim.
dim.
83
1
dim.
dim.
89
dim.
dim.
95
dim.
101

106
f e sempre
sempre più f
più f
112
f marc.
118
123
128
dim.

132
p
dim.
137
141
146
150
dolce
più p

dim.
154
dim.
p dolce
p
159
165
f
f
172
p cresc.
f
178

dim.
dim.
182
p
p
teneramente
p dolce
p
186
191
195
cresc.
f
199
p
dim.
p
p

203
espress.
dolce legg.
207
cresc.
cresc.
211
f
f
216
fp dim.
fp dim.
col. Ped.
222
pp
pp sempre

229
235
vivace
p cresc.
p cresc.
243
246
f
f
f
f
dim.
dim.
250
Ped.
Ped.

sempre più dim.
253
sempre più dim.
p
poco rit.
257
poco rit.
p
dolce sempre
dolce sempre
262
poco rit.
266
poco rit.
a tempo
f
a tempo
f
271

IV.27 and 28 are excerpts from "Pictures at an Exhibition" by Modest Mussorgsky (1839-1881), a Russian composer who was influenced by Russian history and folk material as well as by nineteenth-century Western European musical ideas. His harmonic progressions, his orchestration, and his sense of form have often been criticized; indeed Mussorgsky's opera *Boris Godunov* has been rewritten by several people in order to eliminate "mistakes." More often than not, however, Mussorgsky is merely using the most appropriate means to convey dramatic expression.

The following excerpts are from a group of ten piano pieces which are preceded and connected by the "Promenade." Mussorgsky wrote them in 1874 after seeing an exhibition of paintings by his friend Victor Alexandrovich Hartmann; the pieces bear the titles of the paintings. The "Promenade" theme between movements suggests the movement of the viewer from one painting to another. The piano version given here can be compared to the orchestra version by Ravel (1922).

IV.27. Modest Mussorgsky

"Promenade"

from *Pictures at an Exhibition* (1874)

This version of the Promenade opens the set of pieces. What is the scale basis for the melodic line? How does the phrase structure work with or against the notated metric groupings? Compare the pitch and rhythmic structure of this piece to Bartók's "Dance in Bulgarian Rhythm" (V.17), since both pieces reveal Slavic folk influence.

Allegro giusto, nel modo russico; senza allegrezza, ma poco sostenuto.

IV.28. Modest Mussorgsky

"The Great Gate of Kiev"

from *Pictures at an Exhibition* (1874)

This movement closes the suite. Does it follow any standard formal pattern? Is the opening melodic material related in any way to the "Promenade" theme? This movement was inspired by Hartmann's design for a proposed ceremonial gate in Kiev; Mussorgsky suggests a ceremonial procession by portraying the clanging of bells, the chanting of priests, and the triumphant march of the people. What musical materials does Mussorgsky use for these "effects"?

Allegro alla breve.
Maestoso, con grandezza.

10
15
mf
f
20
cresc.
ff
25
30
p senza
espressione
35
40
dimin.
45
8
f energico
marc. il tema
50

marc. il tema
ff
p
sempre espr.
dimin.
mf
sf
quasi campani
simile

8
cresc.
95
8
f
8
8
100
cresc.
8
105
mf cresc
8
poco a poco più cresc.
110
8

Meno mosso, sempre maestoso.
115
120
125
130
135
140
145
150
ff
mf
cresc.
f
cresc.

Hugo Wolf (1860-1903) is best known for his songs, two of which are given here. Wolf shares Schubert's sensitivity to text setting by creating appropriate accompanimental patterns, but he expands Schubert's harmonic and tonal language to include modal progressions, extended tertian chords, nonfunctional chords, and even sections where the tonal center is in doubt. These songs may also be compared to Berg's songs (V.8a and b).

IV.29. Hugo Wolf

"Der Mond hat eine schwere Klag' erhoben" ("The moon has been seriously complaining")

from *Italienisches Liederbuch* (published 1892)

This collection of songs contains anonymous Italian lyrics which were translated into German by Paul Heyse. Wolf, who, like Schubert and Schumann, often wrote a song in a few hours of inspiration, wrote this song on November 13, 1890. In its simplicity it is a particularly effective setting of the text.

What happens to the material presented in the piano in measures 1-2? How is tonality established? Notice especially the chords in measure 16, where Wolf highlights the one personal reference in the text ("those two eyes of yours, which proved my heart's undoing").

sei - nen Glanz ___ ge - bracht. Als er zu - lezt das Ster - -
pp
p
- nen-heer ge - zählt, da hab' es an der vol - - len Zahl ge - fehlt;
cresc.
f
p
zwei von den schönsten ha - - best du ent - wen - det: die bei - den Au - gen dort,
zart
p sehr weich
pp
die mich ver - blen - det.
ppp

Der Mond hat eine schwere Klag' erhoben
Und vor dem Herrn die Sache kund gemacht:
Er wolle nicht mehr stehn am Himmel droben,
Du habest ihn um seinen Glanz gebracht.

Als er zuletzt das Sternenheer gezählt,
Da hab' es an der vollen Zahl gefehlt;
Zwei von den schönsten habest du entwendet:
Die beiden Augen dort, die mich verblendet.

The moon has been seriously complaining
And before the Lord you are accused of theft:
She feels that you have stolen
Some of the glory of heaven.

When last she counted the multitude of stars,
Some were missing from the great numbers;
Two of the most beautiful had left at your bidding:
Those two eyes of yours, which proved my heart's undoing.

IV.30. Hugo Wolf

"Er ist's"

from *Gedichte von Eduard Mörike* (1888-89)

How does Wolf move from one tonal center to another in measures 1-11? What is the harmonic process in measures 15-30? Can you identify the sonorities that Wolf is using?

10
- nungs - voll das Land.
ppp
15
Veil - chen träu - men
schon,
wol - len bal - de kom - - men.
20
pp
Horch, von fern
ppp

ein lei - ser Har - fen-ton!
25
Früh - - ling, ja du bist's!
Früh - - ling, ja du bist's!
30
Dich hab ich ver-
nom - men! ja du
f
più f
ff
mf molto cresc.

35
bist's!
fff feurig
f
sf
40
sf
45
ff
dim.
Ped.
50
p
dim.
* Ped.

Frühling lässt sein blaues Band
Wieder flattern durch die Lüfte;
Süsse, wohlbekannte Düfte
Streifen ahnungsvoll das Land.

Veilchen träumen schon,
Wollen balde kommen.
Horch, von fern ein leiser Harfenton!

Frühling, ja du bist's!
Dich hab'ich vernommen!
Ja, du bist's!

E. Möricke

The blue ribbon of spring
Flutters again in the air;
Well-known, sweet scents,
Spring's harbingers, float over the countryside.

Violets already dream
Of awakening soon.
Hark, from the distance the sound of a harp!

Yes, spring, it is you!
I have recognized you!
Yes, it is you!

V

Since 1900

This section is necessarily open-ended, since we are living in the midst of musical change. The compositions selected for the first part of this unit represent new ideas present at the turn of the century; several works by Debussy, Ravel, Schoenberg, Berg, Webern, Ives and Stravinsky (each revolutionary in some way) date from this time period (1900-1918). The compositional materials and methods of these composers, as expressed in these works, have had a great effect on the rest of the twentieth century.

Other examples suggest a variety of compositional types, since the twentieth century is a fragmented one and cannot be identified by one musical "style." Hindemith, Britten, and Dello Joio represent the continuation of the tonal tradition. Stravinsky and Bartók create new structures by innovations in both large- and small-scale rhythmic patterning. Handy and Brubeck illustrate in a small way the viability of the American popular tradition and its influence on the "classical" composers of the century. The works of Dallapiccola included here demonstrate a lyrical application of serial procedures. Finally, the works of Crumb and Berio are based on new concepts of structure and timbre, and require new notational procedures.

Since the twentieth century is so varied, there is no one way to analyze its music. In some cases a detailed study of serial organization and pitch structure is necessary. In other pieces timbre and dynamics may be the most important aspects. In all cases the composition should be examined on its own terms, as should any other art work: what are the basic materials and how are they combined to form a whole?

Books that may be helpful in dealing with twentieth-century music include:

AUSTIN, WILLIAM W., *Music in the 20th Century.* New York: W.W. Norton & Co., Inc., 1966. Goes through Stravinsky of 1962.

COPE, DAVID, *New Directions in Music* (2nd ed). Dubuque, Iowa: Wm. C. Brown, 1976. Discussion of newer compositional methods. See also his *New Music Composition* (1977) and *New Music Notation* (1976).

DALLIN, LEON, *Techniques of Twentieth Century Composition* (3rd ed.). Dubuque Iowa: Wm.C. Brown, 1974.

DERI, OTTO, *Exploring Twentieth Century Music.* New York: Holt, Rinehart, and Winston, 1968.

SALZMAN, ERIC, *Twentieth-Century Music: An Introduction* (2nd ed.). Englewood Cliffs, N.J.: Prentice-Hall, 1974.

WENNERSTROM, MARY H., *Anthology of Twentieth-Century Music.* Englewood Cliffs, N.J.: Prentice-Hall, 1969. Selection of twentieth-century works with commentary.

WITTLICH, GARY (ed.), *Aspects of Twentieth-Century Music.* Englewood Cliffs, N.J.: Prentice-Hall, 1975. Six chapters on different elements in twentieth-century music.

V.1 and V.2 are two compositions by Claude Debussy (1862-1918). Debussy, a French composer, is usually associated with the style known as "Impressionism," although he himself did not like that designation. He was influenced by French painters and writers of the late nineteenth century, and some of his works (for example the orchestral piece *Prelude a L'apres-midi d'un faune*) have general programs based on specific pieces of literature. Debussy's work is often analyzed for his use of new sonorities and scales and for his concept of layers.

In addition to important orchestral works, chamber music, and songs, Debussy wrote a large number of piano compositions. Two of his Preludes are included here. There are two books of Preludes, each containing twelve titled compositions.

V.1. Claude Debussy

"La puerta del vino"

No.3 from *Preludes, Book II* (1910-13)

This work is one of many which illustrate the effect Spanish rhythms and colors had on the French composers of the early twentieth century. "La puerta del vino" is one of the gateways in the Alhambra Palace in Granada; Debussy suggests this atmosphere by the continuous use of the "habanera" rhythmic pattern and by a melodic line reminiscent of Spanish or Moorish vocal improvisation.

The piece is centered around the chord in measure 11; what is this chord? How does it compare to the sonority in measure 66? Study the formal structure and the tonal elements in the prelude to see how they interact.

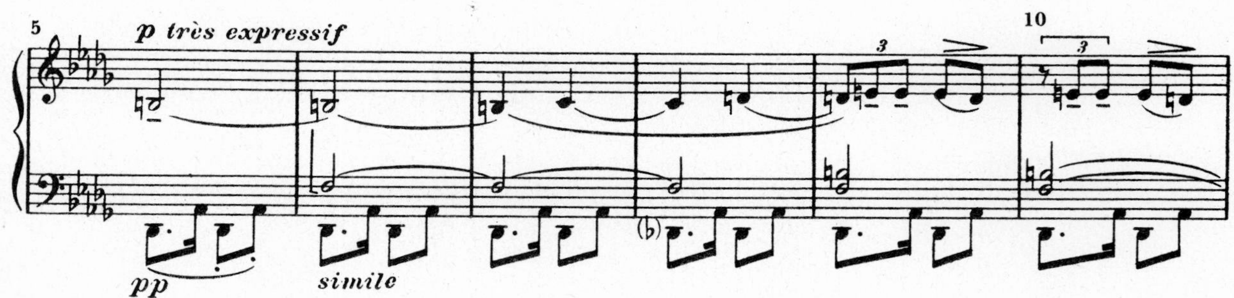

p
15
7
p molto dim.
pp
20
sff
pp
p
Rubato
25
pp
p
più p

30
pp
p marqué
pp sempre
35
p
p
mf
dim.
40
p
au Mouvt
f âpre
f
ff
passionnément
ff
45
mf
dim.

ironique
50
p
gracieux
55
p
p
pp
3
3
3
3
En retenant
60
p
più p
3
65
au Mouvt
pp
70
3
3
simile

(... La puerta del Vino)

V.2. Claude Debussy

"Canope"

No.10 from *Preludes, Book II* (1910-13)

Canopus was an ancient Egyptian city near Alexandria. How does Debussy evoke a "distant atmosphere" in this Prelude? What are the basic small elements in this piece and how do they interact? Does this piece have a tonal center? The chord structures in this piece are all interesting; examine particularly those in measures 11-13, 18-20, and 30.

15
p
p
p
p

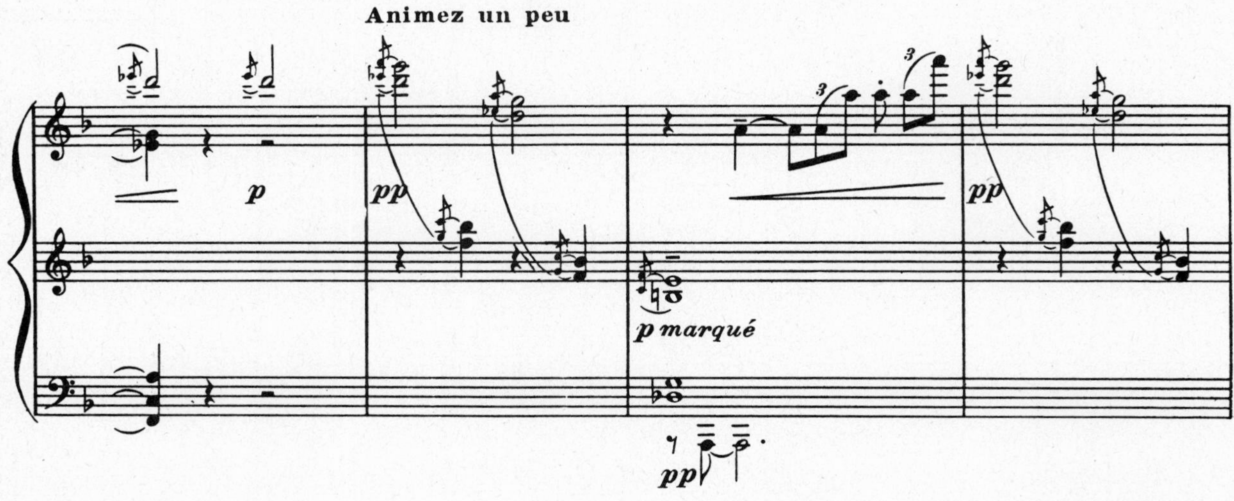
Animez un peu
p
pp
pp
p marqué
pp

20
p marqué
p marqué
pp
pp

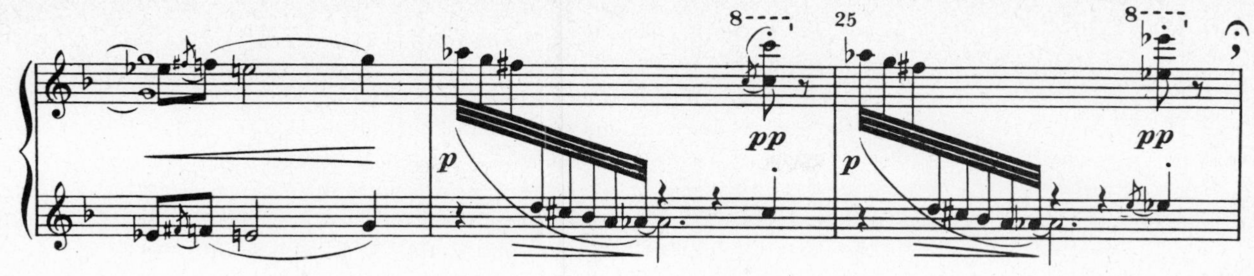
8
25
8
p
pp
p
pp

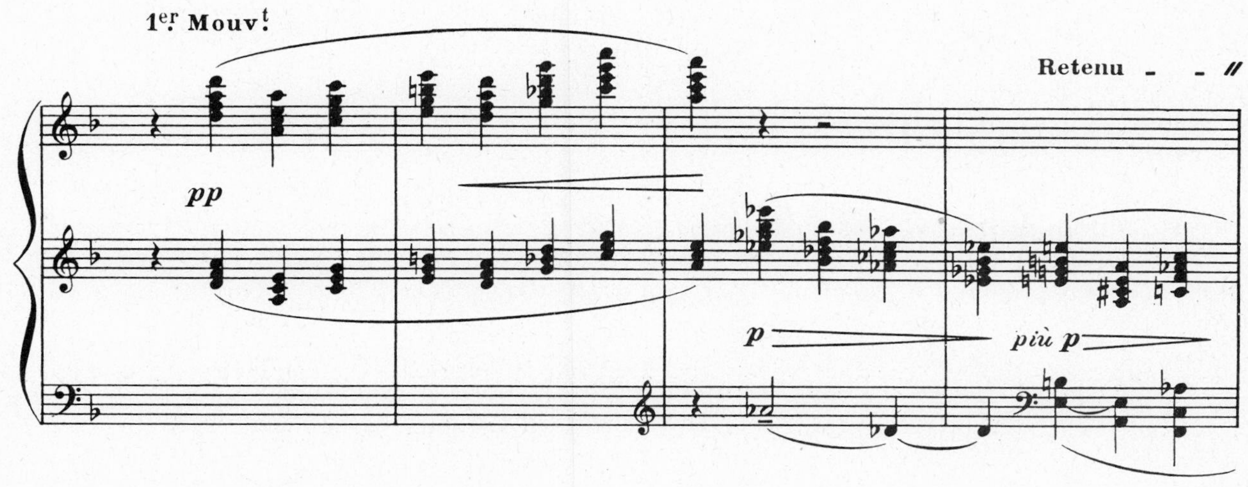
1er Mouvt
Retenu
pp
p
più p

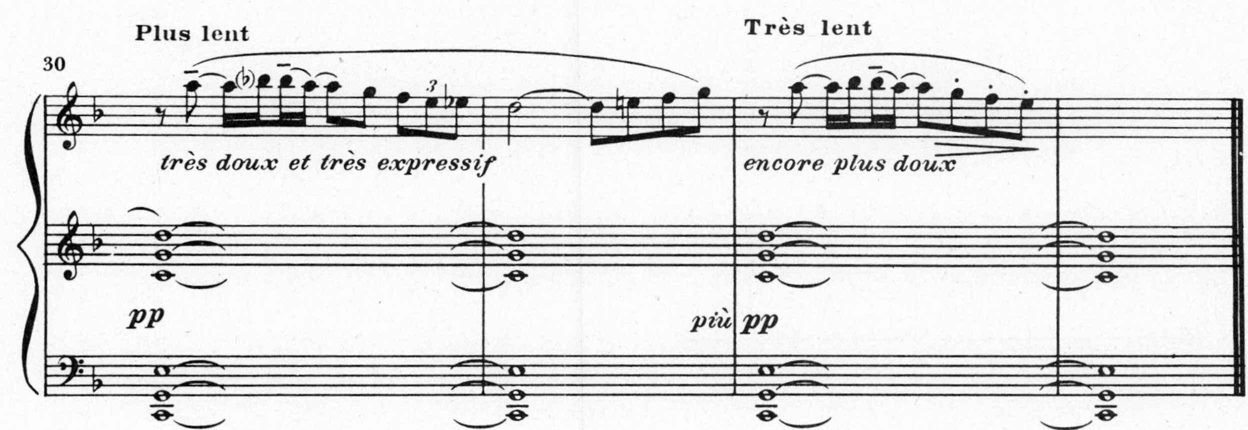
30
Plus lent
Très lent
très doux et très expressif
encore plus doux
pp
più pp

(...Canope)

Maurice Ravel (1875-1937) is a younger contemporary of Debussy; the music of the two composers is often discussed together, although Ravel more frequently followed classical models of form than did Debussy. Ravel, like Debussy, is known for his orchestral works, his chamber music, and his songs, in addition to his rather large number of piano works. The two excerpts here, from *Le Tombeau de Couperin*, are good examples of Ravel's traditional formal patterns combined with an extended harmonic vocabulary. *Le Tombeau de Couperin* is a suite of six pieces (Prelude, Fugue, Forlane, Rigaudon, Menuet, Toccata) in the manner of a Baroque suite. Ravel dedicated each movement to the memory of a friend who died in the First World War. The suite was completed in 1917.

One of Ravel's well-known pieces of orchestral writing is his arrangement of Mussorgsky's *Pictures at an Exhibition* (1922). Compare the sound of Ravel's version with the piano version in IV.27-28.

V.3. Maurice Ravel

Rigaudon

No.4 from *Le Tombeau de Couperin* (1917)

Compare this Rigaudon to Couperin's (II.6). Is Ravel using a standard formal pattern? Is he using functional harmony? Can you determine the underlying tonal plan of measures 1-36? This movement includes several examples of "extended tertian chords" (ninths, elevenths, thirteenths). Identify specific measures in which they occur.

20
più f
25
ff
pp
30
f
35
ff
Moins vif
pp
Ped.
40
45
50
55

soutenu
Sourdine
pp
p
pp
ff
Tempo I°

95
mp
100
ff
ff
mf
105
f
110
più f
115
pp
120
f
125
ff

V.4. Maurice Ravel

Menuet

No.5 from *Le Tombeau de Couperin* (1917)

The middle section of this minuet is entitled "Musette," a reference to a type of Baroque music which imitated the French bagpipe of Couperin's time. How does Ravel suggest the drone characteristics of the bagpipe? The melodic material of measures 1-4 should be traced throughout the piece; can you find various harmonizations of it? How can you describe the final cadence?

Musette
pp
Sourdine
35
40
45
50
p
3 Cordes
mf
55
ff
poco dim.
60
f
mf soutenu
65
pp
Sourdine
70

pp
75
80
p
85
90
mp
95
p expressif
100
pp
Sourdine

pp expressif
105
poco cresc.
p
3 Cordes
110
mf
f
115
mf
120
pp
8
Ralentir beaucoup
125
Très lent
sans faire vibrer

V.5 through V.7 are three compositions by Arnold Schoenberg (1874-1951). V.5 and V.6 are from one of Schoenberg's best known works, *Pierrot Lunaire.* This work, for reciter, piano, flute (or piccolo), clarinet (or bass-clarinet), violin (or viola), and cello is a dramatic setting of twenty-one poems by Albert Giraud, a Belgian poet who published the poems in 1884. The text was translated from French to German by Otto Erich Hartleben and was set by Schoenberg in 1912. The work was written for an actress who first performed in a Pierrot costume on a stage where the instruments were hidden. The composition has been much discussed for its extensive use of *Sprechstimme* (speaking voice), a vocal technique where rhythmic values are determined, but the exact pitches may be varied by sliding up or down to the next pitch, following the contour indicated in the manner of a speech recitation (see the notes marked x in the vocal line). Different performances of the line suggest widely varying interpretations of the vocal pitch parameter.

The piece is arranged in three sets of seven poems; Nos.1 and 8 (the beginning of the first two sets) are given here. The texts suggest the emotional hysteria and subjectivity associated with the term *Expressionism*, an extreme extension of the nineteenth-century idea of personal expression. German visual arts of the first two decades of the century (including paintings by Schoenberg himself) also illustrate expressionistic tendencies and often deal with themes similar to those expressed here: the moon, night, and dark mysterious monsters.

Schoenberg controls the pitch structure not by a key nor by strict serial procedures but by reusing a small group of notes, especially in No.8, which is subtitled "Passacaglia." What are these melodic cells and how are they reused? Study also the musical form of the two pieces, since the text has the repeated structure of a rondeau (or rondel).

These preserial works may be compared with those by Berg (V.8a) and Webern (V.9), two of Schoenberg's pupils. A completely different interpretation of Pierrot may be seen in Schumann's character piece (IV.5).

V.5. Arnold Schoenberg

"Mondestrunken"

No.1 from *Pierrot Lunaire* (1912)

Fl.
G.
Vcl.
am Steg
pizz.
arco
immer pizz.
pp
stacc.
25
Den Wein, den man mit Au - gen trinkt, gießt nachts der Mond in Wo - gen
nie - - der. Der
rit.
Tempo
f molto espress.
30
Dich - ter, den die An - - dacht treibt, be - rauscht sich an dem heil - gen
f espress.
molto rit.
Tran - ke, gen Him - mel wen - det er ver - zückt das Haupt
glissando
pp subito
ppp
35
Tempo
und tau - melnd saugt und schlürft er den Wein, den man mit Au - - gen
pp subito
molto legato
poco rit.
spiccato
39
trinkt.

Mondestrunken

Den Wein, den man mit Augen trinkt,
Giesst nachts der Mond in Wogen nieder,
Und eine Springflut überschwemmt
Den stillen Horizont.

The wine, which one drinks through the eyes,
Pours nightly in torrents from the moon,
And overflows the horizon like a spring flood.

Gelüste, schauerlich und süss,
Durchschwimmen ohne Zahl die Fluten!
Den Wein, den man mit Augen trinkt,
Giesst nachts der Mond in Wogen nieder.

Desires, terrible and sweet,
Are swimming through the flood waters without number!
The wine, which one drinks through the eyes,
Pours nightly in torrents from the moon.

Der Dichter, den die Andacht treibt,
Berauscht sich an dem heilgen Tranke,
Den Himmel wendet er verzückt
Das Haupt und taumelnd saugt und schlürft er
Den Wein, den man mit Augen trinkt.

The poet, in ecstasy,
Grows drunk on the holy drink.
To heaven he turns his head
Rapturously and, reeling, quaffs and slurps
The wine, which one drinks through the eyes.

V.6. Arnold Schoenberg

"Nacht"

No.8 from *Pierrot Lunaire* (1912)

Nacht

Finstre, schwarze Riesenfalter
Töteten der Sonne Glanz.
Ein geschlossnes Zauberbuch,
Ruht der Horizont—verschwiegen.

Aus dem Qualm verlorner Tiefen
Steigt ein Duft, Erinnrung mordend!
Finstre, schwarze Riesenfalter
Töteten der Sonne Glanz.

Und vom Himmel erdenwärts
Senken sich mit schweren Schwingen
Unsichtbar die Ungetüme
Auf die Menschenherzen nieder...
Finstre, schwarze Riesenfalter.

Night

Huge, black, shadowy mothwings
Eclipsed the bright rays of the sun.
Like an unopened magic-book
The horizon broods darkly in silence.

From the mists of deep chasms
Comes a scent—destroying memory!
Huge, black, shadowy mothwings
Eclipsed the bright rays of the sun.

And from Heaven down to earth
Sink unperceived huge monsters
Falling with a heavy motion
On the hearts of all mankind...
Huge, black, shadowy mothwings.

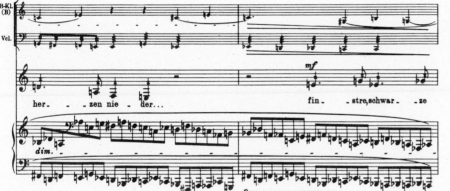

V.7. Arnold Schoenberg

Klavierstück

Op.33a (1929)

This composition is a separate piece for piano and illustrates Schoenberg's approach to serial composition. First, the piece should be studied by examining rhythmic patterns and textures; are there any elements which return? Compare, for instance, measures 32-34 with measures 1-13 and measure 35 with measure 14. Do you see any traditional formal patterns that Schoenberg is using, if in a less obvious way than nineteenth-century composers?

The pitch structure of the piece is based on a 12-tone row, P_0, and a second form of the same row (I_5). These two rows are combinatorial and Schoenberg exploits this property in the composition. The two rows are given below.

Combinatoriality is explained and references are made to this composition in George Perle's *Serial Composition and Atonality* (Berkeley and Los Angeles: University of California Press, 4th ed, 1977). A detailed examination of the tetrachord structure of this piece may be found in Eric Graebner's article, "An Analysis of Schoenberg's Klavierstück, Op.33a" in *Perspectives of New Music* Fall-Winter 1973 (128-140).

6
mf
7
poco rit
8
p
9
a tempo
10
mf
11
poco rit
molto rit
12
fp
p dolce
13
f
Ped
a tempo
14
cantabile
p
15

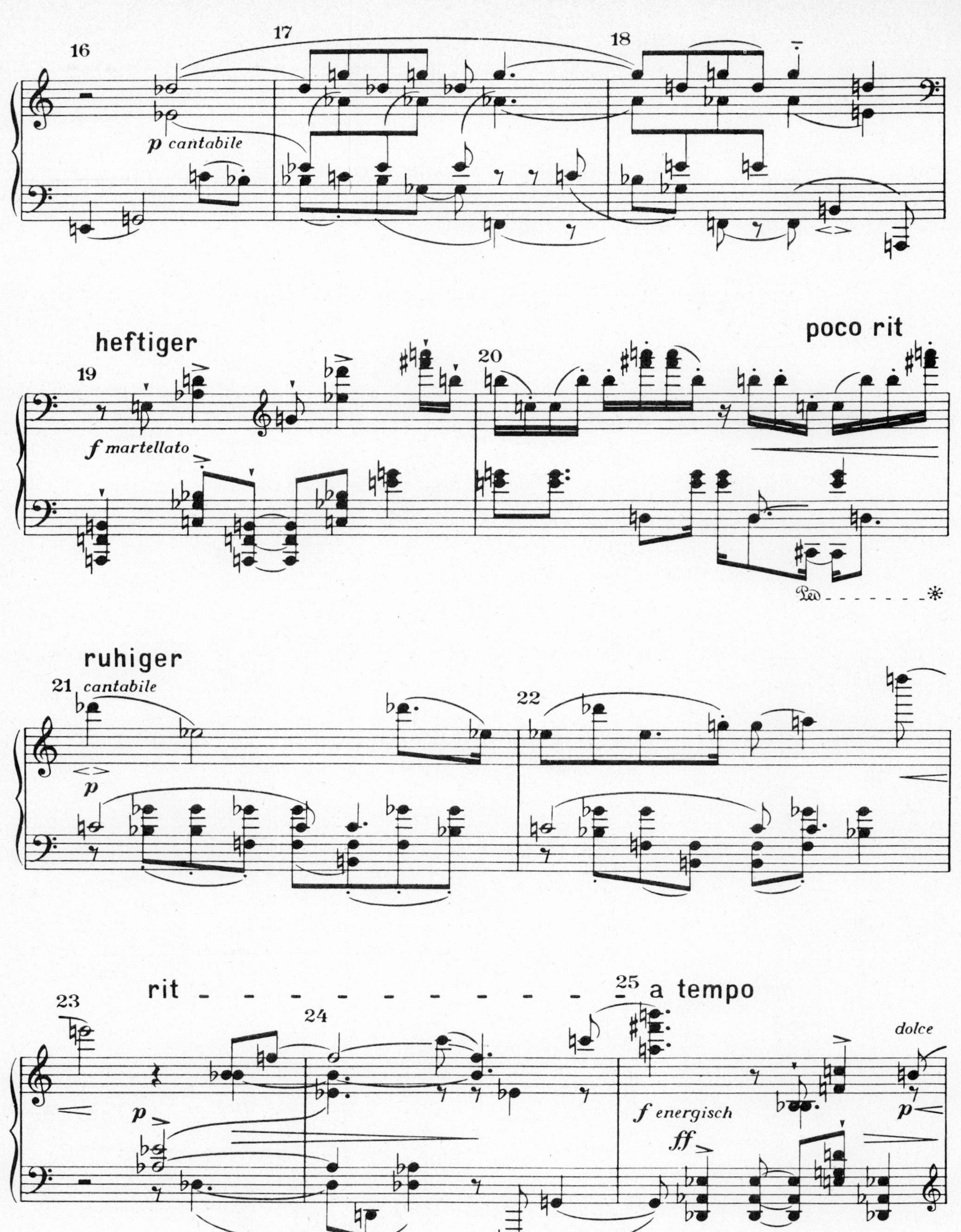
16
17
18
p cantabile
heftiger
poco rit
19
20
f martellato
Ped.
ruhiger
21 cantabile
22
p
23
rit
24
25 a tempo
dolce
p
f energisch
ff
p

26
steigernd
27
scherzando
sf
p martellato
28
f
f
29
8
30
f
31
mp
5
4

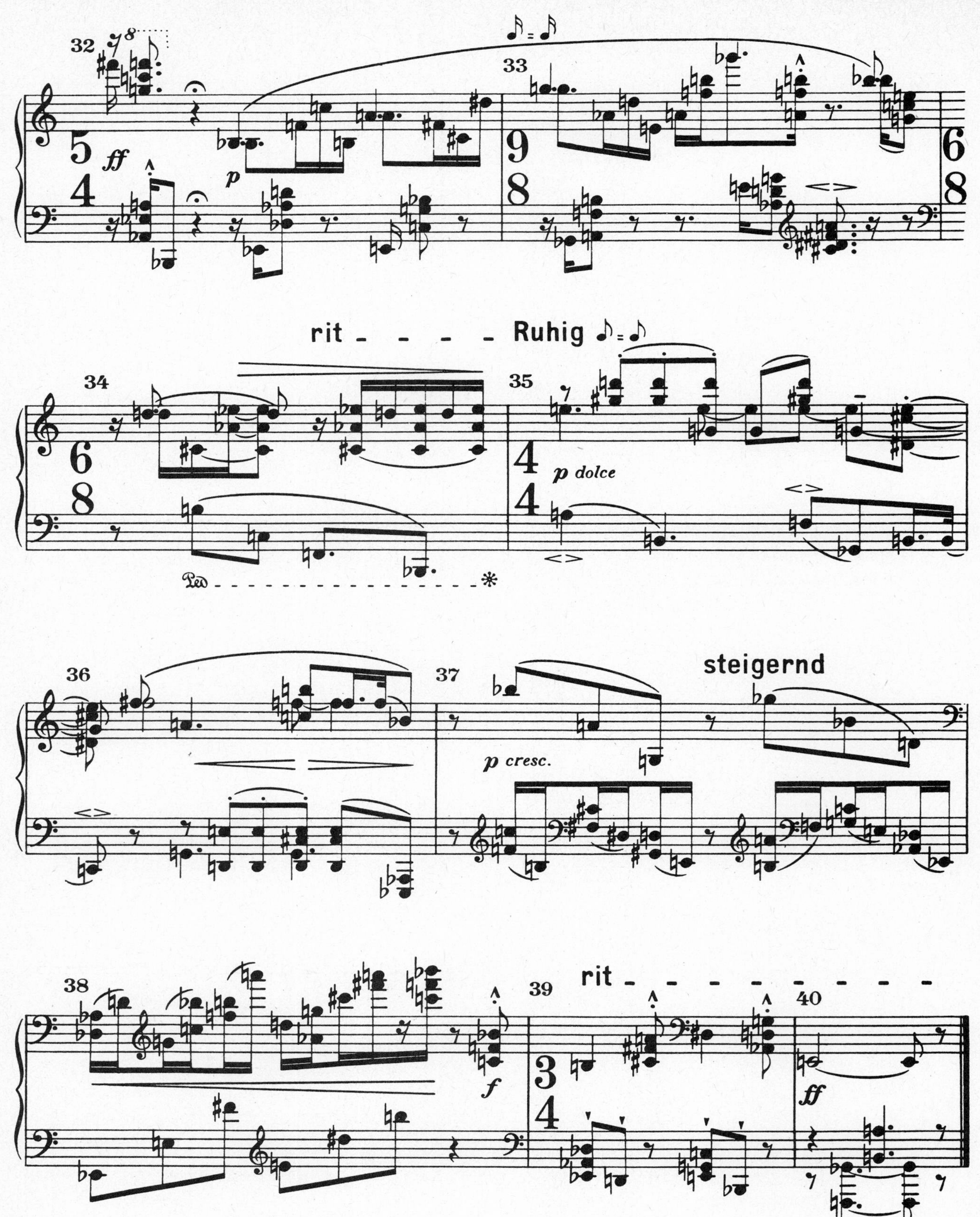
32
8
ff
p
33
5
4
9
8
6
8
rit - - - - - Ruhig
34
35
6
8
4
4
p dolce
Ped
36
37
steigernd
p cresc.
38
39
rit - - - - - - - - - -
40
f
3
4
ff

Alban Berg (1885-1935) was a Viennese composer whose first works grew out of the nineteenth-century romantic tradition. After his studies with Schoenberg, he began to experiment with the twelve-tone method of composition, but in most of Berg's later work this method is not applied strictly throughout. Two settings by Berg of the same text are given in V.8. One dates from 1900, when he was still writing tonally, one from 1925, when he was experimenting with serial composition. The two songs make an interesting comparison with each other and with other songs in the anthology. The songs have been discussed by Willi Reich and, in an appendix to the Universal Edition score, by Hans Redlich.

Version (b) presents a straightforward statement of the row in the vocal line. This row has special properties, and was used by Berg in the first movement of the *Lyric Suite* for string quartet, which he wrote soon after completing this song. In fact, the first violin line opening the suite

may be compared directly with the song. In this sense the song is a study for the suite, in the way that some of Wagner's "Wesendonk" songs were studies for *Tristan und Isolde* (see IV.20).[1]

What are the characteristics of the twelve-tone row in Song (b)?
How is the row used in the vocal line?
How does the piano employ the row? How does it relate to the vocal line?

Compare the two songs for text setting, form, and pitch materials. The poem is by Theodor Storm.

V.8a. Alban Berg

"Schliesse mir die Augen beide"

1900

[1]That the musical and dramatic language of *Tristan* was important to Berg is most clearly demonstrated by a quote from the Prelude to Act I of *Tristan* in the last movement of the *Lyric Suite*.

geht doch al - les, was ich lei - de, un - ter dei - ner Hand zur Ruh.
that my an - guish and my suff'r - ing may find peace in thy sweet touch.
p
5
Und wie lei - se sich der Schmerz Well' um Wel - le schla - fen le - get, wie der letz - te
As my pain flows like the sea___ wave by wave to rest at even - ing, when at last it
begleitend
pp
espr.
p
sempre pp
p
poco cresc.
8
Schlag sich re - get, fül - lest du mein gan - zes Herz, mein gan - zes Herz.
ceas - es beat - ing all my heart is filled by thee, is filled by thee.
8
mp
p
p

V.8b. Alban Berg

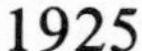

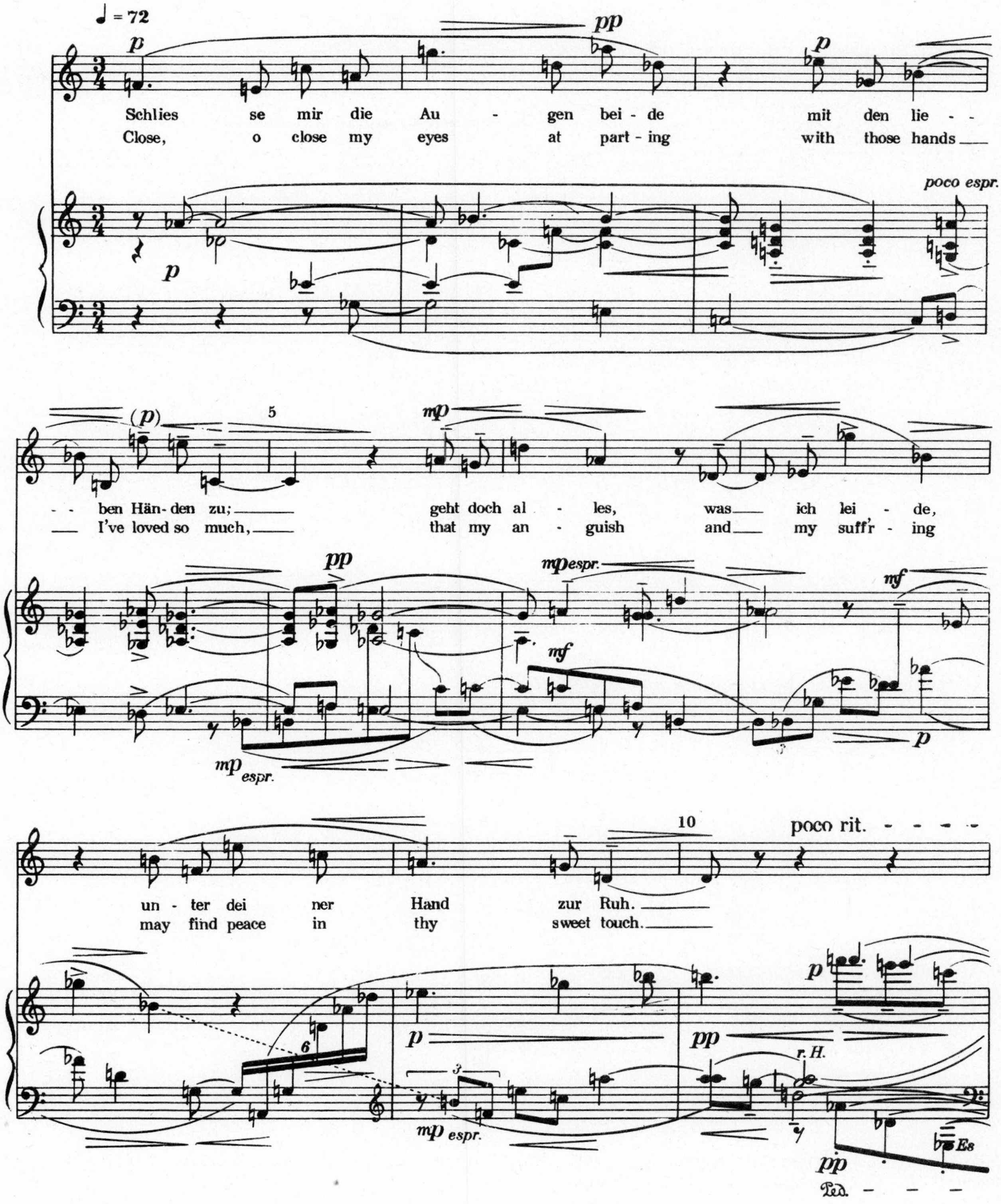

"Schliesse mir die Augen beide"

1925

= 72
Schlies se mir die Au - gen bei - de mit den lie - -
Close, o close my eyes at part - ing with those hands
poco espr.
5
- - ben Hän-den zu; geht doch al - les, was ich lei - de,
I've loved so much, that my an - guish and my suff'r - ing
mp espr.
mp espr.
10
poco rit.
un - ter dei ner Hand zur Ruh.
may find peace in thy sweet touch.
mp espr.
r. H.
Es
Ped.

- - - - a tempo
mp
Und wie lei - se sich der Schmerz
As my pain flows like the sea,
Well' um Wel - le schla - fen
wave by wave to rest at
8
espr.
Cis
mp
p begleitend
Ces
Ped.
15
pp
p
le - get, wie der letz - te Schlag sich re - get, fül - lest
even - ing, when at last it ceas - es beat - ing all my
sempre espress.
pp
p
3
Ped.
pp
poco pesante
cresc.
pp
20
du mein gan zes Herz.
heart is filled by thee.
den Gesang fortsetzend
L.H.
6
poco cresc. ma
sempre tranquillo
espress.
mf
p
(p)
ppp

Anton Webern (1883-1945) was an Austrian composer and, like Berg, a student of Schoenberg. His music, rooted in the Germanic classic and romantic tradition, developed into the concise, sparse style that influenced many of the composers working after the Second World War. However, Webern often spoke of his music in traditional terms such as "antecedent-consequent phrases"; the rhythmic structure and overall formal design should be examined as carefully in these compositions as the pitch structure.

V.9 is an example of Webern's preserial composition. It is based on specific recurring groups of pitches. V.10 is a movement from a large serial composition. These compositions may be compared to preserial and serial works by Schoenberg and Berg (V.5-8).

V.9. Anton Webern

No.3

from Fünf Sätze for String Quartet Op.5 (1909)

This movement illustrates how Webern builds an entire composition from the smallest elements. The C♯ pedal, the melodic cells [0,1,4] and [0,1,5] (represented abstractly in pitches as [C,C♯,E] and [C,C♯,F]), and an idea of texture and form based on contrapuntal development all contribute to an extremely unified piece. Trace the melodic elements throughout the work. How does Webern achieve a sense of finality in the movement?

arco stacc.
col legno
10
pizz.
col legno
col legno
pizz.
pizz.
arco
pizz.
molto rit.
arco
♩= 42
pizz.
pizz.
sehr zart
arco
pizz.
15
tempo (𝅗𝅥 = 84)
poco a
pizz.
arco
poco cresc.

poco accel.
20
arco
mp cresc.
mf
cresc.
f cresc.
arco
mp cresc.
mf cresc.
f
cresc.
mp cresc.
mf cresc.
f cresc.

sehr rasch (𝅗𝅥 = 102)
ff
fff
pizz.
sfff

The *Concerto* for Nine Instruments, Op.24, was composed by Webern in 1934 and was dedicated to Arnold Schoenberg on his sixtieth birthday. It is in three movements (Fast-Slow-Fast); the last movement is given in V.10. The instrumentation is flute-oboe-clarinet; horn-trumpet-trombone; and violin-viola-piano.

The beginning of the first movement is given below. Here the twelve-tone row is presented clearly, divided into trichords; notice also the rhythmic motives associated with each group of three notes. What are the characteristics of the row?

The last movement should be studied not only for the employment of the pitch series but for Webern's careful control of contours, rhythmic patterns, dynamics, articulation, and texture. This almost serial control of elements other than pitch led many composers of the 1940's and 1950's (e.g. Boulez, Stockhausen) to refer to Webern's mature works as part of the source of their work with "total serialism." This particular composition has been discussed by Stockhausen, Leibowitz, and Vlad; an introduction to the work can be found in Walter Kolneder's *Anton Webern*, translated by Humphrey Searle (University of California Press, Berkeley, 1968).

V.10. Anton Webern

Concerto Op.24

third movement (1934)

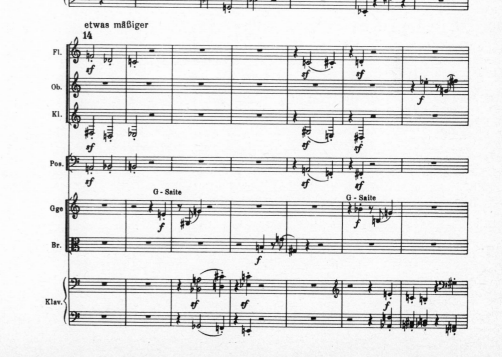

21
Fl.
Ob.
Kl.
Trp.
Pos.
Gge
Br.
Klav.
poco rit. - - - tempo I.
27
Fl.
Ob.
Kl.
Trp.
Gge
Br.
Klav.
34
Fl.
Ob.
Kl.
Gge
Klav.
40
poco rit. - - wieder etwas mäßiger
Kl.
mit Dmpf.
Hr.
Trp.
Pos.
Gge
Klav.

47
Fl.
Kl.
mit Dmpf.
Hr.
Pos.
offen
Gge
Br.
Klav.
53
poco rit. - - - tempo I. sehr flott
Ob.
Kl.
Hr.
Pos.
Gge
Br.
Klav.
59
Hr.
mit Dmpf.
Trp.
Pos.
pizz.
Br.
Klav.
65
Fl.
Ob.
Kl.
Hr.
Trp.
Pos.
pizz.
Gge
Klav.

Igor Stravinsky (1882-1971) is one of the most important composers of the twentieth century. After his early studies in Russia he moved to Paris, where, between 1910-1920, many of his best-known and most influential compositions were written. Excerpts from two of those works are included here. Stravinsky's innovations in rhythm, instrumentation, and form during this decade have been widely discussed; his ideas have influenced many other composers during the century.

During the Second World War Stravinsky moved to the United States and became an American citizen. The *Mass* dates from this period. During the 1950's Stravinsky began to include serial techniques as the basis of his compositions. However, in this area, as in his use of earlier forms and in his parodies of the music of other composers, his music reflects his own unique concept of sound and construction.

V.11. Igor Stravinsky

Danses des Adolescentes

from *Le Sacre du Printemps* (1913)

The Rite of Spring is one of the revolutionary pieces in the history of music. The work is a ballet in two large sections, written by Stravinsky for Diaghilev's *Ballet Russe* and premiered (to the public's dismay) in Paris in 1913. The ballet is based on the stories of Russian pagan rites, where a virgin is sacrificed to the god of spring. The excerpt given here is one of the most familiar parts of the ballet; it occurs in Part I after an introduction.

This excerpt provides an opportunity to study several different aspects of music. Orchestration and the way it reflects Stravinsky's own imaginative ideas combined with his study of Rimsky-Korsakov's music is one area. Because the use of the orchestra is such an important element, this excerpt is given in full score, even though the score is complicated. (Note that measure numbers are omitted and only rehearsal numbers are given.)

Another important aspect is obviously rhythm. Stravinsky is particularly innovative in the way he combines layers of activity to create a larger formal design; the layers of activity, of timbre, and of small melodic units should be traced throughout this excerpt. This section illustrates many other features of Stravinsky's style: narrow-ranged melodic units, ostinatos, and other brief repetitive patterns combine into an interesting mosaic. Compare his use of ostinato and layering to Debussy's compositions (see, e.g. V.1). *The Rite of Spring* has been the subject of an extensive pitch analysis by Allen Forte.

Used by permission of Boosey and Hawkes.

15
Fl. picc. 1. 2.
Cor. ingl.
come sopra
Clar. picc.
Clar. 2. 3. (Sib)
Fag. 1. 2.
1. 2. 3. 4.
Cor.
5. 6. 7. 8.
come sopra
pizz.
Viol. 1.
Viol. 2.
f come sopra
V-le
f come sopra
arco
Celli
f come sopra
Bassi
f come sopra
15
16
Oboi 1. 2.
1. 2.
a 2
2.
Cor. ingl.
Fag. 1. 2.
con sord.
Solo
Tr. 1.
pizz.
Viol. 1.
Viol. 2.
V-le
pizz.
Celli
poco meno
pizz.
Bassi
16

17
Fl. picc.
1.
2.
Fl. gr.
Flatterzunge
ff
Fl. in Sol
3 Oboi
a 2
sempre simile
Cor. ingl.
Clar. picc.
sim.
Clar. 1.(La)
Clar.(Si♭)
Fag. 1.2.
Cor. 4.
con sord.
picc. in Re
Trombe
1.2.3.4. in Do
Viol. 1.
mf
Viol. 2.
pizz.
V-le
Celli
sf meno f
Bassi

18
Fl. picc.
Fl. gr.
Fl. in Sol
3 Oboi
Cor. ingl.
Clar. picc.
Clar. 1. (La)
Clar. (Sib)
Fag. 1. 2.
8 Corni
picc. in Re
Trombe
1.2.3.4. in Do
Viol. 1.
Viol. 2.
V-le
Celli
Bassi
sim.
a 2
muta in Mi♭
muta in Si♭
4º senza sord.
sempre
senza sord.
arco
sempre simile
non div.
sempre sim.
unis.
non div. come sopra
come sopra
18

19
a 2
Fag. 1.2. 3.
C-Fag.1.
Cor.
Viol.1.
V-le
Celli
Bassi
p sub.
f
19
20
a 2
più f
Trombone 1.
mf
20
21
Fl.1.
Oboi 1.2.
21

22
23
1.
Fl. picc.
2.
Fl. gr. 1.
Oboi. 1. 2.
Cor. ingl.
sim.
Clar. 2. 3. (Sib)
Fag. 2.
1. 2. 5. 6.
Cor.
3. 4. 7. 8.
Tr. picc. (Re)
Tr. 1. (Do)
Solo
stacc.
marc.
Tr-boni. 1 2
Tube. 1. 2.
Timp.
Gr. C.
Viol. Solo.
Viol. 1.
pizz.
arco
Viol. 2.
V-le.
Celli.
Bassi.
22
23

24
Cor. ingl.
Solo
marc.
sim.
Clar. 2.3.(Sib)
1.2.
Fag.
3.4.
Tr. 1. (Do)
2 Viol. Soli
sul Sol
p sub.
Viol. 1.
Viol. 2.
V-le
col legno sino al segno
Celli
pizz.
col legno sino al segno
25
Fl. gr. 1.
Solo
Cor. 1. 2.
Solo
mp (mais en dehors)
sempre simile

26
Fl. gr. 1.
Oboi 1. 2.
Soli
mf
1. 2.
Fag.
3. 4.
Cor. 1.
Tr. 1. (Do)
Solo
mf
2 Viol. Solo
Viol. 1.
Viol. 2.
V-le
Celli
26
27
Fl. gr. 2.
Fl. in Sol
Solo
f
mf
Clar. 2.3. (Sib)
p
1. 2.
Fag
3. 4.
Cor. 5.
Solo
mf
Solo con sord.
senza sord.
Tr. 2. (Do)
2. Viol. Solo
Viol. 1.
Viol. 2. div.
V-le
Celli
27

28
Fl.gr.
1.
2.
Fl.in Sol
Clar.picc.(Mib)
Clar.(Sib) 2.
1.
3.
Clar.basso
Fag.
1.2.
3.4.
C-Fag.
Cor 5.
Tr-boni 1.2.
Timp.
1.2.
3.
2 Viol.Solo.
Viol.1.
Viol.2. div.
V-le.
Celli.
Bassi.
mf
f
pp
tr
pizz.
28

29
Fl. picc.
Fl. gr.
Fl. in Sol.
Oboi 1. 2.
stacc.
Clar. picc. (Mi♭)
Clar. (Si♭)
Clar. basso
Fag.
C-Fag.
Tr. (Do)
mp cantabile
Tr-boni 1. 2.
Timp.
Triang.
bag. en bois
Cymb. antique
Pult 5. 6. 7. 8.
Tutti
div. en 2
Viol. 1.
Viol. 2.
V-le. div. en 3.
arco
marcatiss. e molto cantabile
3 Soli
Celli
gli altri
Bassi
29

30
Fl. picc. 1. 2.
Fl. gr. 1. 2.
Fl. in Sol
Oboi 1. 2. 3.
mp
Cor. ingl. 1. 2.
2° cor. ingl. to Ob. 4°
Clar. picc. (Mib)
Clar. (Sib) 1. 2. 3.
Clar. basso
Fag. 1. 2. 3. 4.
4° Fag. to C. Fag 2°
Cor. 1. 2. 3. 4. 5. 6. 7. 8.
Tr. (Do) 1. 2. 3. 4.
Tr-boni 1. 2.
Timp. 1. 2. 3.
Triang bag. en bois
Cymb. antique
Viol. 1. div. en 2.
p sub. e stacc.
Viol. 2. div. en 2.
pizz.
p sub.
pizz.
V-le. div. en 3.
sur le sol
4 Sole
p sub
Tutte le altre
pizz
3 Celli Soli
Celli gli altri
p sub.
Bassi
p sub.
30

Clar. picc. (Mi♭)
(in Re)
Clar. (Si♭) 1.
2. 3.
Clar. basso
sempre sf
Viol. 1.
Viol. 2.
4 Soli V-le.
le altre
3 Soli Celli
gli altri
Bassi
meno f
cresc.
sf
31
Solo
mf grazioso
Fl. picc. 1.
Oboi 1. 2.
3.
Cor. ingl. 1
C-Fag. 1. 2.
a 2
Cor. 4.
Viol. 1.
div. pizz.
sff
Viol. 2.
(pizz.) div.
V-le.
div. pizz.
Celli
pizz.

32
Fl.picc. 1.2.
Fl.gr.
Fl.in Sol
Oboi
Cor. ingl.
Clar.picc.(Re)
Clar.(Sib)
Fag. 3.
C-Fag. 1.2.
a 2
Cor.
Tr. (Do)
Viol. 1.
arco
Viol. 2.
V-le.
mf cresc
Celli
Bassi
f sempre
32

33
Fl. picc. 1. 2.
Fl. gr. 1. 2.
Flatterzunge
Fl. in Sol
(Flatterzunge)
sempre sim.
Oboi 1. 2. 3. 4.
Cor. ingl.
Clar. picc. (Re)
Clar. (Sib) 1. 2. 3.
Fag. 1. 2. 3.
a 2
sempre dim.
C-Fag. 1. 2.
Cor. 1. 2. 3. 4. 5. 6. 7. 8.
Tr. picc. (Re)
Tr. (Do) 1. 2. 3. 4.
Tube
Viol. 1.
arco
Viol. 2.
sempre sim.
V-le
Celli
pizz.
Bassi
33

34
Fl. picc. 1.2.
sempre sim.
Fl. gr.
(Flatterzunge)
Fl. in Sol
Oboi
2.3.4.
Cŏr. ingl.
stacc.
Clar. picc. (Re)
(Flatterzunge)
Clar. (Si♭)
Flatterzunge
Flatter-zunge
(Flatterzunge)
Clar. basso
Fag. 1.2.3.
a 3
C-Fag. 1.2.
a 2
1.2.3.4.
Cor.
5.6.7.8.
Tr. picc. (Re)
Tr. (Do)
Tr-boni.
Tube
poco più f
Viol. 1.
f assai
Viol. 2.
f assai
V-le
Celli
arco
sim.
Bassi
34

35
Fl. picc. 1.2.
Fl. gr.
sempre sim.
Fl. in Sol
Oboi
2.3.4.
Cor. ingl.
Clar. picc. (Re)
Clar. (Si♭)
Clar. basso
Fag. 1.2.3.
C-Fag. 1.2.
a 2
1.2.3.4.
Cor.
5.6.7.8.
Tr. picc. (Re)
4. Tr. (Do)
Tr-boni
Tube
poco più f
secco
Timp.
Viol. 1.
Viol. 2.
4 Pos.
V-le
Celli
Bassi
35

36
Fl. picc. 1.2.
Fl. gr.
Fl. in Sol
Oboi
2.3.4.
Cor. ingl.
Clar. picc. (Re)
Clar. (Sib)
Clar. basso
a 3
Fag. 1.2.3.
a 2
C-Fag. 1.2.
2° C. Fag to Fag 4°
gliss.
Cor. 3.4.
5.6.7.8.
Tr. picc. (Re)
4 Tr. (Do)
Tr-boni
come sopra
Tube
Timp.
Viol. 1.
Viol. 2.
V-le
Celli
Bassi
36

V.12. Igor Stravinsky

Three Dances

from *L'Histoire du Soldat (The Soldier's Tale)* (1918)

L'Histoire du Soldat is a story that is told by a narrator and acted and danced against a musical background. It is more familiar in the suite version, which consists of a group of musical pieces extracted from the dramatic version. In this composition the performance forces are greatly reduced from the huge requirements of *The Rite of Spring*; Stravinsky returns to a Baroque conception of chamber music and even includes a "Great Chorale" in the suite.

Although there is a radical difference in surface appearances between V.11 and V.12, the compositional techniques are similar: an imaginative use of rhythm, repeated units, and small-ranged melodic lines. In the course of the three dances, Stravinsky changes his material from a tango to a waltz to ragtime. What is the basic material in all three dances? How are the dances similar? How do they differ? The movement can also be studied for the influence on Stravinsky of American ragtime (see V.25, for example).

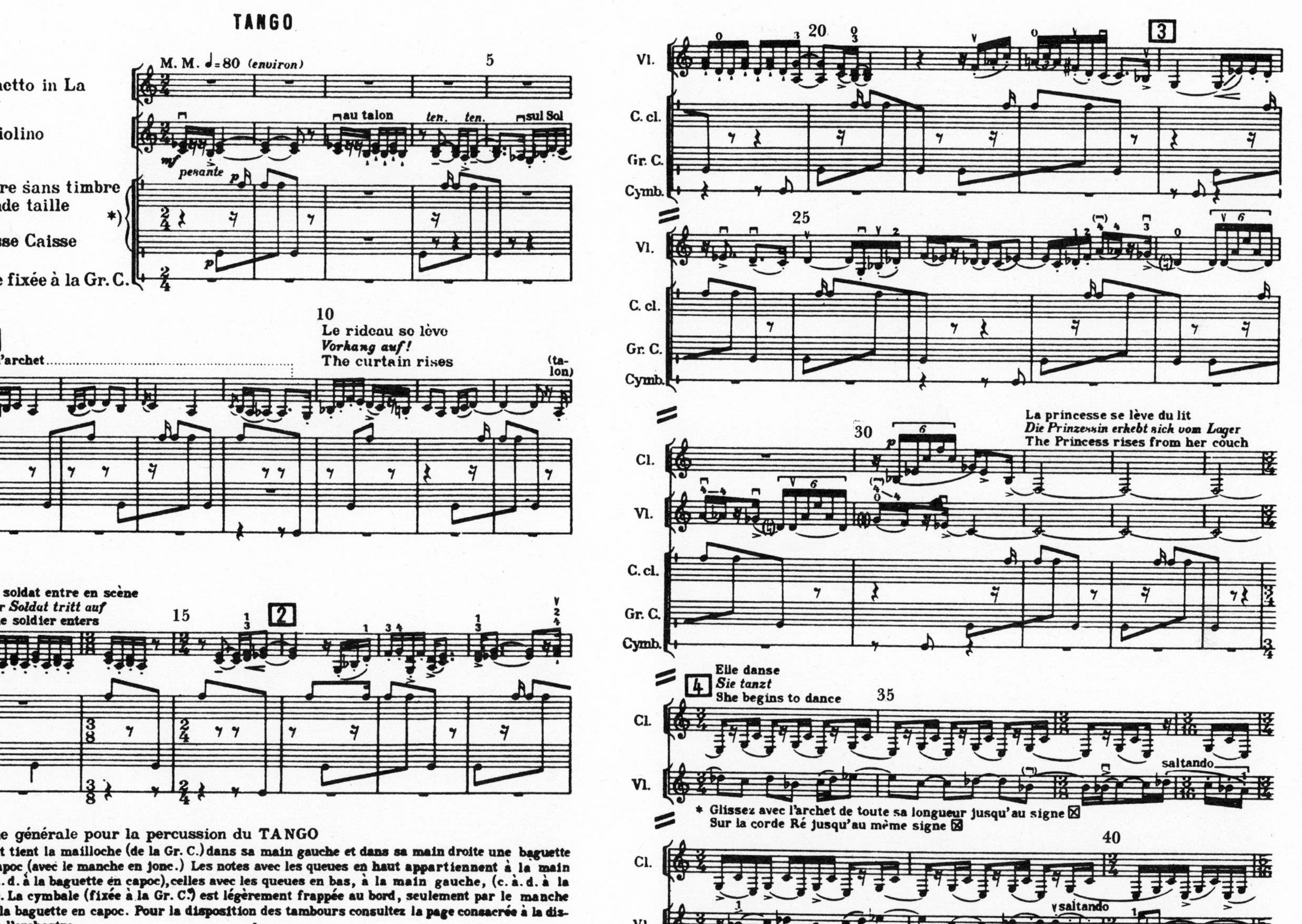
TANGO
M. M. ♩= 80 (environ)
Clarinetto in La
Violino
Caisse claire sans timbre grande taille
Grosse Caisse
une Cymbale fixée à la Gr. C.
pesante
au talon
ten.
ten.
sul Sol
1
tout l'archet
Le rideau se lève
Vorhang auf!
The curtain rises
(talon)
Vl.
C. cl.
Gr. C.
Cymb.
Le soldat entre en scène
Der Soldat tritt auf
The soldier enters
2
3
La princesse se lève du lit
Die Prinzessin erhebt sich vom Lager
The Princess rises from her couch
Cl.
4
Elle danse
Sie tanzt
She begins to dance
saltando
* Glissez avec l'archet de toute sa longueur jusqu'au signe ⊠
Sur la corde Ré jusqu'au même signe ⊠
* Exception faite des endroits marqués par le „saltando"
*) Remarque générale pour la percussion du TANGO
L'exécutant tient la mailloche (de la Gr. C.) dans sa main gauche et dans sa main droite une baguette à tête de capoc (avec le manche en jonc.) Les notes avec les queues en haut appartiennent à la main droite (c. à. d. à la baguette en capoc), celles avec les queues en bas, à la main gauche, (c. à. d. à la mailloche). La cymbale (fixée à la Gr. C.) est légèrement frappée au bord, seulement par le manche en jonc de la baguette en capoc. Pour la disposition des tambours consultez la page consacrée à la disposition de l'orchestre
J.

5
Cl.
Vl.
C. cl.
Gr. C.
sul Sol
45
6
je - té
manière d'exécution
Cymb.
50
je
té
7
55
laissez vibrer
8
60
Poco più mosso ♩= 92 - 96
sur la corde Sol
*) Glissez avec l'archet de toute sa longueur jusqu'au signe
saltando
2 C. cl.
petite taille
grande taille
65
9
Du milieu de l'archet jusqu'au signe
70
VALSE / WALZER / WALTZ
10
75
♪ = ♩ = 184 - 192
Clarinetto in La
Fagotto
pp leggierissimo
Cornet à pistons in La
Violino
mf leggiero
Contrabasso
pizz.
arco
p
80
Fg.
C. B.
sempre simile
*) Exception faite des endroits marqués par le „saltando"
J.

Fg.
Vl.
C.B.
Cl.
C.à P.
poco pesante
sempre
p sempre simile
arco
pizz.
pp sub.
sur la touche
glissez avec l'archet de toute sa longueur
p sempre
sempre sim.
court, du talon
leggierissimo
come sopra
(pizz.)
sempre simile
pizz. de la m. g.
IVa pos.
marcato (en dehors)

*) Toute cette percussion est (légèrement) frappée avec la tringle du triangle. Le triangle est tenu de la main gauche de l'exécutant; à sa droite, se trouvent (très près) l'un en face de l'autre, la C. cl. et le Tamb. de basque (posés de champ, ce qui est plus commode pour l'exécutant;) à sa gauche la Grosse caisse.

J.

26
200
Cl.
Fg.
Trb.
Trgl.
T.d.b.
C.cl.
Gr.C.
Vl.
sempre
27
205
210
marc.
sim.
28
215
29
220
sempre
pizz.
J.
30
225
f sempre
f molto
31
230
staccatissimo
f marcato
f en dehors
meno f
arco
p secco
C.B.
32
235
240
p leggiero
C.à P.
con sord.
glissando
pizz.
(laissez vibrer)

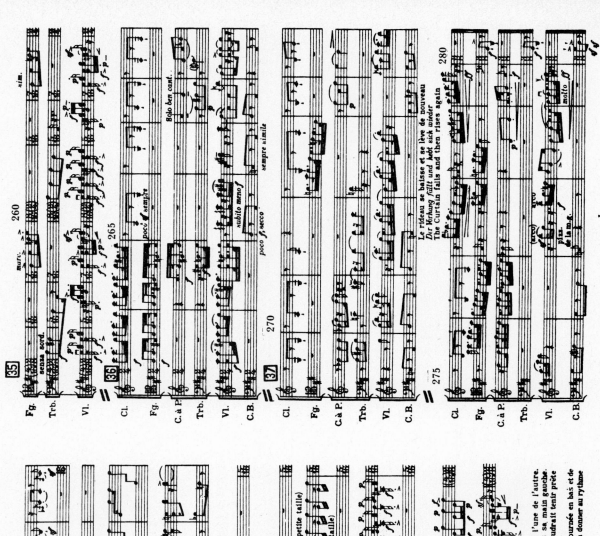

35
260
marc.
sim.
Fg.
senza sord.
Trb.
Vl.
36
265
Cl.
poco ff sempre
Fg.
C. à P.
Solo ben cant.
Trb.
Vl.
subito meno f
C. B.
poco f, secco
sempre simile
37
270
Cl.
Fg.
C. à P.
Trb.
Vl.
C. B.

Le rideau se baisse et se lève de nouveau
Der Vorhang fällt und hebt sich wieder
The Curtain falls and then rises again

275
280
Cl.
Fg.
C. à P.
Trb.
Vl.
(arco)
arco
pizz. de la m. g.
molto ff
C. B.

*) La Gr. C. se trouve à gauche et les 2 C. cl. juste en face de l'exécutant, et très près l'une de l'autre. Frappez ces instruments avec une baguette à tête en capoc que l'exécutant tient dans sa main gauche. Dans sa main droite il tient une baguette mince à petite tête en éponge (qu'il lui faudrait tenir prête pour le Nº 34)

**) Exécuter avec la bag. a tête d'éponge dont l'exécutant prendra soin de tenir la tête tournée en bas et de la manier rien qu' avec les doigts (le bras restant parfaitemente immobile) de façon à donner au rythme une allure mécanique et précise

J.

In V.13 Stravinsky looks back not to Baroque models but to Renaissance polyphony. His *Mass* (1948) is a setting of the standard five movements of the Ordinary of the Mass. It is written for four-part chorus (Stravinsky suggests that children's voices should be employed for the top two lines) and double wind quintet. The instrumentation of two oboes and English horn, two bassoons, two trumpets, and three trombones illustrates Stravinsky's fondness for unusual combinations, particularly those involving unusual wind groups.

How does this Kyrie compare with the Kyries of Renaissance masses given in this anthology (I.17, I.18, and I.24)? Is Stravinsky using any of the same compositional procedures? Do you see any of the techniques which occur in V.11 and V.12?

V.13. Igor Stravinsky

Kyrie

from *Mass* (1948)

*) Children's voices should be employed.

ste, Chri ste e lei son. Chri
Chri-ste, Chri ste e lei son.
p stacc.
p stacc.-marc.
ste,..... Chri ste, Chri ste, Christe e-lei son,
Chri ste, Chri ste,
Chri ste, Christe e–
Chri ste,
e lei-son, e-lei-son, e-lei son e lei son.
lei son, e-lei-son, e lei son.
Ky-ri-e, Ky-ri e,... Ky-ri–
Ky-ri-e, Ky rie, Ky-ri-e, Ky ri–
D.
A.
T.
B.
Ob. I.II
Fag. I
Tr. I in B♭
Trb.
C.I.
Fag.
Tr. in B♭
Ob.
Trb. I

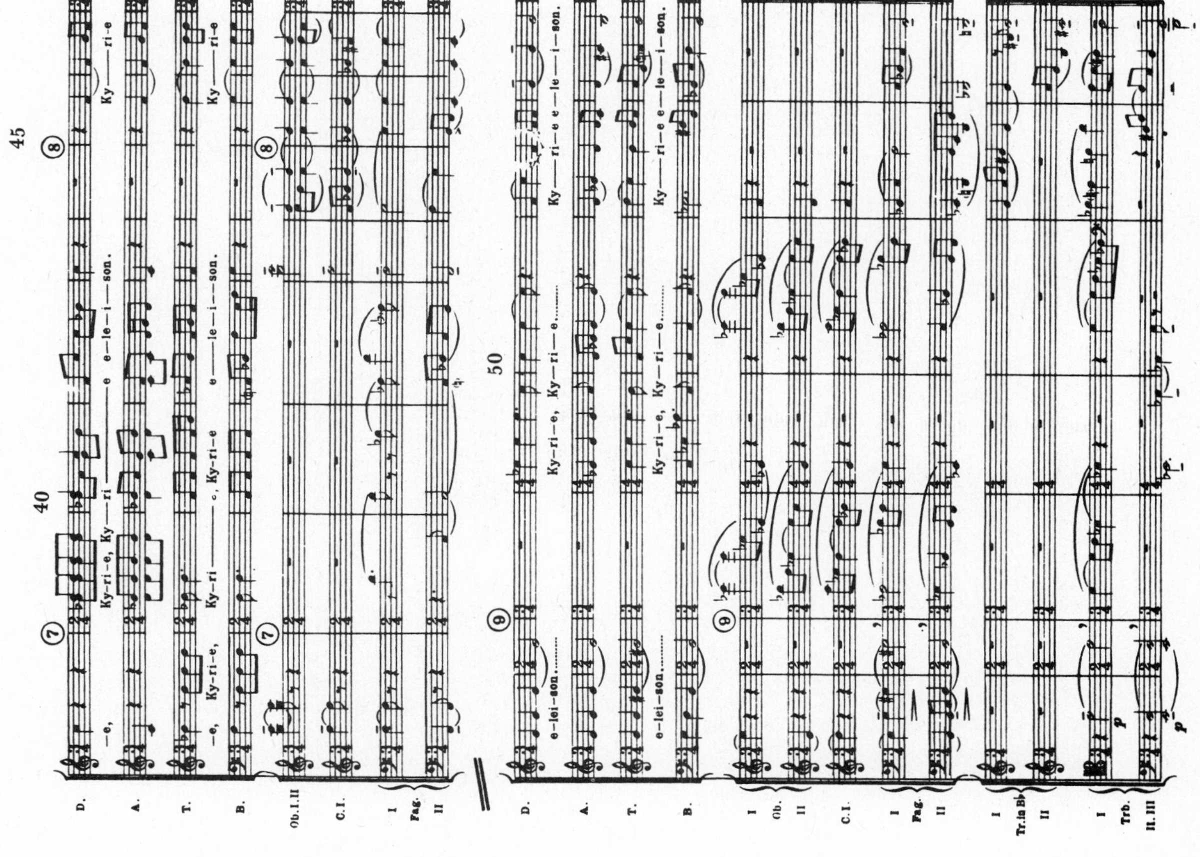
D.
A.
T.
B.
Ob. I. II
C. I.
Fag.
Ob.
Tr. in B♭
Trb.
Ky-ri-e, Ky-ri
e-lei-son
Ky-ri-e, Ky-ri-e
e-le-i-son.

Charles Ives (1874-1954), an American composer, was born in Danbury, Connecticut. Many of his innovations in harmony, texture, and form anticipated later developments in Europe. He is well known for his quotation of American folk songs and hymns and for his superposition of often extremely disparate layers of sound. He expressed in his music and in his writings (*Essays Before a Sonata*) many of the ideas of Emerson and Thoreau.

"The Housatonic at Stockbridge" is the last movement of an orchestral set entitled *Three Places in New England*, completed between 1906 and 1914. The title refers to the Housatonic River at Stockbridge, Massachusetts and was suggested, Ives says, "by a Sunday morning walk that Mrs. Ives and I took near Stockbridge the summer after we were married. We walked in the meadows along the River and heard the distant singing from the Church across the River. The mist had not entirely left the river bed, and the colors, the running water, the banks and trees were something that one would always remember."[2] The song, written in 1921, is an attempt to reproduce this atmosphere with voice and piano. Study particularly the harmonic structures and the textural layers of this composition. Is there a tonal center? How would you analyze the cadence at the end of the song? Listen to the orchestral version and compare the density of the texture to the song.

V.14. Charles Ives

The Housatonic at Stockbridge

(1921)

The poem is by Robert Underwood Johnson.

* ***NOTE:*** The small notes in the right hand may be omitted, but if played should be scarcely audible. This song was originally written as a movement in a set of pieces for orchestra, in which it was intended that the upper strings, muted, be listened to separately or sub-conciously- as a kind of distant background of mists seen through the trees or over a river valley-their parts bearing little or no relation to the tonality, etc. of the tune. It is difficult to reproduce this effect with piano.

[2] Henry and Sidney Cowell, *Charles Ives and His Music* (Oxford University Press, London, 1969), p.65

5
mp
Con - tented ri - ver ! in thy
10
dream - - y realm The cloud - y wil - low and the
mp
ppp
mp
plu - my elm: Thou
ppp
mf
r.h.
l.h.
pp
r.h.
f
pp
rit.

15
mp
beau - ti - ful! From ev - 'ry dream - y hill what
pp a tempo
ppp
eye but wan - ders with thee at thy will,
20
mp
Con - ten - ted ri - ver!
pppp
mp
ppp
p

25
And yet o - ver-shy
To mask thy beau - ty from the ea - ger eye;
Hast thou a thought to hide— from field and— town?
In some deep—
3
3
pp
cur - rent of the sun - lit brown
30
pp
mf

a little faster
............Ah! there's a res - tive rip-ple, and the swift red leaves Septem-ber's
in a gradually animated way
mf
35
firstlings faster drift;........Wouldst thou a-way, dear stream? Come, whis-per near! I al-so of much
mf
f
cresc.
rest - ing have a fear: Let me to -
8
ff

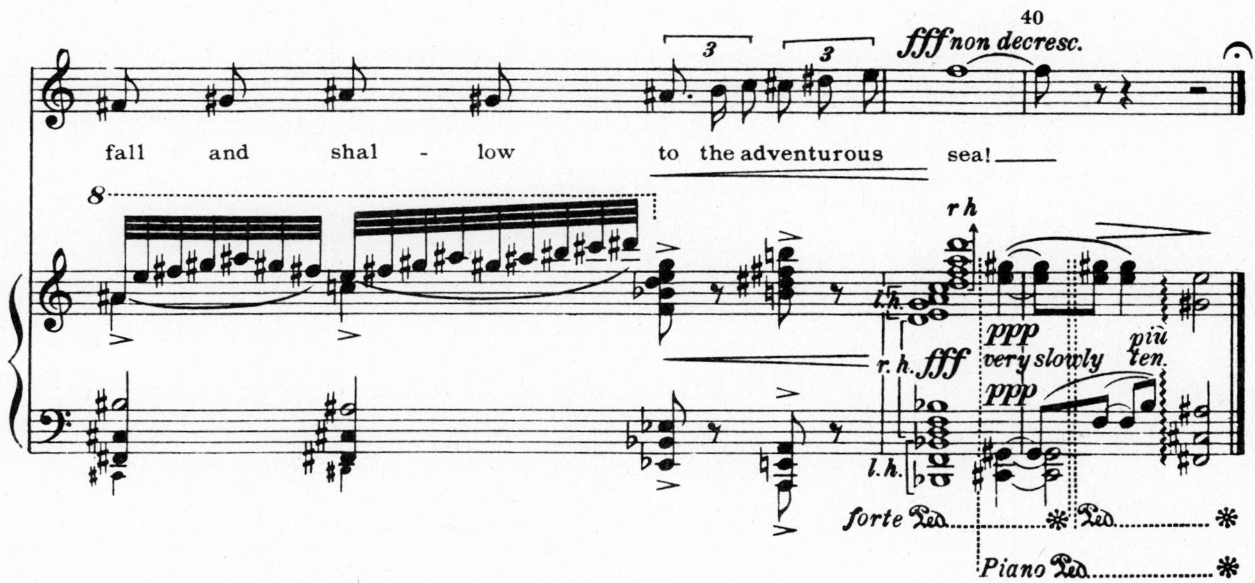

V.15 through V.18 are compositions by Béla Bartók (1881-1945), a Hungarian pianist and composer who came to the United States during the Second World War. Much of Bartók's music reflects his interest in Slavic folk music; he published several books and articles on his folksong research in Hungary and neighboring countries.

V.15 through V.17 are from *Mikrokosmos*, a collection of 153 pieces for piano that illustrate Bartók's interest in the development of piano technique (they range from very easy to complex) and in the compositional working-out of a limited bit of material. In these ways they parallel the aims of Bach's collection of two-part inventions and three-part sinfonias (see II.8-9). V.18 is a movement from one of Bartók's chamber works.

V.15. Béla Bartók

"Chromatic Invention"

No.91 from *Mikrokosmos* (1926-37)

What is the basic melodic idea of this piece? How does Bartók's working-out of the idea compare to Bach's treatment of material? (Compare, for example, II.8).

V.16. Béla Bartók

"From the Island of Bali"

No.109 from *Mikrokosmos* (1926-37)

What is the relationship between the two voices in measures 1-4? How is this relationship continued or changed in the course of the piece? What is the basis for the selection of pitch materials in this composition? This work should also be studied for the relationship of one section to another.

20
25
poco allarg.
30
sf
(prol. Ped.)
Andante
p, dolce
m.s.
dim.
35
poco rit.
40
a tempo
pp
(prol. Ped.)
[1 min. 56 sec.]

V.17. Béla Bartók

"Dance in Bulgarian Rhythm No.2"

No.149 from *Mikrokosmos* (1926-37)

How does Bartók establish the groupings suggested in the meter signature? What collection of pitches occurs at the opening of the piece (study particularly measures 1-12)? Are there any functional implications in the harmonic motion of the composition?

cresc.
f martell.
25
sf
marc.
30
mf
dim.
sff
35
mp
p
40

45
mp
50
mf
rit.
55
a tempo
f
p
più p
(Ped.)
60
pp
[1 min. 10 sec.]

The six string quartets of Bartók rank as a major contribution to chamber music in the twentieth century. They require the same sort of study that is necessary to penetrate Beethoven's late quartets: detailed analysis of small motivic structure, developmental techniques, and the proportional relationships of sections. The first movement of the Fourth String Quartet, written in 1928 and premiered in Budapest in 1929, is given in V.18. This movement should be compared with Beethoven's (III.18); they are similar in their development of large architectural form from a minimum of material.

The Fourth Quartet has five movements, arranged symmetrically in an arch. Movements I and V are both large-scale Allegro movements. Movement III is a slow middle movement, surrounded by a Prestissimo second movement (played entirely with mutes) and an Allegretto fourth movement, performed pizzicato. The first movement of this quartet has been studied in many articles and books for its terse pitch and rhythmic material. Study especially measures 5-7, noting the rhythmic and pitch motive in the cello in measure 7 and the vertical sonorities formed at the end of measure 5 and the beginning of measure 6. What creates contrast in this movement? Where does return occur, and how is it prepared?

The following sources may prove useful:

LENDVAI, ERNO, *Béla Bartók; An Analysis of His Music* (London: Kahn and Averill, 1971). Discusses Bartók's application of the golden mean.

MASON, COLIN, "An Essay in Analysis, Tonality, Symmetry, and Latent Serialism in Bartók's Fourth Quartet," *Music Review* XVIII, 1957. 189ff.

PERLE, GEORGE, "Symmetrical Formations in the String Quartets of Béla Bartók," *Music Review* XVI, 1955, No.4. 300-12.

TRAVIS, ROY, "Tonal Coherence in the First Movement of Bartók's Fourth String Quartet," *Music Forum* II, 1970, 298-371. Very detailed study of pitch structure.

TREITLER, LEO, "Harmonic Procedure in the Fourth Quartet of Bartók," *Journal of Music Theory* III, no.2, 1959, 292-98.

V.18. Béla Bartók

String Quartet No.4

first movement (1928)

25
cresc.
pp
f marc.
30
più f
menof
sf
ff
35
menof
simile
pesante
cresc.
40
cresc.
45
marc.

50
55
60
65

70
75
cresc.
80
simile
ruvido
85
sempre simile

90
sempre sf
poco sf
95
100
meno f
II
IV
III
105
110

115
meno f
meno f
più f
più f
120
B & H 9043
125
marcato
Più mosso, ♩=120
sf marcatiss. con brio
sf marcatiss. con brio
sf con brio
sf marcatiss. con brio
B & H 9043

130
135
140
145
150
cresc.

155
simile
160
Pesante, ♩ = 100
marc.

V.19 and V.20 are two excerpts from Paul Hindemith's *Ludus Tonalis (Game of Tones).* Hindemith (1895-1963) was a composer who believed strongly in tonality and in well-crafted, practical compositions. He composed sonatas and chamber pieces for almost every conceivable instrument, and was an influential teacher and theorist of the first part of the twentieth century.

Ludus Tonalis is subtitled "Studies in Counterpoint, Tonal Organization, and Piano Playing." It thus reflects the goals of previous collections, such as Bach's *Well-Tempered Clavier* (see II.10-II.15). The work begins with a Praeludium and closes with a Postludium. In between are twelve fugues, separated by eleven interludes. The fugues follow Hindemith's "Series 1" as explained in his *Craft of Musical Composition,* Volume I: an ordering of twelve pitches to show their closeness to a "progenitor tone." Beginning with C, the fugues follow the order of G, F, A, E, E♭, A♭, D, B♭, D♭, B, and F♯, ending with the tone most distantly removed from C. Fugue No.2 in G is given here, together with the Interlude which immediately follows it.

V.19. Paul Hindemith

Fugue No.2 in G

from *Ludus Tonalis* (1942)

What is the structure of the subject of this fugue? Trace the subject through the fugue. Does Hindemith change the metric placement of the subject? Compare this fugue with the ones from Bach's *Well-Tempered Clavier* (II.10 and II.11).

20
p
cresc.
25
mf
30
pp
35
mf
f
40
pp

45
mf
50
p subito
cresc.
55
f
60
mp
cresc.
65
mf
cresc.
f

V.20. Paul Hindemith

Interlude

from *Ludus Tonalis* (1942)

Is this interlude in a key? Do you see any functional basis for its tonal structure? Under what formal category can this interlude be classified?

Benjamin Britten (1913-1976) was an English composer who is well known for both his orchestral writing and for his extensive vocal music, including choral works and operas. V.21 presents two short excerpts from *The Young Person's Guide to the Orchestra*, a large-scale orchestral piece which can be performed with or without narrator.

The work is a set of variations on the beginning of Purcell's Rondo, given in II.2, suggesting Britten's fondness for the earlier English composer. After a statement by the full orchestra, the theme is played again by each section (woodwinds, brass, strings, and percussion); the variations show off individual instruments in the order in which they appear on an orchestral score. Britten then derives a fugue subject from Purcell's composition, and after working out the subject, combines it with Purcell's original material.

The first statement of the theme and the opening of the fugue are given here. How does the melodic structure of the fugue subject relate to Purcell's Rondo? What process is Britten following to determine the entry pitch of each statement of the subject?

V.21 a. Benjamin Britten

Theme

from *The Young Person's Guide to the Orchestra*, Op.34 (1946)

*) Cut to [2] if commentary is not spoken

10
Picc.
Flts. I & II
Oboes I & II
Clts. in B♭ I & II
Bsns. I & II
Hns. in F I & II
III & IV
Trpts. in C I & II
Trombs. I & II
III & Tuba
Timp.
Xyl.
S.D.
Cym.
B.D.
Harp
The WOODWIND are superior varieties of the penny-whistle. They are made of wood.
Vln. I
Vln. II
Vla.
'Cello
Bass
pp
ff
dim.
*) Bars marked 2 if commentary is not spoken.

V.21b. Benjamin Britten

Fugue (opening)

from *The Young Person's Guide to the Orchestra*, Op.34 (1946)

V.22. Benjamin Britten

"Dirge"

from *Serenade*, Op.31 (1943)

This is one movement from a composition written for tenor voice, horn, and strings. The work begins with a Prologue and ends with an Epilogue, both for solo horn. The other movements set texts by various poets, including Tennyson and Keats. The text for "Dirge" is an anonymous one from the fifteenth century.

First, study the pitch and rhythmic structure of the vocal line. What process is Britten using in this line throughout the composition? Second, study the instrumental parts. They are following a process separate from that of the voice line. What is their relationship of parts? Do they establish a tonal center? Does this support or conflict with the center established by the voice? What elements create a large-scale formal design in this work?

Voice
Hn. in F
Vln. I
Vln. II
Vla.
'Cello
Bass
Sit thee down and put them on;.......... And Christe re - ceive thy saule...... If
cresc.
fp
20
hos'n and shoon thou ne'er gav'st nane, E-very nighte and alle, The
mf marc.
whinnes sall prick thee to the bare bane;........ And Christe re - ceive thy saule........ From
f pesante
25
Whin - ny - muir when thou may'st pass, E-ver-y nighte and alle, To
sfp
f stacc. e pesante sempre

30
Voice
Brig o' Dread thou com'st at last; .... And Christe re - ceive thy saule.... From
Hn. in F
Vln. I
Vln. II
Vla.
'Cello
Bass
cresc.
sfp
f stacc. e pesante
pizz.
arco
Brig o' Dread when thou may'st pass, E-ver-y nighte and alle, To
molto f largamente
(veloce)
ffp
ff
pizz.
arco
f marc.
35
Purg-a-to-ry fire thou com'st at last; .... And Christe re - - ceive thy saule....... If
ffp
cresc.
f marc.
e - ver thou gav'st meat or drink, E-ver-y nighte and alle, The
dim.
sempre più p
p
mf

40
Voice
Hn. in F
Vln. I
Vln. II
Vla.
'Cello
Bass
fire sall ne-ver make thee shrink;.. And Christe re - ceive thy saule.............. If
pizz.
45
meat or drink thou ne'er gav'st nane, E-ver-y nighte and alle, The
arco
fire will burn thee to the bare bane;.... And Christe re - ceive thy saule.................. This ae nighte,
div.
pp dim.
p distinto
50
senza ritardando
this ae nighte, E-ver-y nighte and alle, Fire and fleet and candle-lighte, And Christe re-ceive thy saule....
unis. pizz.
meno f ma sempre distinto
dim.
pizz.

V.23 is a set of variations on a theme derived from the Gregorian chant given in I.1 (the Kyrie "De Angelis"). It is the first movement of Piano Sonata No.3 by Norman Dello Joio (b.1913); the other movements of the sonata are "Presto e leggiero," "Adagio," and "Allegro vivo e ritmico." This movement illustrates Dello Joio's fondness for variation techniques and the influence of chant on his melodic writing; it also illustrates sonorities and harmonic procedures typical of the tonal composers of the twentieth century. Dello Joio, an American, has been active as a teacher and as the head of several important educational projects and schools.

How does the theme make use of the Gregorian chant? What happens to this melodic material in the variations? How do these variations compare with other sets in the anthology (see study guide)?

V.23. Norman Dello Joio

Piano Sonata No.3

first movement (Theme and variations) (1947)

rall.
pp
Var. I (♩. = 80)
p secco e leggiero
p
mf
marcato il basso
f
p

Var. II (♩. = 66)
mf ed amabile
p ben cantando

Var. III (𝅗𝅥 = 176)
martellato
ff e marcatissimo

Var. IV (♩. = 56)
90
mf e con sentimento
cant.
calando
a tempo
95
100
p
mf
105
rit. poco
cantabile
110
ritardando e decrescendo
p

Var. V (𝅗𝅥 = 55)
115
con calore ma non f
mf
p
poco rall.
a tempo
pp
120
125
sonoro
mf
f
con intensità
f
130
f
f

cantabile
mf
135
p
p
140
pp
pp
attacca (𝅗𝅥 = 80)
p
rall. poco a poco
145
pp

V.24 through V.26 are three short examples of the blues, a native American style derived from black folksongs which, at least by 1910, was recognized as a separate kind of music. Although the blues as an artistic expression is a composite of words, emotion, and form, what has become known as the "blues progression" is a fairly standard harmonic framework over which the piece develops. The progression upon which the twelve-bar blues is generally based is given in skeletal form in V.24. In its essential parts, it includes only tonic, dominant, and subdominant chords, but the progression is so flexible that all sorts of substitutions of sonority or of root are possible. The principle here is the same as that of the sixteenth-century patterns given in I.28 and expanded in I.29 and I.30; the two sets of patterns may be compared for similarities in structure.

V.24.

Twelve-bar blues pattern.

The blues were developed into interesting and complex compositions by many composers in the twentieth century. One of the earliest was W.C.Handy (1873-1958), who, by his playing and teaching, brought the blues to the attention of the American public. Ragtime and the blues influenced many American and European composers of classical music; see, for instance, Stravinsky's "Ragtime" (V.12). Handy's most famous composition is the *St. Louis Blues*; the one given here, from 1913, illustrates elements of both ragtime and the blues. The first two large sections are given here. They are followed by two sections in C major.

What are the rhythmic characteristics of ragtime that are evident here? Which of those characteristics does Stravinsky use? Which parts of this piece follow the twelve-bar blues pattern? What substitute chords are used? What other chords and harmonic patterns are used? The blues and Handy's work can be further studied in *Blues: An Anthology* (New York: Macmillan Company, 1972), edited by W.C. Handy (1926), revised by Jerry Silverman (1972).

V.25. W.C.Handy

Jogo Blues

opening (1913)

Con Spirito
ff
20
25
1
2
30
mf
35
40

A more recent manifestation of the blues is given in V.26. This is the beginning of "Far More Blue" by Dave Brubeck (b.1920-) from his blues suite, *Time Further Out*. This suite is a collection of eight pieces inspired by a painting by Miró; each piece is based on the twelve-bar blues pattern or a variation of it. The excerpt given here is the theme and the first improvisation; since the basis of Brubeck's writing is jazz improvisation, a performance of this piece will not necessarily correspond to the notated version. The improvisation should be viewed as suggesting possible variational procedures on the pattern. Many of the pieces in Brubeck's suite, like this one, are written in meters other than the conventional $\frac{2}{4}$ or $\frac{4}{4}$.

How is the blues pattern stated in this work? What sorts of harmonic substitutions and additions are present? Listen to Brubeck's performance of the whole work (Columbia CL 1690 and CS 8490); how many times is the pattern stated? What elements is the group using for improvisation?

The version given here was transcribed from the recording by Howard Brubeck.

V.26. Dave Brubeck

"Far More Blue"

Theme and first improvisation, from *Time Further Out* (1961-62)

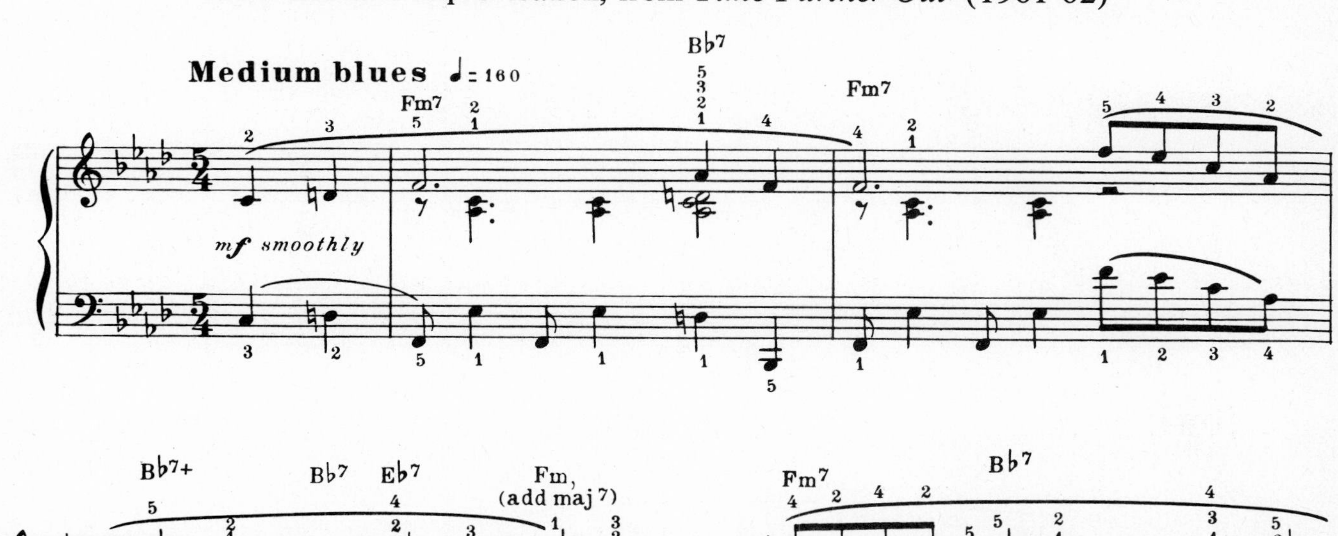

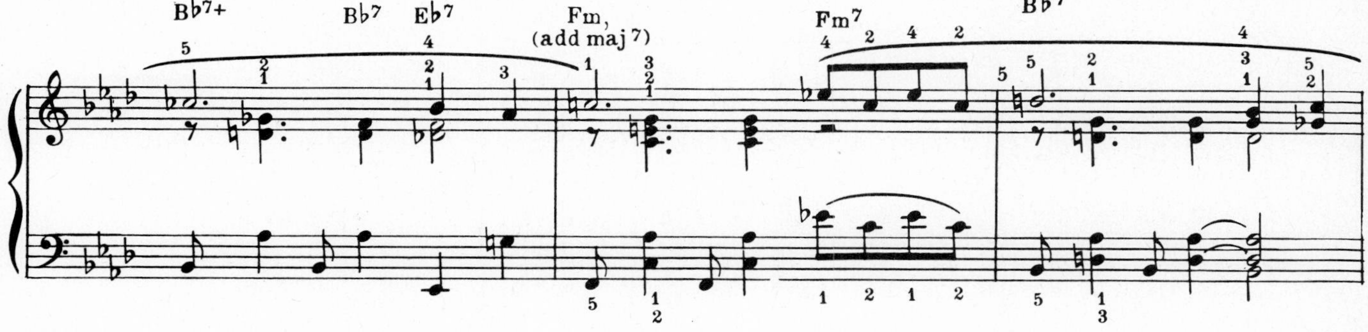

Eb7
C7
Fm7
G7
C7
Fm7
Bbm6
C7
10
Bbm6
Bbm7
Bbm6
C7
Fm, maj7
1st Improvisation
Fm7
Bb7
Fm7
mf
15
Bb7
Eb7
Fm7

B♭7
E♭7
C7
Fm7
G7
C7
20
Fm7
Gm7
C7
Gm7
C7
Gm7
C7
Fm7
C
2nd Improvisation
25
Fm7
B♭7
Fm
B♭7
E♭7

Examples V.27 through V.29 are three excerpts from Dallapiccola's *Quaderno musicale di Annalibera (Musical Notebook for* [his daughter] *Annalibera).* The eleven pieces in the composition are based on an all-interval row, first stated as: A♯, B, E♭, G♭, A♭, D, D♭, F, G, C, A, E. This work also exists in an orchestral version as *Variations for Orchestra.*

What are the musical characteristics of the row? What sonorities and melodic patterns does it suggest? How is the row presented in each of these examples? The melodic line in V.29, measures 1-4, actually makes use of the all-interval property of the row, including one occurrence of each interval from a minor second through a major seventh.

In addition to studying the serial procedures in these excerpts, one might compare Dallapiccola's compositional methods with those of Bach. In many ways the *Quaderno* is an "Homage à Bach"; Dallapiccola quotes Bach's name extensively in the first section ("Simbolo") and chooses titles reminiscent of Bach's various notebooks and contrapuncti (compare Bach's *Art of Fugue*). Do you see any justification in calling these pieces variations of each other? Are there other elements common to the three movements besides the all-interval row?

Dallapiccola (1904-1975) was an Italian composer known for his lyric use of serialism. He has written many chamber works and works for chorus and orchestra; one of these, the *Canti di liberazione*, uses the same row as the *Quaderno*.

V.27. Luigi Dallapiccola

"Linee"

No.4 from *Quaderno musicale di Annalibera* (1953)

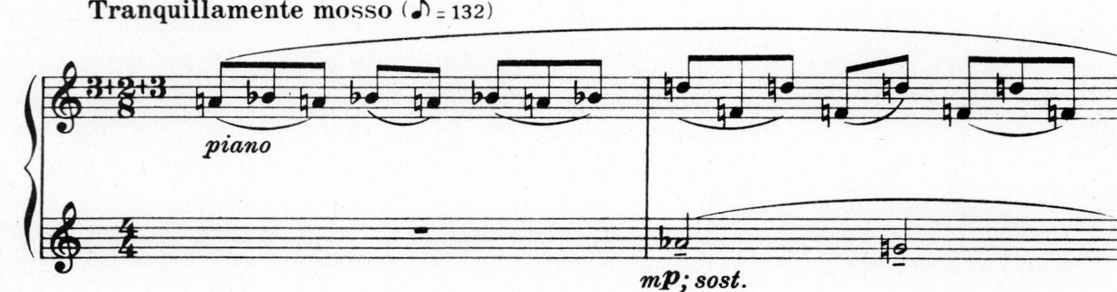

V.28. Luigi Dallapiccola

"Contrapunctus Secundus"

No.5 from *Quaderno musicale di Annalibera* (1953)

How do the lines relate to each other in this piece? Compare it with Bach's Goldberg Variation No. 15 (II.18).

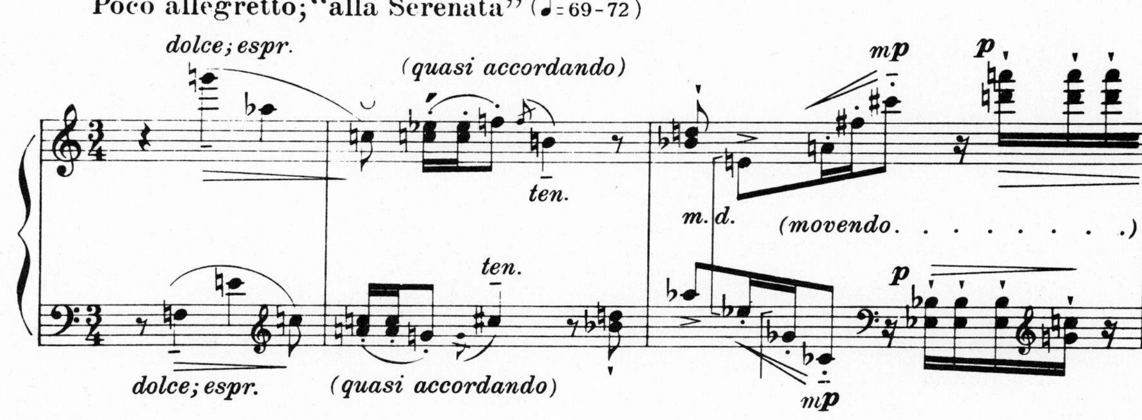

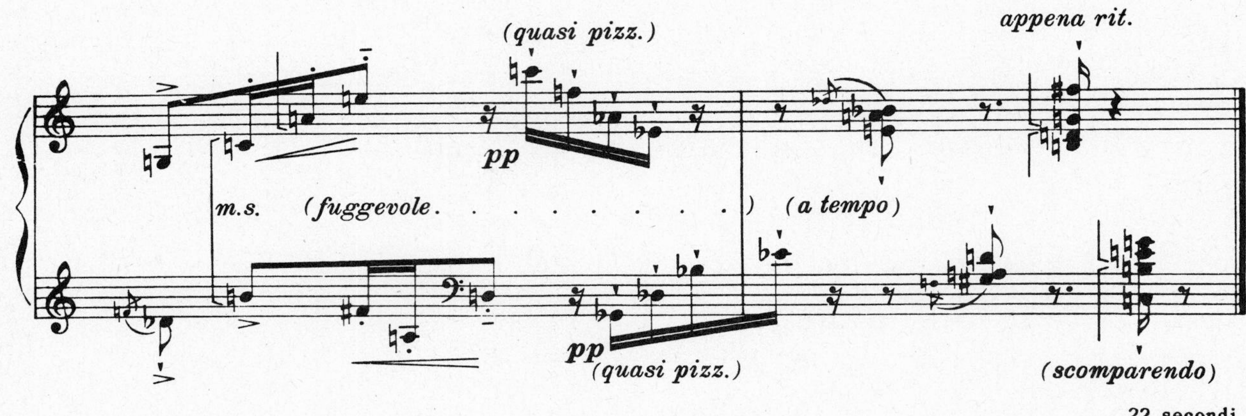

22 secondi

V.29. Luigi Dallapiccola

"Fregi"

No.6 from *Quaderno musicale di Annalibera* (1953)

Molto lento; con espressione parlante (♪. = 76)

1 min. 10 secondi

George Crumb (b. 1929) is an American composer who has written many works for unusual chamber ensembles. All of his works exploit color; timbral quality, dynamics, and articulation are very important to his sense of structure. Even the positioning of the performers is important, as can be seen in this diagram for *Ancient Voices of Children.*

STAGE POSITIONING

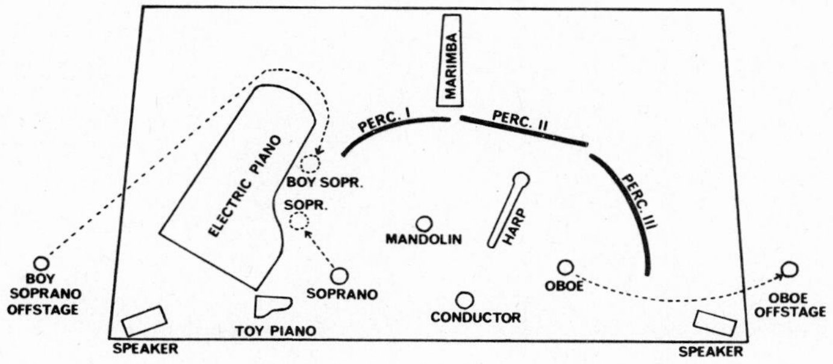

This work for soprano, boy soprano, oboe, mandolin, harp, electric piano, toy piano, and percussion has five sections based on texts by Federico Garcia Lorca. Section I is followed by, and Section V preceded by, separate instrumental "dances," thus creating an arch arrangement for the whole composition. This arch is intensified by the return in Section V of material from Section I and by the climax of activity in Section III. Section V is given here complete. Crumb has mentioned his admiration for Mahler; compare the opening of this section with the opening of the last movement of Mahler's *Lied von der Erde.*

In order to aid in reading the score, Crumb's complete notes for performance are given below.

V.30a. George Crumb

Performance Notes

from *Ancient Voices of Children*

PERFORMANCE NOTES

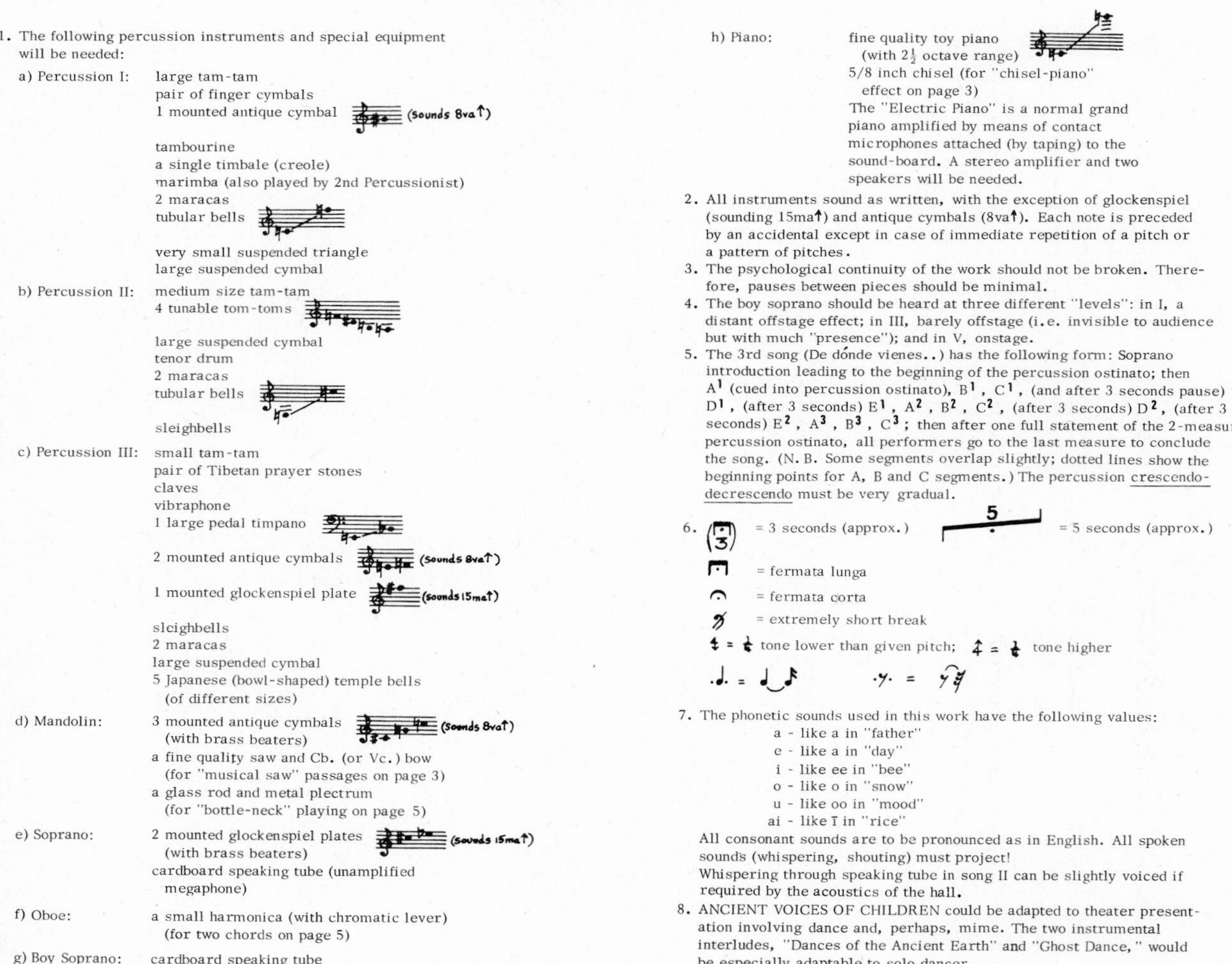

1. The following percussion instruments and special equipment will be needed:

a) Percussion I: large tam-tam; pair of finger cymbals; 1 mounted antique cymbal (sounds 8va↑); tambourine; a single timbale (creole); marimba (also played by 2nd Percussionist); 2 maracas; tubular bells; very small suspended triangle; large suspended cymbal

b) Percussion II: medium size tam-tam; 4 tunable tom-toms; large suspended cymbal; tenor drum; 2 maracas; tubular bells; sleighbells

c) Percussion III: small tam-tam; pair of Tibetan prayer stones; claves; vibraphone; 1 large pedal timpano; 2 mounted antique cymbals (sounds 8va↑); 1 mounted glockenspiel plate (sounds 15ma↑); sleighbells; 2 maracas; large suspended cymbal; 5 Japanese (bowl-shaped) temple bells (of different sizes)

d) Mandolin: 3 mounted antique cymbals (with brass beaters) (sounds 8va↑); a fine quality saw and Cb. (or Vc.) bow (for "musical saw" passages on page 3); a glass rod and metal plectrum (for "bottle-neck" playing on page 5)

e) Soprano: 2 mounted glockenspiel plates (with brass beaters) (sounds 15ma↑); cardboard speaking tube (unamplified megaphone)

f) Oboe: a small harmonica (with chromatic lever) (for two chords on page 5)

g) Boy Soprano: cardboard speaking tube

h) Piano: fine quality toy piano (with $2\frac{1}{2}$ octave range); 5/8 inch chisel (for "chisel-piano" effect on page 3)
The "Electric Piano" is a normal grand piano amplified by means of contact microphones attached (by taping) to the sound-board. A stereo amplifier and two speakers will be needed.

2. All instruments sound as written, with the exception of glockenspiel (sounding 15ma↑) and antique cymbals (8va↑). Each note is preceded by an accidental except in case of immediate repetition of a pitch or a pattern of pitches.
3. The psychological continuity of the work should not be broken. Therefore, pauses between pieces should be minimal.
4. The boy soprano should be heard at three different "levels": in I, a distant offstage effect; in III, barely offstage (i.e. invisible to audience but with much "presence"); and in V, onstage.
5. The 3rd song (De dónde vienes..) has the following form: Soprano introduction leading to the beginning of the percussion ostinato; then A^1 (cued into percussion ostinato), B^1, C^1, (and after 3 seconds pause) D^1, (after 3 seconds) E^1, A^2, B^2, C^2, (after 3 seconds) D^2, (after 3 seconds) E^2, A^3, B^3, C^3; then after one full statement of the 2-measure percussion ostinato, all performers go to the last measure to conclude the song. (N. B. Some segments overlap slightly; dotted lines show the beginning points for A, B and C segments.) The percussion crescendo-decrescendo must be very gradual.
6. (3) = 3 seconds (approx.) 5 = 5 seconds (approx.)
   = fermata lunga
   = fermata corta
   = extremely short break
   = tone lower than given pitch; = tone higher
7. The phonetic sounds used in this work have the following values:
   a - like a in "father"
   e - like a in "day"
   i - like ee in "bee"
   o - like o in "snow"
   u - like oo in "mood"
   ai - like ī in "rice"
   All consonant sounds are to be pronounced as in English. All spoken sounds (whispering, shouting) must project!
   Whispering through speaking tube in song II can be slightly voiced if required by the acoustics of the hall.
8. ANCIENT VOICES OF CHILDREN could be adapted to theater presentation involving dance and, perhaps, mime. The two instrumental interludes, "Dances of the Ancient Earth" and "Ghost Dance," would be especially adaptable to solo dancer.

V.30b. George Crumb

"Se ha llenado de luces mi corazón de seda"

from *Ancient Voices of Children.* (1970)

The poetry of Lorca has inspired much of Crumb's work. In his notes on this composition, Crumb mentions that his original compositional inspiration was from the last part of the text given below.

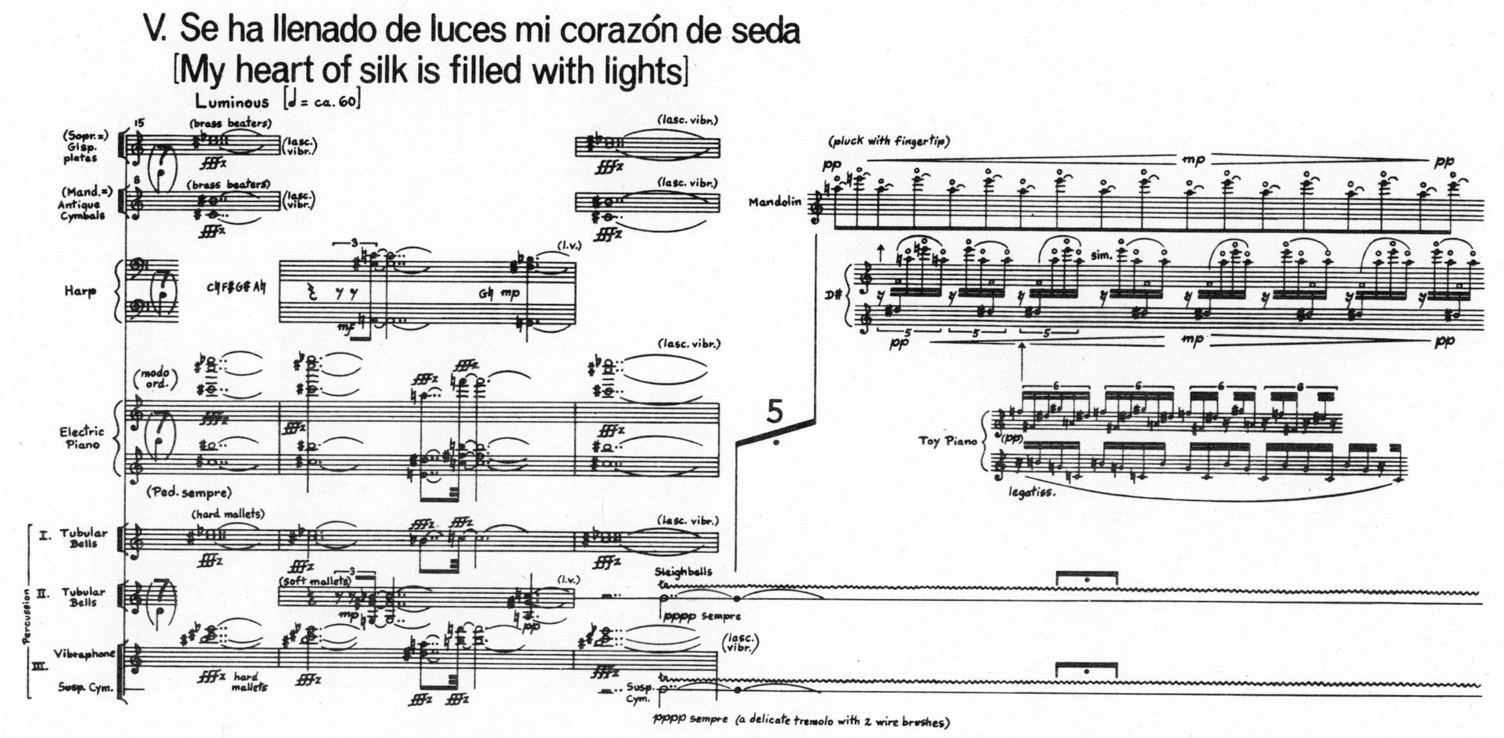

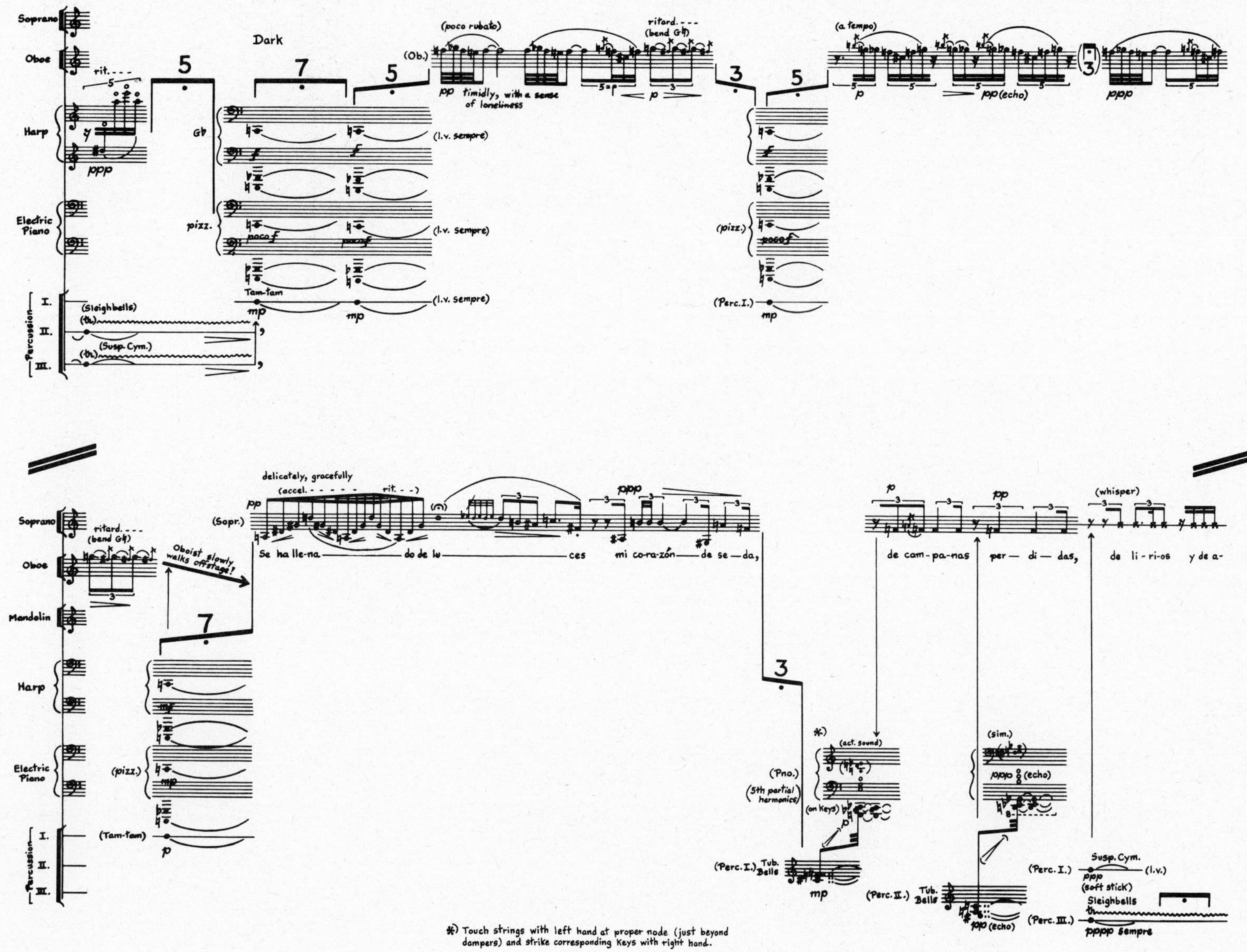

*) Touch strings with left hand at proper node (just beyond dampers) and strike corresponding Keys with right hand.

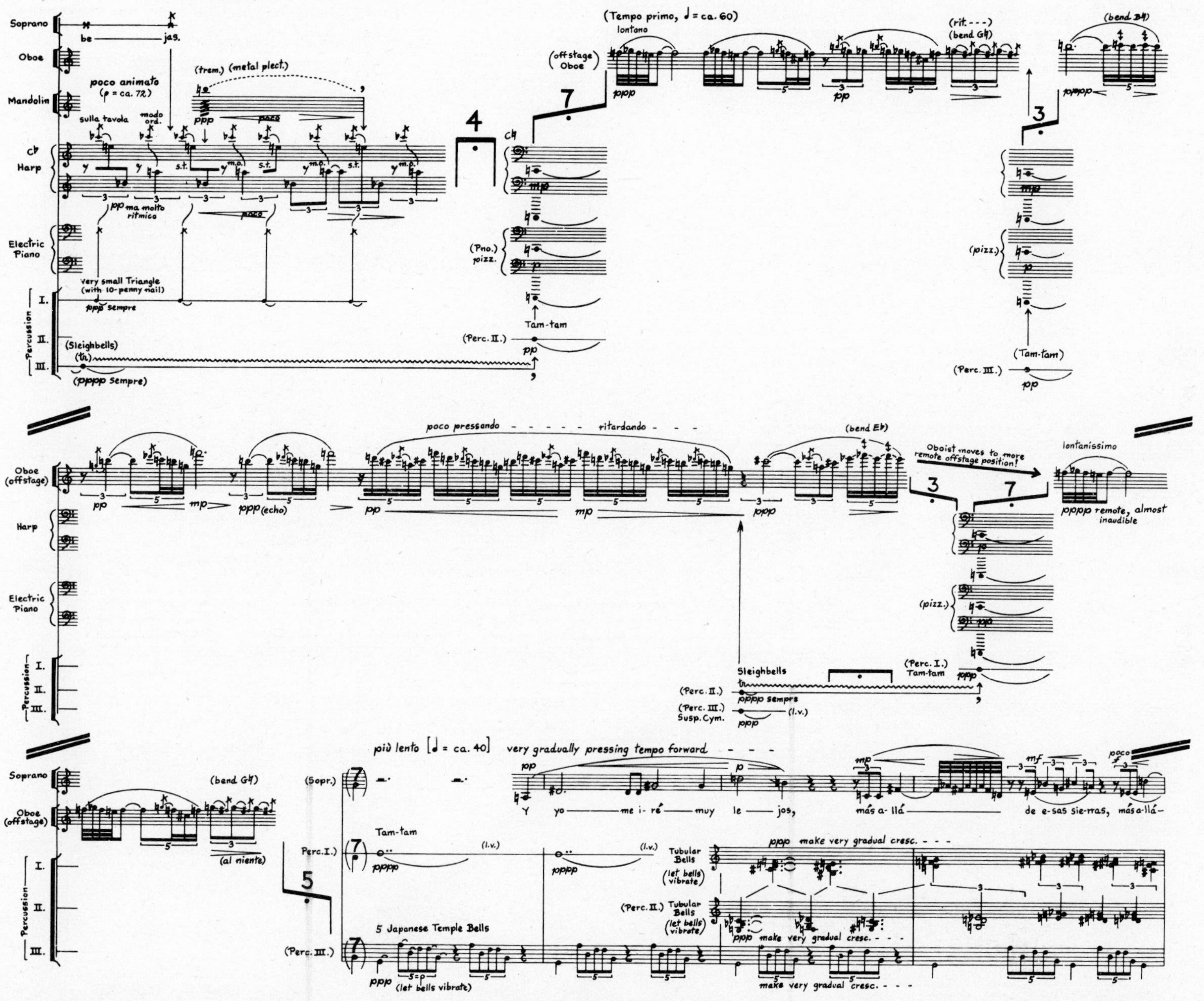
Soprano
Oboe
Mandolin
Harp
Electric Piano
Percussion
be — jas.
poco animato (♩ = ca. 72)
sulla tavola
modo ord.
(trem.) (metal plect.)
pp ma molto ritmico
Very small Triangle (with 10-penny nail)
ppp sempre
(Sleighbells)
(pppp sempre)
(Pno.) pizz.
Tam-tam
(Perc. II.)
(offstage Oboe)
(Tempo primo, ♩ = ca. 60)
lontano
(rit. - - -)
(bend G♮)
(bend B♮)
(pizz.)
(Tam-tam)
(Perc. III.)
Oboe (offstage)
poco pressando - - - - - ritardando - - -
(echo)
(bend E♭)
Oboist moves to more remote offstage position!
lontanissimo
pppp remote, almost inaudible
Sleighbells
(Perc. II.)
pppp sempre
(Perc. III.) Susp. Cym.
(l.v.)
(Perc. I.) Tam-tam
(bend G♮)
(al niente)
(Sopr.)
più lento [♩ = ca. 40] very gradually pressing tempo forward - - -
Y yo — me i-ré — muy le — jos, más a-llá — de e-sas sie-rras, más a-llá-
Perc. I.
Tam-tam
(l.v.)
Tubular Bells (let bells vibrate)
ppp make very gradual cresc. - - -
(Perc. II.) Tubular Bells (let bells vibrate)
ppp make very gradual cresc. - - -
(Perc. III.)
5 Japanese Temple Bells
ppp (let bells vibrate)
make very gradual cresc. - - -

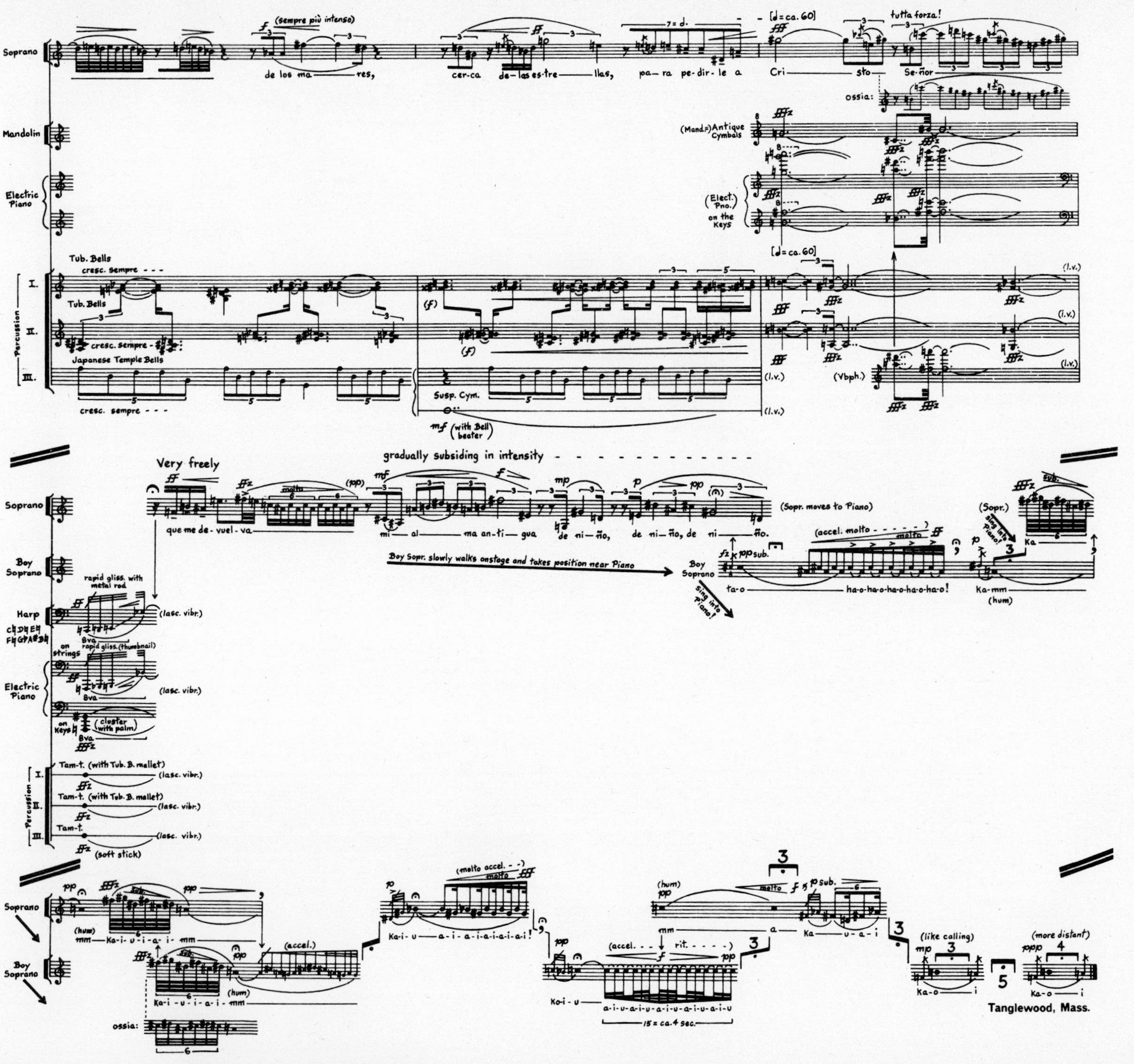
Soprano
Mandolin
Electric Piano
Percussion I. II. III.
(sempre più intenso)
de los ma— res,
cerca de las estre— llas,
para pe-dir-le a
Cri— sto— Se-ñor
tutta forza!
ossia:
(Mand.=) Antique Cymbals
(Elect. Pno. on the Keys)
Tub. Bells
cresc. sempre
Japanese Temple Bells
Susp. Cym.
(with Bell beater)
(Vbph.)
(l.v.)
Very freely
gradually subsiding in intensity
que me de-vuel-va
mi— al— ma an-ti— gua de ni— ño, de ni— ño, de ni— ño.
(Sopr. moves to Piano)
Boy Soprano
Boy Sopr. slowly walks onstage and takes position near Piano
Sing into Piano!
(accel. molto)
ta-o— ha-o-ha-o-ha-o-ha-o!
Ka-mm (hum)
Harp
rapid gliss. with metal rod
(lasc. vibr.)
on strings
rapid gliss. (thumbnail)
on Keys
(cluster with palm)
Tam-t. (with Tub. B. mallet)
Tam-t.
(soft stick)
(hum)
mm— Ka-i-u-i-a-i-mm
Ka-i-u-i-a-i-mm
(accel.)
(molto accel.)
Ka-i-u— a-i-a-i-a-i-a-i!
Ko-i-u— a-i-u-a-i-u-a-i-u-a-i-u-a-i-u
(accel. rit.)
15 = ca. 4 sec.
mm— a— Ka— u-a-i
(like calling)
Ka-o— i
(more distant)
Ka-o— i
Tanglewood, Mass.

V.

Se ha llenado de luces
mi corazón de seda,
de campanas perdidas,
de lirios y de abejas.
Y yo me iré muy lejos,
más allá de esas sierras,
más allá de los mares,
cerca de las estrellas,
para pedirle a Cristo
Señor que me devuelva
mi alma antigua de niño.

Federico García Lorca.

My heart of silk
is filled with lights,
with lost bells,
with lilies, and with bees,
and I will go very far,
farther than those hills,
farther than the seas,
close to the stars,
to ask Christ the Lord
to give me back
my ancient soul of a child.

Translated J.L. Gili

Luciano Berio is an Italian composer, born in 1925. He studied with Dallapiccola and later founded an electronic studio in Milan. He has taught at various schools in the United States. In 1958 he began the composition of a series of sequenzas. Each is for a solo performer and involves great virtuosity, in some cases incorporating elements of theater into the performance. Sequenza VII for Oboe (1969), given in V.31, is preceded by sequenzas for flute, harp, voice, piano, trombone, and viola.

This work illustrates various new notational procedures common to the second half of the twentieth century. Berio does not explain any of his notation, but many of his symbols are now standard.[3] The piece proceeds across each line in time units measured in seconds. The entire composition is accompanied by some sound source continually producing a B natural.

The opening of the work, where the oboe colors the B, is a good illustration of *Klangfarbenmelodie* (melody built out of tone color), a concept used by Schoenberg and others earlier in the century. How is the rest of the work structured by pitch, rhythm, dynamics, and color?

[3]The most complete source of information for modern notational practices is *Music Notation in the Twentieth Century* by Kurt Stone (W.W. Norton and Co., New York, 1980). Many of the symbols in this piece are explained in this book.

V.31. Luciano Berio

Sequenza VII for Oboe

(1969)

*) A B♮ must sound throughout the piece. The sound-source should preferably not be visible; this can be an oscillator, a clarinet, a pre-taped oboe, or something else. The intensity should be kept to a minimum, with quite small variations. The B♮ should give the impression of lending a slight resonance to the solo oboe.

Der Ton h' muß während der gesamten Dauer des Stuckes klingen. Die Tonquelle soll moglichst unsichtbar sein; diese kann ein Oszillator, eine Klarinette, eine vorher aufgenommene Oboe, oder anderes sein. Die Intensität muß äußerst gering sein, mit ganz leichten Schwankungen. Das h muß sich wie ein schwaches Echo der Solo-Oboe anhören.

2"
1,8"
1,5"
1,3"
1,3"
1"
1"
1"
NB. as short as possible/so schnell wie möglich

Study Guide

This section is intended to provide general directions for the study of pieces in this anthology. It is not intended to be comprehensive, nor to suggest any particular methodology. The questions should be viewed as points of departure for a thorough analysis of both the structural and the stylistic elements of the compositions. Suggested works in each category are generally arranged from simpler examples to more complex ones. The index should also be consulted for references to specific items.

I. Melody

Melodic stucture can be studied in monophonic examples as well as in clearly defined melodies which occur in thicker textures. Points to consider:

Pitch

1. What pitches are used in the melody? Do they form a traditional scale?
2. Is there a tonic note or center? If so, how is it established?
3. Are there any chromatic notes? How are they used?
4. If no traditional pattern is used, can the pitch content be analyzed in terms of small groups of intervals?

Rhythm and meter

1. Is a metric grouping established?
2. What rhythmic patterns recur? How do the rhythmic patterns relate to the meter?

Shape

1. What is the range of the melody?
2. Does it have a well-defined contour?

Structure

1. Where are the melodic cadences? How do the cadential notes relate to the tonality of the melody?
2. How do the phrases relate to each other? Are there examples of repetition, variation, contrast?
3. Are there small motives or melodic units that are being varied?
4. Can the melody be reduced to an underlying pitch framework? Conversely, how is the basic framework elaborated in the melody?

Other elements

Consider dynamics, text setting, timbre, etc.

Classification by scale basis

So many of the compositions in the anthology are based on the major and minor scale that only those which are not are referenced here.

Example Number	*Title*	*Page*
I.1	Chant, Kyrie from Missa "De Angelis" (Mass VIII)	2
I.2	Chant, "Victimae paschali laudes," Sequence	3

I.3	Chant "Alma redemptoris Mater," Antiphon	4
I.4	Chant, "Ave regina caelorum," Antiphon	5
I.5	Chant, "Veni sponsa Christi," Antiphon	5
I.6	Chant, "Pange lingua gloriosi," Hymn	6
I.8	Wizlaw von Rugen, "Nach der senenden claghe mů̊z ich singhen"	8
I.9	Wizlaw von Rugen, "Ic parrêre dî dorch mîne trôwe"	9
I.11	Machaut, "Foy porter"	12
I.14	Chant, "Ave maris stella," Hymn	20
I.29, top line	Traditional, "Greensleeves"	66
II.41a, b	Luther, "Christ ist erstanden"/"Christ lag in Todesbanden"	160
IV.27, top line (m. 1-6)	Mussorgsky, "Promenade" from *Pictures at an Exhibition*	391
V.17, top line (m. 1-13)	Bartók, "Dance in Bulgarian Rhythm No.2," No. 149 from *Mikrokosmos*	481
V.16 (e.g. m. 12-16)	Bartók, "From the Island of Bali," No. 109 from *Mikrokosmos*	479
V.22, m. 1-6	Britten, Dirge from *Serenade,* Op. 31	501

Structure

The above melodies should also be studied for elements other than pitch. The following lines or clearly defined units from homophonic or polyphonic textures are suggested for complete melodic study.

Example Number	*Title*	*Page*
I.7	Moniot D'Arras, "Ce fu en mai"	6
III.9, theme; top line	W. A. Mozart, String Quartet in D minor, K. 421 (E417b), fourth movement.	212
III.4, m. 1-26, top line	F.J. Haydn, String Quartet in G major, Op. 54 No. 1, fourth movement	181
II.24, top line, Aria	G.F. Handel, Aria con Variazione from Suite in B♭ major	121
III.6, voice line, m. 37-51	W.A. Mozart, Recitative and Aria from *Don Giovanni* ("In quali eccessi, O Numi – Mi tradì quell' alma ingrata")	200
III.23, vocal line, m. 3-27, 29-60	F. Schubert, "Der Müller und der Bach" from Die schöne Müllerin	290
IV.28, top line, m. 1-22	M. Mussorgsky, "The Great Gate of Kiev" from *Pictures at an Exhibition*	392–93
IV.16, top line, m. 1-16	F. Chopin, Mazurka in A minor, Op. 7 No. 2	341
V.20, top line, m. 1-10	P. Hindemith, Interlude in G from *Ludus Tonalis*	496
V.26, top line, m. 1-12	D. Brubeck, "Far More Blue"	515–16
IV.8, vocal line, m. 2-13	R. Schumann, "Widmung," from *Myrthen*, Op. 25 No. 1	318–19
IV.21, vocal line, m. 27-64	G. Verdi, "Celeste Aida" from *Aida*	361–64
II.21	Bach, Courante from Suite for Violoncello No. 1 in G major (study the polyphonic implications)	118–19
IV.1, m. 72-111	Berlioz, *Symphonie Fantastique*, first movement	304–5

IV.19 (beginning of Scene I)	Wagner, Prelude to and opening of Act I from *Tristan und Isolde*	356–57
IV.20 (beginning of Scene I)	Wagner, Prelude to and opening of Act III from *Tristan und Isolde*	458–59
V.30, solo vocal and oboe lines	Crumb, "Se ha llenado de luces mi corazón de seda" from *Ancient Voices of Children*	523–26
V.31	Berio, Sequenza VII	528–29

II. Counterpoint

Counterpoint involves the combination of somewhat independent lines.

Points to consider:

1. What creates independence between the lines?
2. Is one line more important than another?
3. How do the lines relate to each other intervallically? What intervals or chords are used at opening and closing points? In between?
4. Is a tonal center established? Is it the same in all parts?
5. What is the rhythmic relationship between the lines? Do they trade rhythmic activity?
6. Is imitation present?
   a. If so, between which voices?
   b. At what pitch interval?
   c. At what time distance?
   d. Is it strict canonic imitation?
7. How does each line develop? Does it use small melodic motives?
8. Are any contrapuntal techniques used? Check for inversion, augmentation, diminution, etc.
9. Do the lines switch places in the texture? (invertible counterpoint)
10. Is countermaterial used consistently?
11. Is there more than one important melodic idea presented?
12. How are phrases constructed? What creates cadences?
13. Is there a sectional plan in the piece? An underlying tonal plan, texture plan, etc.?
14. How is an overall form created in the composition?

Obviously many of the homophonic examples in the anthology not cited here contain contrapuntal passages or can be studied for contrapuntal aspects of voice leading.

Two-part writing

A. Nonimitative:

Example number	*Title*	*Page*
I.13	Landini, "Giovine vagha, i'non senti"	18
II.6	Couperin, Premier livre, deuxième ordre, Rigaudon	85
II.17	Bach, Goldberg Variations, Variation 8	112
III.15	Beethoven, Eroica Variations, "A due"	244
B. Imitative:		
I.21	Lassus, "Justus cor suum"	46
II.8	Bach, Two-part invention in B♭ major	88
V.15	Bartók, "Chromatic Invention," No. 91 from *Mikrokosmos*	478
V.16	Bartók, "From the Island of Bali," No. 109 from *Mikrokosmos*	479
V.23, Var. 3	Dello Joio, Piano Sonata No. 3, first movement	508
C. Canon:		
II.25, Var. 62	Handel, Chaconne in G major	123

Example number	*Title*	*Page*
III.15, Var. 7	Beethoven, Eroica Variations Op. 35	249
II.19 (over 3rd part)	Bach, Goldberg Variations, Variation 18	116
II.18 (over 3rd part)	Bach, Goldberg Variations, Variation 15	114
IV.25, Var. 6	Brahms, Theme and Variations 1-8 from *Variations and Fugue on a Theme by Handel*	378
V.28	Dallapiccola, "Contrapunctus Secundus," No. 5 from *Quaderno musicale di Annalibera*	519
Three-part writing		
A. Nonimitative:		
I.10	Anonymous, Motet "Ave, regina celorum - Alma redemptoris mater - Alma"	10
I.12	Machaut, Motet "Bone pastor Guillerme-Bone pastor, qui pastores-Bone pastor"	13
I.14	Dunstable, "Ave maris stella"	20
II.23	Bach, Gavotte from French Suite in E major, No. 6	120
II.16 (somewhat imitative)	Bach, Aria from Goldberg Variations	111
B. Imitative:		
I.15	Dufay, "Bon jour, bon mois"	21
I.22	Lassus, "Cantate Domino"	48
II.4	Corelli, Sonata V, Op. 2, Allemande	82
II.9	Bach, Three-part Sinfonia in F minor	89
C. Fugue:		
II.11	Bach, Fugue XXI in B♭ major from *The Well-Tempered Clavier,* Book I	96
II.10	Bach, Fugue XV in G major from *The Well-Tempered Clavier*, Book I	91
V.19	Hindemith, Fugue No. 2 in G from *Ludus Tonalis*	493
II.13 (more than one subject)	Bach, Fugue XIV in F♯ minor from *The Well-Tempered Clavier*, Book II	100
D. Canon:		
I.20 (plus cantus firmus)	Josquin des Prez, "Vive le roy"	44
Four-part writing (or more than 4 voices)		
A. Nonimitative:		
I.17	Dufay, "Missa L'homme armé," Kyrie	23
II.14 (somewhat imitative)	Bach, Prelude XVI in G minor from *The Well-Tempered Clavier*, Book II	104
B. Imitative:		
I.18	Josquin des Prez, "Missa Pange Lingua," Kyrie	28
I.23	Palestrina, "Veni sponsa Christi"	51
I.24	Palestrina, "Missa Veni sponsa Christi," Kyrie	54
I.19	Josquin des Prez, "Alma redemptoris Mater/Ave regina coelorum"	31
II.20	Bach, Goldberg Variations, Variation 30	117
II.28	Handel, Allegro, ma non troppo, from Concerto Grosso, Op. 6 No. 2 in F major	130
IV.12	Mendelssohn, "Help, Lord!" from *Elijah*	330
V.13	Stravinsky, Kyrie from *Mass*	469
V.6	Schoenberg, "Nacht," No. 8 from *Pierrot Lunaire*	426

C. Fugue:

II.7	Fischer, Fugue in E major from *Ariadne musica*	87
II.15	Bach, Fugue XVI in G minor from *The Well-Tempered Clavier*, Book II	106
II.12	Bach, Fugue IX in E major from *The Well-Tempered Clavier*, Book II	98
III.3 (more than one subject)	Haydn, String quartet in F minor, Op. 20 No. 5, fourth movement	178
V.21b	Britten, Fugue from *The Young Person's Guide to the Orchestra*	500
V.22	Britten, Dirge from *Serenade*, Op. 31	501

III. Harmony

Almost every work in this anthology may be studied for its harmonic (vertical) component. Since a complete cross-referencing is impossible, the pieces listed here are only the clearest examples of certain general types of chords. The index references specific types of chords and key changes. Clear homophonic textures were selected as much as possible, since such textures facilitate the study of harmony as a separate element. In all cases the other elements of the composition, particularly the melodic and rhythmic elements, should be considered as they relate to the harmonic element.

Points to consider:

1. What sorts of sonorities (chords) are used? (triads, sevenths, nontertian chords, etc.)
2. How are the chords related to each other? What are the patterns of root movement between chords?
3. Do the chords follow a large functional pattern? Do they have a harmonic direction? Are some chords more important than others? (Check, for instance, for sonorities functioning as passing and neighboring chords.)
4. What sonorities are used for cadential patterns? How do the cadence chords (usually a group of two or three) relate to each other?
5. How does the succession of chords relate to the rhythm and meter of the composition? What is the prevailing harmonic rhythm? Does this harmonic rhythm change at cadence points?
6. Does the movement of the harmony help to establish the meter or work against it? What is the metric arrangement of the cadences?
7. Is a tonal center established? How? What sort of plan do the cadence chords follow?
8. Are there changes of tonal center? How do these changes relate to the overall tonic?
9. Are there changes of mode, for example is there a mixture of chords from parallel major and minor scales?
10. How do factors such as spacing, textural placement, and dynamics influence the harmony?

Selected examples in the categories "Diatonic Chords" (triads and sevenths), "Extended tertian chords," and "Chromatic chords" are given below. "Chromatic chords" include secondary dominants (all kinds of dominant embellishments such as major-minor sevenths, diminished sevenths, etc.), augmented sixths, Neapolitans, other altered chords, and less functional chromatic chords. There is also a listing of compositions which use nontertian chords.

Diatonic Chords.

Some of these examples also contain a few embellishing dominants. Specific types of diatonic chords are referenced in the index.

Extended Tertian Chords

Also includes some altered tertian chords and some chromatic chords.

Chromatic chords

Functional chromatic chords or chords related by chromatic voice leading. Specific types of chromatic chords are referenced in the index.

IV.13	Chopin, Prelude in C minor, Op. 28 No. 20	337
IV.16	Chopin, Mazurka in A minor, Op. 7 No. 2	341
IV.17	Chopin, Mazurka in G major, Op. 67 No. 1	343
IV.18	Chopin, Nocturne in C♯ minor, Op. 27 No. 1	345
IV.23	Brahms, Intermezzo in A minor, Op. 76 No. 7	369
IV.26, especially m. 1-21	Brahms, Violin Sonata in A major, Op. 100, first movement	380
IV.30	Wolf, "Er ist's"	400
V.8a	Berg, "Schliesse mir die Augen beide"	433

Nontertian chords

V.6	Schoenberg, "Nacht," No. 8 from *Pierrot Lunaire*	426
V.7, opening	Schoenberg, *Klavierstück* Op. 33a	428
V.11	Stravinsky, *Le Sacre du Printemps*, Part I (Danses des Adolescentes)	445
V.14	Ives, "The Housatonic at Stockbridge"	472
V.23, Var. 5	Dello Joio, Piano Sonata No. 3, first movement	510–11
V.10	Webern, Concerto Op. 24, third movement	441

IV. Variations

Variational procedures occur in all sorts of ways in musical compositions. Some pieces are structured with a clear-cut theme, followed by sectional variations. In other works, a repeated melodic, rhythmic, or harmonic pattern is the unifying basis. Almost every composition manifests variation of material; only pieces which follow a regular process are listed here.

Points to consider:

1. What is the basic material, or theme, of the work? Is it, for example, a melodic/rhythmic line, a harmonic pattern, a phrase structure, or tonal plan?
2. How is this material retained throughout the composition? Are any changes applied to the material itself (is it decorated, stated in diminution, etc.)?
3. How is the context around the material changed? Consider such things as texture, harmony, and rhythmic activity.
4. How many times is the basic material stated? Do these statements divide the composition into sections?
5. Is there any transitional material which is not a complete statement of the basic material? How is it related to the rest of the composition?
6. Does the composition suggest groupings of variations? Is there an overall formal pattern, such as A B A? If so, how does the composer accomplish these groupings? Are there returns of earlier variations?

Repeated rhythmic/melodic line and/or repeated harmonic progression

Example Number	*Title*	*Page*
II.1 (ground bass)	Monteverdi, "Pur ti miro," duet from *L'incoronazione di Poppea*	72
II.25 (chaconne)	Handel, Chaconne in G major	122
II.3 (ground bass)	Purcell, "Chaconne" from *King Arthur*	78
II.16 (chaconne, ground)	Bach, Aria from Goldberg Variations	111
I.29 (chaconne)	Traditional, "Greensleeves"	66
I.30 (chaconne)	Terzi, "Pass'e mezzo per b molle in trei modi" and "Trei parti di gagliarde"	67
I.10 (isorhythmic/ isomelodic)	Anonymous, Motet "Ave, regina celorum - Alma redemptoris mater - Alma"	10
I.12 (isorhythmic/ isomelodic)	Machaut, "Bone pastor Guillerme - Bone pastor, qui pastores - Bone pastor"	13

V.25 (chaconne)	Handy, "Jogo Blues"	513
V.26 (chaconne)	Brubeck, "Far More Blue"	515
V.22 (repeated melody)	Britten, Dirge from *Serenade*, Op. 31	501

Theme and variations.

II.24	Handel, Aria con Variazione from Suite in B♭ major (Variation 1 only)	121
II. 16-20	Bach, Aria from Goldberg Variations, Variations 8, 15, 18, 30	111–17
III.9	Mozart, String Quartet in D minor K. 421 (E. 417b), fourth movement	212
III.15	Beethoven, Theme and Variations 1-8 from Fifteen Variations in E♭ Major, Op. 35 ("Eroica")	244
IV.25	Brahms, Theme and Variations 1-8 from *Variations and Fugue on a Theme by Handel*	375
V.23	Dello Joio, Piano Sonata No. 3, first movement	505

Treatment of a cantus firmus

Strictly speaking, one statement of a cantus firmus (usually a preexistent line) does not qualify a piece as a "variation," which assumes several different statements of the same material. However, cantus firmus treatment is often studied in a survey of variational techniques because one can frequently compare several different settings of the same cantus firmus and thus observe variant treatments.

Points to consider for these pieces

1. What is the one-line cantus firmus?
2. In which voice or voices does it occur?
3. How is it presented? (in long notes, decorated, rhythm changes, etc.)
4. How do the other voices of the texture relate to the cantus firmus? Do they use motives from it? Follow their own procedure?
5. Is there more than one statement of the cantus firmus?
6. Does the composition divide into sections? If so, how are the sections related?

For study comparison, all the pieces in the anthology which use a cantus firmus, either preexistent or newly composed, are listed here. Many of the compositions are not "variations" as such, but in all cases the integration of the melodic line into a texture may be studied.

Treatment of a cantus firmus

Example Number	*Title*	*Page*
1) Decorated melody:		
I.14	Dunstable, "Ave maris Stella"	20
II.40b	Bach, "Nun komm, der Heiden Heiland" (S. 659)	158
V.23, theme	Dello Joio, Piano Sonata No. 3, first movement	505
2) Long-note presentation:		
II.41c	Bach, "Christ lag in Todesbanden" (Cantata No. 4, Verse 3)	162
I.20	Josquin des Prez, "Vive le roy"	44
I.17	Dufay, "Missa L'homme armé," Kyrie	23
3) Imitative:		
I.18	Josquin des Prez, "Missa Pange Lingua," Kyrie	28
I.23 (also illustrates parody)	Palestrina, "Veni sponsa Christi"	51
I.24 (also illus trates parody)	Palestrina, "Missa Veni sponsa Christi," Kyrie	54
I.19	Josquin des Prez, "Alma redemptoris Mater/Ave regina coelorum"	31

II.20	Bach, Goldberg Variations, Variation 30	117
II.41d	Bach, "Christ lag in Todesbanden" (Cantata No. 4, verse 5)	164

4) Four-part harmonizations:

I.29	Traditional, "Greensleeves"	66
II.30a	Traditional, "Von Himmel hoch" (Choral Book)	139
II.30b	Scheidt, "Von Himmel hoch"	139
II.31a	Traditional, "Wachet auf" (Chorale Book)	141
II.31b	Bach, "Wachet auf", (371, #179)	141
II.32a	Traditional, "Nun danket alle Gott" (Chorale Book)	146
II.32b	Bach, "Nun danket alle Gott" (371, #32)	146
II.33a	Pachelbel, "Jesu, meine Freude"	148
II.33b	Bach, "Jesu, meine Fruede" (371, #263)	149
II.34	Bach, "Wie schön leuchtet der Morgenstern" (371, #278)	150
II.35	Bach, "Ach, bleib bei uns, Herr Jesu Christ" (371, #177)	151
II.36	Bach, "In dulci jubilo" (371, #143)	152
II.37b	Bach, "Sei gegrüsset" (371, #172)	154
II.40a	Scheidt, "Nun komm, der Heiden Heiland"	157
II.41e	Bach, "Christ lag in Todesbanden" (Cantata No. 4, Verse 7)	169

Pieces which illustrate a more abstract transformation of material are listed below. While perhaps not technically variations (although Dallapiccola named his work in one version "Variations for Orchestra"), they employ various transformations of melodic/rhythmic material that may be related to the general idea of variation. What is being retained and changed in each piece?

Example Number	*Title*	*Page*
IV.1, 2	Berlioz, *Symphonie Fantastique,* first and second movements	301,307
IV.5, 6, 7	Schumann, "Pierrot" No. 2, "Arlequin" No. 3; and "Valse noble," No. 4 from *Carnaval*	314,316, 317
V.27, 28, 29	Dallapiccola, "Linee," No. 4; "Contrapunctus Secundus" No. 5; and "Fregi" No. 6 from *Quaderno musicale di Annalibera*	518,519, 520
V.12	Stravinsky, Three Dances from *L'Histoire du Soldat*	462
IV.19, 20	Wagner, Prelude to and opening of Acts I and III from *Tristan und Isolde*	351,357
V.6	Schoenberg, "Nacht" No. 8 from *Pierrot Lunaire* (subtitled "Passacaglia")	426

V. Sectional Forms

Sectional form is a general name given to forms which have basically clearly defined and separable parts. In contrast to developmental forms, where one half or part depends on the other, sectional forms such as ternary (ABA) or rondo can be more easily divided into independent units. However, many of the characteristics of developmental forms (working out of material, transitional sections) are often combined with a simple sectional design, and thus compositions cannot be placed into a mold.

Points to consider:

1. What delineates sections? Are there changes of key, tempo, melodic material, texture, etc.?

2. What is the internal phrase structure of each section?
3. How are the sections connected? Is there any transitional material?
4. How many sections can be clearly identified? How do they relate to each other?
5. Does a section return exactly within the piece? Does it return in some sort of varied way?
6. What creates contrast between the sections? Are any elements retained from part to part?
7. What is the key scheme or cadential pattern of the work? How do the keys relate to each other?
8. Are there any developmental aspects?

A wide variety of sectional plans is possible. The list which follows includes a number of pieces in the anthology which fall most clearly into conventional categories. Many pieces which are similar to these formal models are not listed, but can be discussed in terms of their similarities and differences to the usual formal plan.

Example Number	*Title*	*Page*
Strophic		
II.31b	Bach, "Wachet auf"	141
II.33b	Bach, "Jesu, meine Freude"	149
IV.9	Schumann, "Im wunderschönen Monat Mai," No. 1 from *Dichterliebe*	323
Ternary (A B A) and Da Capo Aria		
II.1	Monteverdi, "Pur ti miro," duet from *L'incoronazione di Poppea*	72
IV.3	Schumann, "An important event," No. 6 from *Scenes from Childhood*	312
II.26	Handel, "L'amerò?—È gelosia" from *Serse*	124
III.14	Beethoven, String Quartet in G major, Op. 18 No. 2 second movement	240
IV.16	Chopin, Mazurka in A minor, Op.7 No.2	341
IV.17	Chopin, Mazurka in G major, Op.67 No.1	343
IV.8	Schumann, "Widmung," from *Myrthen*, Op. 25 No. 1	318
IV.18	Chopin, Nocturne in C♯ minor, Op. 27 No.1	345
IV.22	Brahms, Intermezzo in A major, Op. 76 No. 6	366
IV.24	Brahms, Romance in F major, Op. 118 No. 5	371
V.3	Ravel, Rigaudon from *Le Tombeau de Couperin*	414
Minuet/Trio		
The internal forms of the minuet and trio are often binary.		
III.2	Haydn, Menuet and Trio from Divertimento in C major (Hoboken XVI. 1)	176
III.12	Beethoven, Piano Sonata in E major, Op. 14 No. 1, second movement	233
III.19 (Scherzo)	Beethoven, String Quartet in B♭ major, Op. 130, second movement	281
V.4	Ravel, Menuet from *Le Tombeau de Couperin*	418
Rondo (A B A xxx A)		
II.2	Purcell, Rondo	75
III.6	Mozart, Recitative and Aria from *Don Giovanni* ("In quali eccessi, O Numi— Mi tradì quell' alma ingrata")	198

III.24	Schubert, "Entr'acte" from *Rosamunde*	294
III.4	Haydn, String Quartet in G major, Op. 54 No. 1, fourth movement	181
III.13 (sonata-rondo)	Beethoven, Piano Sonata in E major, Op. 14 No. 1, third movement	235
IV.28	Mussorgsky, "The Great Gate of Kiev" from *Pictures at an Exhibition*	392

Medieval and Renaissance "formes fixes" (virelai, rondeau, etc.)

I.7	Moniot d'Arras, "Ce fu en mai"	6
I.8	Wizlaw von Rugen, "Nach der senenden claghe můz ich singhen"	8
I.9	Wizlaw von Rugen, "Ic parrêre dî dorch mîne trôwe"	9
I.11	Machaut, "Foy porter"	12
I.13	Landini, "Giovine vagha, i'non sentî"	18
I.15	Dufay, "Bon jour, bon mois"	21

VI. Developmental Forms

The idea of development of material is present to some degree in almost any composition. The continuous presentation of new material results in chaos; static repetition leads to boredom. However, the term "developmental forms" usually refers to those compositions where development of material is a basic part of a formal design either in a separate section of the movement or throughout as an integral compositional process. (Contrapuntal forms are generally not included, however.) In all cases the sections of developmental forms are not complete without each other, in contrast to the independence of the sections in sectional forms. However, form in music is a very elusive property and many compositions exhibit properties of several different types of form. These properties should be discusssed and compared instead of ignored by forcing the work into a formal prototype.

Points to consider:

1. What determines the large sections of the work? (Usually tonality is important)
2. What is the basic material of the composition? Melodic lines? Rhythmic patterns? Chord progressions?
3. How is the material first presented?
4. How is it changed in the course of the composition? Is there a separate development section?
5. What elements are returned at the end of the movement? Does a key area return?
6. Is it important to identify a second key area? Second thematic material?
7. Is there an introduction? A coda?
8. How are sections connected? by transitional material or by abrupt changes?

The compositions listed below range from very simple binary examples to complex sonata-allegro (sonata-movement) forms. Many of the internal forms in minuet/trio compositions also illustrate the binary pattern (see the listing in "Sectional forms").

Binary

Example Number	*Title*	*Page*
II.4	Corelli, Sonata V, Op. 2, Allemande	82
II.5	Corelli Sonata V, Op. 2, Sarabande	83
II.24, aria	Handel, Aria con Variazione from Suite in B♭ major	121
II.22	Bach, Sarabande from French Suite in E major, No. 6.	119
II.23	Bach, Gavotte from French Suite in E major, No. 6	120
III.15, theme	Beethoven, Eroica Variations Op.35	245

II.16	Bach, Aria from Goldberg Variations	111
V.20	Hindemith, Interlude from *Ludus Tonalis*	496
II.29 (compare with sonata-allegro)	Scarlatti, Sonata K. 412 (L. 182) in G major	134
IV.23 (framed by an introduction and coda)	Brahms, Intermezzo in A minor, Op. 76 No. 7	369
V.27 (what is "2-part" in these compositions?)	Dallapiccola, "Linee," No. 4 from *Quaderno musicale di Annalibera*	518
V.29	Dallapiccola, "Fregi," No. 6 from *Quaderno musicale di Annalibera*	520
Sonata-movement		
III.8	Mozart, Sonata in D major K. 284 (E. 205b), first movement	206
III.11	Beethoven, Piano Sonata in E major, Op. 14 No. 1, first movement	227
III.1	C.P.E. Bach, Sonata III in F minor, first movement	172
III.7	Mozart, Sonata in F major, K.280 (E. 189e), second movement	204
III.5 (slow introduction)	Haydn, Symphony No. 100 in G major ("Military"), first movement	185
III.10 (concerto)	Mozart, Concerto for Horn and Orchestra in E♭ major K.447 (E.447), first movement	217
III.16	Beethoven, Piano Sonata in F minor Op. 57, ("Appassionata"), first movement	250
III.17	Beethoven, Piano Sonata in E♭ major, Op. 81a, first movement	264
IV.26	Brahms, Violin Sonata in A major, Op. 100 first movement	380
III.18	Beethoven, String Quartet in B♭ major, Op. 130, first movement	270
V.18	Bartók, String quartet No. 4, first movement	485

VII. Serial and Atonal Compositions

Several of the compositions in the fifth section of the anthology are based on serial technique.

Points to consider:

1. What is the basic tone row?
2. How is it constructed? What intervals are used?
3. Does the row itself have any particular characteristics? Is it symmetrical, all-interval, etc.?
4. How does the composition use the row? In melodic lines? In chords? Are several row forms combined?
5. What are the audible organizing features of the composition? A certain texture, rhythmic pattern, melodic shape?
6. Are any of the elements of the row audible? Do interval patterns or row forms contribute clearly to the melodic, harmonic, or formal structure?

A suggested order for study:

Example Number	Title	Page
V.27	Dallapiccola, "Linee," No. 4 from *Quaderno musicale di Annalibera*	518
V.28	Dallapiccola, "Contrapunctus Secundus," No. 5 from *Quaderno musicale di Annalibera*	519
V.29	Dallapiccola, "Fregi," No. 6 from *Quaderno musicale di Annalibera*	520
V.8b	Berg, "Schliesse mir die Augen beide"	435
V.7	Schoenberg, *Klavierstück* Op. 33a	428
V.10	Webern, Concerto Op. 24, third movement	441

Many of the compositions in Section V are not based on the serial technique, nor are they centered around a particular tonic. Sometimes, however, they gravitate to a particular chord. Pitch organization often depends on small sets of notes which are stated melodically and harmonically and provide a degree of unity for the composition. A few of these compositions are listed below. In each case, what is the basis for the pitch organization? Are there recurring chords or melodic units? Are there important pitch-class sets?

V.15	Bartók, "Chromatic Invention" No. 91 from *Mikrokosmos*	478
V.16	Bartók, "From the Island of Bali," No. 109 from *Mikrokosmos*	479
V.9	Webern, No. 3 from *Funf Sätze* Op. 5 for String Quartet	437
V.6	Schoenberg, "Nacht," No. 8 from *Pierrot Lunaire*	426
V.5	Schoenberg, "Mondestrunken," No. 1 from *Pierrot Lunaire*	432
V.11	Stravinsky, *Le Sacre du Printemps*, Part I (Danses des Adolescentes)	444

VIII. Special Projects for Study

Figured bass realization

The following examples of figured bass may be realized at the keyboard or in three- or four-part written excercises.

II.4	Corelli, Sonata V, Op. 2, Allemande	82
II.5	Corelli, Sonata V, Op. 2, Sarabande	83
II.26, recitative	Handel, "L'amerò?—É gelosia" from *Serse*	124
II.37a	Bach, "Sei gegrüsset"	153
II.38	Bach, "So gibst du nun, mein Jesu, gute Nacht"	155
II.39	Bach, "O Jesulein süss"	156

Examples in Section II of unfigured bass may also be realized (see, for example, a model in the Monteverdi excerpt, II.1).

Score reading

The following examples are printed in open score. They can be used for score reading practice at the keyboard (play as many lines as possible) or for written exercises in transposition and piano reduction.

Example Number	Title	Page
1) Pieces using open score with treble and bass clefs only:		
3 voices:		
I.10	Anonymous, Motet, "Ave, regina celorum - Alma Redemptoris mater - Alma"	10

Sources

Most of the sources, including all copyrighted ones, are identified with the music. The compositions by J.S. Bach, Beethoven, Brahms, Orlando di Lasso, Mozart, Schubert, and Schumann are taken from the Breitkopf und Härtel editions of the complete works, published in Leipzig in the late nineteenth century. Other sources taken from specific editions are given below.

Bach, J.S. *Well-Tempered Clavier* Vols. I & II. Peters, ed. by F. Kroll.

——— *389 Chorale Melodies,* Belwin.

Chopin, Frederic. *Sämtliche Klavier-Werke,* ed. Hermann Scholtz. C.F. Peters, Leipzig. (n.d.)

Corelli, Arcangelo. *Les Oeuvres de Arcangelo Corelli,* ed. J. Joachim and F. Chrysander. London: Augener, 1890.

Des Prez, Josquin, *Werken,* ed. by A. Smijers. Nederlandse Muziekgeschiedenis, 1931, 1952, 1963.

Haydn, F.J. Works in Eulenburg scores (London, n.d.). Ed. W. Altman, H.C. Robbins Landon, C.A. Martienssen.

Mendelssohn, Felix. *Elijah.* G. Schirmer, New York (n.d.).

Mozart, W.A. *Don Giovanni.* English version by Natalie Macfarren. G. Schirmer, New York, 1900.

Mussorgsky, Modest. *Pictures at an Exhibition,* ed. Walter Niemann. Peters (n.d.).

Purcell, Henry, *Harpsichord Music* Vol. VI. Ed. William Barclay Squire. Novello, Ewer, and Co., London 1895.

——— *King Arthur*, Vol. 26, Novello.

Wagner, Richard. *Tristan und Isolde*, ed. R. Kleinmichel (Leipzig: Breitkopf und Härtel, n.d.).

Wolf, Hugo. *Italienisches Liederbuch.*

——— *Songs on Poems by Moericke.* International Music Company (n.d.).

Composers in Chronological Order

1200

Moniot d'Arras (13th century)
Wizlaw von Rugen (1268-1325)

1300

Guillaume de Machaut (1300-1377)
Francesco Landino (1325-1397)
John Dunstable (c. 1380-1453)

1400

Guillaume Dufay (c. 1400-1474)
Josquin des Prez (c. 1440-1521)

1500

Jacob Arcadelt (c. 1505-1560)
Pierluigi da Palestrina (1525-1594)
Orlando di Lasso (1532-1594)

1550

Don Carlo Gesualdo (c. 1560-1613)
John Dowland (1562-1626)
Claudio Monteverdi (1567-1643)
Samuel Scheidt (1587-1654)
Giovanni Terzi (f. 1593)

1650

Johann Pachelbel (1653-1706)
Arcangelo Corelli (1653-1713)
Henry Purcell (1659-1695)
J.K.F. Fischer (c. 1665-1746)
François Couperin (1668-1733)
J.S. Bach (1685-1750)
Domenico Scarlatti (1685-1757)
George Frideric Handel (1685-1759)

1700

C.P.E. Bach (1714-1788)
Franz Joseph Haydn (1732-1809)

1750

W.A. Mozart (1756-1791)
Ludwig van Beethoven (1770-1827)
Franz Schubert (1797-1828)

1800

Hector Berlioz (1803-1869)
Felix Mendelssohn (1809-1847)
Frédéric Chopin (1810-1849)
Robert Schumann (1810-1856)
Richard Wagner (1813-1883)
Giuseppe Verdi (1813-1901)
Johannes Brahms (1833-1897)
Modest Mussorgsky (1839-1881)

1850

Hugo Wolf (1860-1903)
Claude Debussy (1862-1918)
W.C. Handy (1873-1958)
Arnold Schoenberg (1874-1951)
Charles Ives (1874-1954)
Maurice Ravel (1875-1937)
Béla Bartók (1881-1945)
Igor Stravinsky (1882-1971)
Anton Webern (1883-1945)
Alban Berg (1885-1935)
Paul Hindemith (1895-1963)

1900

Luigi Dallapiccola (1904-1975)
Benjamin Britten (1913-1976)
Norman Dello Joio (b. 1913)
Dave Brubeck (b. 1920)
Luciano Berio (b. 1925)
George Crumb (b. 1929)

Index

This index references terms, compositional techniques, and specific musical elements by page and measure number (if necessary). Page numbers are given first; measure numbers are given in parentheses. For complete works, the first page of the example is given. Some of the references are to the graded lists of compositions in the study guide. In some cases the beginning measure of an item is given, with *ff* indicating that it continues in the following measures. Usually only the first example of an item in a composition is referenced; the work should be examined for other examples of the same element.

References are complete, except in the case of frequent musical procedures. In those cases a few of the most striking examples were selected; there are more in the anthology. Certain very common elements (authentic cadences, passing and neighbor tones) are not referenced.

Cadence types are listed under Cadence. Chord types and functions are listed under Chords. Key changes are listed under Modulation. For both chords and keys, small roman numerals (e.g. ii, iii) represent minor and large roman numerals (e.g. II, III) represent major. Types of works included in the anthology are referenced under Media and under separate entries such as symphony, concerto, and sonata.

A

B

C

D

N

O

P

Q

R